DEAL WITH IT!

DEAL WITH IT!

A Whole New Approach to Your Body, Brain, and Life as a gURL

by the creators of

esther drill
heather mcdonald
rebecca odes

POCKET BOOKS

New York   London   Toronto   Sydney   Tokyo   Singapore

An <u>Original</u> Publication of POCKET BOOKS

 POCKET BOOKS, a division of Simon & Schuster, Inc.
1230 Avenue of the Americas, New York, NY 10020

ISBN: 0-671-04157-6

First Pocket Books trade paperback printing September 1999

10 9 8 7 6 5 4 3 2

POCKET and colophon are registered trademarks of
Simon & Schuster, Inc.

Book design by Georgia Rucker
Cover illustration by Rebecca Odes

Printed in England

For orders other than by individual consumers, Pocket Books grants a discount on the purchase of **10 or more** copies of single titles for special markets or premium use. For further details, please write to the Vice-President of Special Markets, Pocket Books, 1230 Avenue of the Americas, New York, NY 10020.

For information on how individual consumers can place orders, please write to Mail Order Department, Simon & Schuster, Inc., 200 Old Tappan Road, Old Tappan, NJ 07675.

The author of this book is not a physician and the ideas, procedures, and suggestions in this book are not intended as a substitute for the medical advice of a trained health professional. All matters regarding your health require medical supervision. Consult your physician before adopting the suggestions in this book, as well as about any condition that may require diagnosis or medical attention. The author and publisher disclaim any liability arising directly or indirectly from the use of this book.

For gURL
Executive Editor: Esther Drill
Creative Director: Rebecca Odes
Director of Community: Heather McDonald
Excerpts: Zoe Balsam, Cathy McDonald,
    Eve Meltzer, Naomi Odes
Additional Writing: Joan A. Odes ACSW, LCSW

For Roundtable Press, Inc.
Directors: Julie Merberg, Marsha Melnick,
    Susan E. Meyer
Contributors: Janet Allon, Lisa Sussman
Project Editors: Elizabeth Bogner,
    Meredith Wolf Schizer
Designer: Georgia Rucker
Production: Laura Smyth

Thank you! Thank you! Thank you!

This book has been an enormous undertaking—more so than we could have imagined—and we have had so much help along the way.

Many thanks to:

The incredible Georgia Rucker, the best designer a book could ask for, in both talent and temperament.

Julie Merberg and Meredith Wolf Schizer, without whose hard work there would be no book at all.

Our families for supporting us, gURL, and DEAL WITH IT! from the beginning.

Our friends and lovers for their support, understanding, and input, especially: Hila Dar, Craig Kanarick, Rhonda Lieberman, Julia Meltzer, Ignazio Moresco, Kimberly Peirce, Michael Seeber, Julie Shapiro, Louis Spitzer.

The fabulous gURLstaff, for holding down the fort and putting up with the chaos.

The girls of the gURL connection for their inspiration, insight, continual feedback, and respectful debates.

All our friends at iTurf, dELiA*s, and the Interactive Telecommunications Program at NYU, especially Stephen Kahn, Alex Navarro, Renny Gleeson, and Red Burns.

P.S. Georgia would like to thank Michael Tritter, her family, and pals.

Advisory Board

Gila Leiter, M.D. Ob/Gyn., Assistant Clinical Professor Mt. Sinai School of Medicine; Attending at Mt. Sinai Hospital; Fellow, American College of Obstetricians and Gynecologists; American Society of Reproductive Medicine; New York Gynecological Society

Frederyka Shabry, M.D., Director of Child Psychiatry, Coney Island Hospital, New York; Clinical Assistant Professor at SUNY Health Science Center at Brooklyn

We would like to thank the following individuals and organizations, all of whom gave generously of their time and expertise for this book:

American College of Obstetricians and Gynecologists (ACOG); American Psychological Association; Professor Susan Basow, psychology professor at Lafayette College; Michele Bernstein, M.S.W., Jewish Family and Vocational Service; The Center for Reproductive Law and Policy; Covenant House; Rebecca Drill, Ph.D.; Families and Friends of Lesbians and Gays (PFLAG); Food and Drug Administration (FDA); Rita Freedman, psychologist; Dr. Roberta Garside, plastic surgeon; Dr. Florence Haseltine, National Institutes of Health (NIH); National Abortion Federation; National Clearinghouse for Alcohol and Drug Information; National Eating Disorders Organization; New York Cares; Parents Magazine; Planned Parenthood Federation of America; Planned Parenthood of New York; Rock the Vote; Karen Sheldon; SAFE (Self-Abuse Finally Ends); Sexuality Information Education Council of the United States (SIECUS); and Youth Volunteer Corps of America.

BRAIN 165

LIFE 215

This book grew out of our website, gURL.com, but its seeds were planted when we were teenagers. Two of us grew up together (Rebecca and Esther) and navigated the murky waters of adolescence side by side. We met Heather in graduate school where we started gURL. We wanted to do something for girls that came from our own personal experiences to show that there is not just one right way of doing things or one right way to be.

Our experience with the site has put us in touch with hundreds of thousands of teenage girls talking about what matters to them in their own voices. Hearing what they had to say convinced us that there was a need for a new kind of book about being a girl, one that's smart, funny, approachable, and tuned in to the things girls really want to know.

This book is divided into four parts: Body, Sexuality, Brain, and Life. The categories are a natural way of approaching different parts of yourself—although there are so many other interesting ways of defining, dividing, and understanding who you are. We try to give each topic a thorough and thoroughly entertaining treatment with plenty of conversation and commentary from the girls on our site. We left the snippets of conversations mostly as they were written online because we wanted them to be real (though all screen names have been changed for privacy reasons). The girls on our site have different backgrounds, ages, and points of view, and what they have to say covers a wide range of ideas and perspectives.

Adolescence is both a personal and a universal experience. The changes you're going through are major, and they are different for everyone. At the same time, every girl is dealing with it everywhere. From the changes in your body to the challenges you face, we think this book will provide you with the honest information and valuable resources you need.* We hope it will provide you with a new way of looking at what it means to be a gURL.

REBECCA   HEATHER   Esther

* Most of the chapters in this book are followed by a resource section listing national organizations, online resources, and books you can turn to for more information on subjects of particular interest to you. Our site at www.dealwithit.com has links to all of the online resources listed here, as well as many others you may find helpful.

gURL.com, the website that spawned this book, was founded in 1996, as a school project. It began as an irreverent online magazine, and has developed into the leading website for teenage girls. In addition to regularly updated articles, gURL offers games, chat rooms, posting boards, daily polls, free e-mail, free homepage hosting, and a whole lot more. Come visit us online!

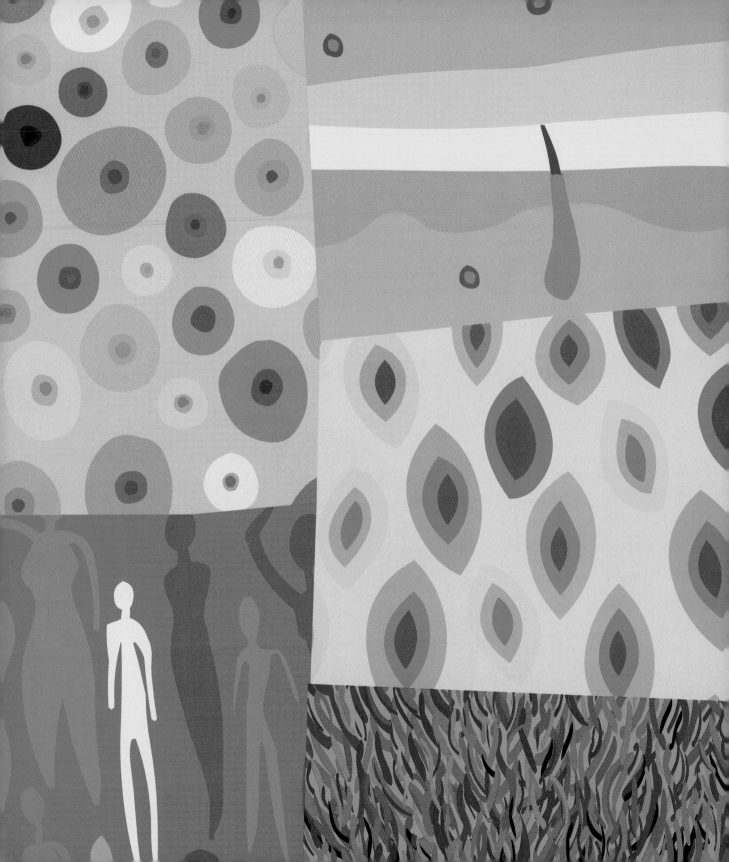

PART 1

body

You and your body are inseparable. You live, grow and evolve together.

Adolescence brings dramatic changes to your body—boobs, periods, pimples, body hair, and more... Hormones, chemicals that are produced in your brain and ovaries, are working behind the scenes of these developments.

Everyone's body changes differently and at its own pace. The way your own body develops may seem exciting, embarrassing, irritating, or anxiety-producing.

The particular changes you are going through obviously affect how you feel and relate to your body as well as to the bodies around you. Understanding what's happening to you and why is a necessary step in beginning to understand and be comfortable with yourself.

Chapter 1

Boobs get a lot of attention. There's a certain amount of biological motivation for this—breasts are the first source of human nourishment—but that's only the beginning.

The stress on boobs in our society creates a lot of stress for girls who are growing them. You don't have much control over your breast development and the outcome can be unpredictable.

When boobs start popping up left and right, they can be hard to ignore. Whatever your specific situation, shape, or size, your boobs are bound to be an important part of your female identity.

boobs boobies hooters jugs knockers
tits titties melons kasabas hoojies
bosom ta-tas twins knobs honkers
bonkers caldoons mammies bazongas

GROWING THEM

Breasts start to grow in response to an increase in the hormone estrogen, which causes the growth of mammary glands (which produce milk) and also signals cushions of fat to grow and surround those glands. Much of the volume of the breast comes from these cushions of fat. Also inside the breast is a network of milk ducts connected to the milk-producing glands, which are ready to send milk out of the nipple when it comes time to nurse a baby.

There are roughly five stages of breast development. Everyone goes through them at her own rate. Some girls may go through the whole process in a couple of months and can actually seem to bypass whole stages; others can take almost 10 years to get from the beginning to the (relatively) final product.

Stage 1 The first stage usually starts between ages 8 and 11 (although it can come earlier or later). During this stage, there are no visible signs of development. Inside the body, though, puberty is beginning. The ovaries enlarge and estrogen begins to circulate.

Stage 2 The first visible thing that happens is the nipple and the areola (the skin around the nipple) get larger and maybe a bit darker. They may also feel tender or ache a little. It can hurt to sleep on your stomach or wear certain clothes.

Next, milk ducts and fat tissue form a little, round, dense, disklike mound under each nipple and areola, making them stick out. One disk might form before the other, even as much as a year earlier. These disks can often feel like lumps.

Stage 3 Fat deposits now start to fill out the area around the nipple and areola. At this stage, many girls' breasts appear pointy. The amount of fat and where it grows vary and will determine the size and shape of your breasts. This is the time when many girls think about wearing a bra.

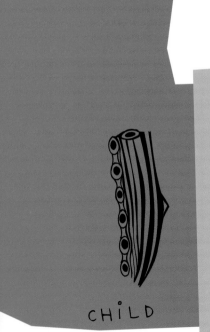

CHILD

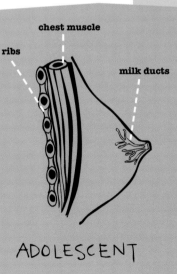

ribs
chest muscle
milk ducts

ADOLESCENT

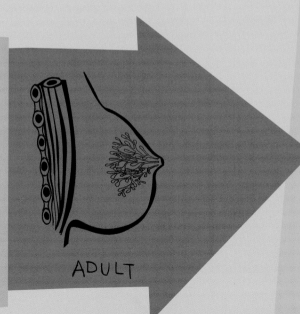

ADULT

Stage 4 Not everyone goes through Stage 4. If you do, you will observe that your nipple and areola begin to form a separate mound at the end of your breast and get bigger and more pronounced. Some women keep this characteristic permanently. The breasts continue to fill out and grow larger. (If you didn't get your period during stage 3, you probably will now.)

Stage 5 By the time you reach stage 5, what you see could be what you get. Breast size can change during a woman's adult life, however. This is generally due to body weight changes or hormonal factors (birth control pills, pregnancy), although there are a significant number of women whose breasts continue to change throughout their twenties.

SHAPES AND SIZES

Breasts come in all shapes and sizes. There is no one normal boob profile. And nobody notices the idiosyncrasies of your boobs like you do. The timing of your boob development makes no difference in what they end up looking like. Breasts also go through cyclical changes with the menstrual cycle. They tend to get a little fuller and more sensitive leading up to the period and stay pretty tender until the period is over. After the period they settle down to their less-full form.

> I think girls obsess waaaay too much about breast size. No one seems to be satisfied with what size theirs are. What's the big deal anyway?
> **— poKey**

Asymmetry

Your whole body (eyes, ears, etc.) is asymmetrical and chances are that there are some subtle differences between your two breasts, too. In some people it's enough to be noticeable, but almost never dramatically so. In rare instances, a right and left boob may vary a cup size or more. Very occasionally a girl will wear a prosthesis or even have surgery to even out a severe difference in size. Generally, though, it's one of those things that is a lot less noticeable to everyone else in the world than to the bearer of the boobs in question.

> One of my breasts is smaller than the other. My mother says it's normal, but I don't think she understands. It's not just a little bit smaller, it's noticeably smaller and different-looking. It is less developed, I suppose, because the nipple is smaller and more like from when I was younger than my other nipple.
> **— lanaturner**

Nipples

Nipples also come in all shapes, colors, and sizes. Some nipples are particularly sensitive to outside stimuli.

> I know the stiff-nippled syndrome well. You can try to get a thicker bra or just try turning the other way.
> **— TaraGirl**

> This sounds really weird, but when I'm in class and I get cold my nipples get hard. And boys think I'm getting horny. It's so embarrassing.
> **— mayip**

5

the boob files

large

Just because my breasts are bigger than the rest of my friends' who are virtually FLAT doesn't mean they have to tease me about it! When I was younger I used to pray for a big bust. Now I pray for a small one. Am I a loser, or am I totally CONFUSED?
- **goaliegirl**

It seems like everyone hates their chest except guys. But being big-chested, at my school I could be sitting with one friend, looking at the ground kicking rocks and all the guys would think "what a slut" just because I have big breasts ...I'm sick of it!
- **spiderLeg**

I'm 16 right now, but I've had this problem ever since I was 9. I'm an early bloomer who is cursed with big, heavy boobs that bug the freak out of me. I can hardly run, they make me look fat, and I always have to be very careful about what I wear.
- **ACME**

I'm 16 and a mere 34A. I don't even wear a bra half the time. I only got my period in the beginning of my sophomore year, so they'll probably grow later, but I really don't care anymore. It used to bother me in junior high when all my friends were acquiring new curves and I wasn't, because guys were all excited about the new breasts to ogle at and I was left out, but now I'm sort of glad I'm flat. Sports are painless, as is walking up and down stairs. So if you're flat, look at the assets that come along with that (small) package, not the drawbacks.- **hildE**

I have large breasts. They're not small, or medium. They're large. They're not on the small side of large or the large side of medium. They're just large. And they're not the kind that look large in a tight shirt or the kind that look large in a loose shirt. They're just large.

Now, I've known this for a while, and yet people keep reminding me as if it's some sort of secret, or revelation. Boys in high school thought they were the first ones to discover it so they had no problem screaming down the hallway, "Hey you know something, you got big tits!" Thanks.

In Europe, men on the streets reminded me by staring directly at my chest with tremendous smiling faces. Sometimes they'd even say "hello." To my tits.

I am almost 16 and a 38C...I know girls who aren't satisfied with their breasts don't believe it, but I don't like being so big-chested. The looks, the comments, it can be just as big a pain as being flat! You really can't win either way, and it certainly isn't something you should worry about. - **SadieSuperStar**

6

I am not exactly big-breasted. In fact, they're pretty small. But it seems guys only like girls who are big, at least where I live. They only ask "big" girls out. It's like if you don't have big boobs, you're not anything. What the hell?
— **MeoWPoWer**

Guys are, for some reason, fascinated with girls with big breasts—trust me, I'm a 38C or D, depending on the bra. But most guys won't base a date on breast size. Ultimately, not all guys are scum and will choose you for who you are. Those who don't are immature and by they time they grow up, you'll have found someone better.
— **Heady**

lopsided

Every boob-bearing individual knows that no two boobs are alike. Even within one seemingly identical pair, you should be able to find some noteworthy differences: a little more droop here, a bit of extra perk there, a radical contour shift to the right, an off-center nipple on the left. Because no two boobs really belong to one another, it seems there would always emerge a favorite, a first among equals.

At least that is how it is for me. My two boobs are sisters, sure, but let's just say they are more like fraternal twins, not born of the same egg.

Sometimes I wonder how it is that two boobs could be so different, how could one be so distinguished and the other, so mediocre.

small

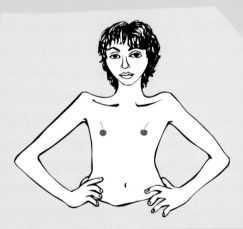

Forsaking all cleavage, these breasts have challenged me to trust that my voluptuous personality and mind are my most winning assets. Never floppy, bouncy or squishy, these breasts have encouraged me to be firm, athletic and strong. Like an iron shield, they stop bimboys in their tracks.

My breasts are the espresso to the double cappuccino boobs of this world. They may be little, but they pack a punch.

My left boob is a bit smaller than my right boob, and I was just wondering if there were any exercises or anything to even it out. I don't want to wear a pad in one and not in the other, 'cause people in my grade notice that kind of thing.— **paps**

Almost everyone has one boob that's bigger than the other. Don't worry about it. You're probably just being paranoid because people put so much emphasis on boobs these days. It's not like girls can help their breast size.
— **Lanku**

boobs

There's a long historical tradition of women making more or less of their bustlines than nature provides.

Breast enhancers

"Breast enhancers," which aren't that different from the actual implants inserted during surgery, are worn on the outside of the body and are available for purchase in the backs of magazines and at drugstores, promising every girl the silhouette she has always wanted. These products are obviously safer and cheaper than actual implants, but they don't change the way you look without a bra on.

Breast implants

First of all, no one NEEDS breast implants. Women may feel that their life enjoyment is being diminished by an insufficient cup size. But that's kind of a limited way of thinking—do you really want to give that much power to two lumps of fat sitting on your chest?

The decision of whether to alter your body for a cosmetic reason is a serious and personal one. Some women have had terrible health problems as a result of getting breast implants, although scientifically the jury is still out on whether they are dangerous. In any event, it's a good idea to wait a while before taking such a drastic step. Most reputable plastic surgeons won't even consider breast implants on a woman younger than 18. The way people feel about their bodies changes over time, and making a big, unnatural, permanent change now might be something you could later regret. Besides, you might still be growing.

Having bigger boobs won't change the kind of person you are, and if it does make more boys notice you, it might not be for the reason you want them to.

Breast reduction

Some women are physically challenged by the large size of their breasts. These problems can include chronic neck and back pain; poor posture; rashes; pain, and discomfort during exercise; and bra straps that actually cut grooves in their shoulders. Some of these women opt for breast reduction surgery to have some of their breast tissue removed. Women who have had breast reduction are said to be about the happiest plastic surgery patients afterward. But reduction surgery can leave significant scarring—usually in an inverted T-shape from the nipple to the underside of the breast—and may affect breast-feeding later.

boys like boobs (all different kinds)

boobs
in
society

There are plenty of reasons people like breasts, and focus on them accordingly. Some trace it back to infant oral fixations. Others think it may be the round shapes that are pleasing to the senses. Breasts are the most visible sexual organs. While other sexual organs are developing at the same time, they are (generally) kept under wraps and are not able to be seen. Breasts, on the other hand, make themselves known. Boobs certainly get their fair share of media attention, and the recent explosion of public breast enlargements makes them more obvious than ever. Historically, though, a variety of sizes and shapes of breasts have been considered ideal. Not all cultures share the American fixation on boobs, either. Many European countries present a more integrated view of the female body, and women appear topless on public beaches and in advertisements. On a more personal level, different people are attracted to different breast attributes (just as some people may have a preference for a certain eye color). But many people seem to think that breasts in general are pretty great, whatever the particulars may be.

Guys do stare at breasts. I asked my friend what it is about guys and breasts and he said, "Well, you know...breasts are just cool." And I said, "Hey, if you like them so much you should get your own pair." Then he said, "If I could, I would, and I would play with them all day. I don't see why girls don't play with their breasts." He just confused me even more!!
—hazelQ

You have big breasts and they laugh at you. If you have small breasts they laugh at you too. No matter what you do you can't win with boys (hmmm??) **- SamC**

All women experience some such fibro-cystic changes: lumpiness, tenderness, swelling. Eventually, you should get to know your own patterns of lumpiness.

Lumps and bumps

The vast majority of lumps and bumps in the breast, at any age, are harmless. Breast budding in the early stages of breast develop-ment can often feel like a lump. At certain times of the month, especially before their periods, some women develop cysts—small fluid-containing sacs. They are usually found near the armpits, can hurt a little, and disappear within a few days.

Show your doctor any lump that does not disappear within a few days; it is probably nothing to worry about. Breast cancer is obviously a scary and serious disease, which affects one in eight women over the course of a lifetime. But it is extremely, extremely rare in teenagers.

> There is a small weird lump left of the nipple on my left breast. I don't know what it is, and I dont want to ask my mom. I was wondering how young you have to be to get breast cancer? My family kind of has a history of it and I am scared that this lump might be it. I am only 14, but I just don't know how early is early for breast cancer.
> — **sleepie**

Fibrocystic breasts

Many girls and women develop lumpiness in their breasts due to hormonal changes during their menstrual cycle. Women with fibrocystic breasts have denser fibrous material in between the fatty deposits in their breasts, so it's more likely to become tangled up into knots. Fibrocystic lumps are not cancerous, although the first time you notice them, you may want to have them checked out.

Breast pain

Most girls experience some occasional breast pain—most often before a period or dur-ing the early stages of breast development. If the pain is really plaguing you, happens at irregular times not linked to your cycle, or is much more pro-nounced in one breast, it's worth mentioning to your doctor, who may suggest cutting down on caffeine or taking vitamin E supplements and prim-rose oil.

Discharge or bleeding

Some discharge from the nipple can be brought on by hormonal fluctuations, but both discharge and bleeding that lasts for more than a week should be checked out with a doctor.

Chafed nipples

Nipples stick out and can rub against your clothes and sometimes get irritated, dry, and cracked, and even bleed a bit. Wearing soft fabrics or natural fibers can help. It can also help to put ointment, lanolin preparations, or even flavor-free lip balm on irritated areas.

Inverted nipples

Some nipples do not stick out; instead, they appear to stick in (inverted nipples). This is not uncommon. Some nipples may go from "innies" to "outies" during the course of development. Once your breasts are fully developed, usually at age 18, any sudden changes should be reported to your doctor.

My nipples are weird. Sometimes they are inverted and I wanna know why! I'm embarrassed to let a guy see me. Why do they do that, and can I fix it? **— patsychic**

Lots of girls have inverted nipples. Any guy who thinks they're weird has some strange ideas.
— rhodarules

Hairy nipples

Some girls grow a few dark hairs around the areola, the area surrounding the nipple. You may be tempted to tweeze them, but that could lead to ingrown hairs and infection. They can be trimmed or zapped with electrolysis—or left hanging.

Stretch marks

When boobs, or any parts of the body, grow fast, the skin has to stretch to keep up. Sometimes the skin is not quite elastic enough to do that, and purplish lines, called stretch marks, may appear where the skin has been stretched. These are not uncommon, and they do fade with time, although not always entirely.

how to give a breast self-exam

Breast cancer, though not a big concern to teenagers, is a prospect that all adult women need to be aware of. There are all sorts of studies linking breast cancer with heredity, diet, hormonal imbalances, and lifestyle. New treatments and medical breakthroughs hold some promise in eventually defeating this disease, but nothing beats early detection. That's why your first line of defense against breast cancer is monthly self-examination. You can start as soon as your breasts are fully developed.

Breast self-exams should be done at the same time of the month every month, right after your period ends, when the breasts are neither tender nor swollen.

1. Lie down on your back; put your right arm over your head and a pillow under your right shoulder.

2. With the three middle fingers of your left hand, feel for lumps or thickened tissue in your right breast, using a firm circular motion radiating out from the nipple. Press hard enough to familiarize yourself with how your breast feels, but not so hard that it hurts.

3. Repeat steps 1 and 2 for your left breast.

4. Standing and looking in a mirror, check your breasts for any surface anomalies like puckering, dimpling, or swelling. Do this with your arms at your sides, with them stretched above your head, and with your hands on your hips while flexing your chest muscles.

BRAS

Whether or when to wear a bra is an entirely personal decision. Some, especially larger-breasted women, find they are more comfortable with their boobs strapped in and supported, since there's less jiggling and bouncing that way. Many women also find it more comfortable to wear a bra when jogging or doing other kinds of exercise. Some women are more comfortable going braless.

The jury is still out about whether wearing a bra in fact prevents eventual sagging. Some experts say it can help preserve some of the elasticity of the tissue and the ligaments that hold the breast up. But others say that over the long haul, gravity, wear and tear, motherhood, and changes in size brought on by weight gain and loss all take their toll, no matter how often a woman has worn a bra.

The shape of a nipple—which can stiffen if it's cold or aroused—is less visible underneath a bra, if that's something you care about.

Girls usually experiment to figure out which kind of bra suits them. Bras can make your boobs look bigger or smaller or otherwise different. There's a veritable smorgasbord of silhouette-altering brassieres at your disposal.

SOFT CUP BRA

UNDERWIRE

The soft-cup bra (with or without underwire) is the most au naturel bra option. The right one can make you look braless, but still supported. They come in varying fabrics and thicknesses. The stretch soft-cup bra is the least boob-altering of bras. This bra will allow more nipple exposure than most, especially if it's seamless.

If your boobs are bigger than a C cup, though, you might find that you prefer the sculpting and support of the underwire version.

PUSH-UP BRA

The push-up bra uses shaping and some padding to shove your boobs up and together, creating super-dramatic cleavage and a pretty serious profile. It gives the wearer a look that's reminiscent of the fifties silhouette, Marilyn Monroe style.

PADDED BRA

Padded bras are designed to make you look bigger and come in many varieties. They usually contain substantially more padding than push-ups, and the padding tends to cover the breast rather than move it into a more obviously visible position.

DEMI BRA

The demi bra is a type of underwire bra that is cut just above the nipple. This bra can be excellent for low-cut necklines. Big boobs can sort of spill out the top, creating a quadruple boob effect.

SPORTS BRA

Sports bras have an obvious purpose, and a huge number of different options are available. It's really important (especially for girls with medium to large boobs) to get a sports bra that is both supportive and comfortable. Sports bras can sometimes smush boobs together. If this bugs you, look for one that has some distinction between the two cups and isn't just made like a tight tank top.

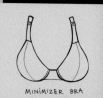

MINIMIZER BRA

The minimizer bra is specially designed to make large boobs look smaller. Usually made of relatively thick fabric, the bra basically compresses your breasts so they don't stick out as much. Minimizers generally have substantial back and straps.

National Organizations

American Medical Women's Association (AMWA) provides information on all aspects of women's health, including maintaining healthy breasts. Address: 801 North Fairfax St., Suite 400, Alexandria, VA 22314. Phone: 703-838-0500. Website: http://www.amwa-doc.org.

Breast Cancer Information Clearinghouse (BCIC), NYSERNet, Inc., 200 Elwood Davis Rd., Suite 103, Liverpool, NY 13088. Phone: 315-453-2912, ext. 225.

National Alliance of Breast Cancer Organizations (NABCO) provides information to anyone with questions about breast cancer. Address: 9 East 37th St., 10th floor, New York, NY 10016. Phone: 800-719-9154. Website: http://www.nabco.org.

National Women's Health Network is a nonprofit organization that seeks to provide women with a greater voice in the health care system. Address: 514 Tenth St., NW, Suite 400, Washington, DC 20004. Phone: 202-347-1140 for information regarding legislation.

Society for the Study of Breast Disease, 3409 Worth, Suite 300, Sammons Tower, Dallas, TX 75246. Phone: 214-821-2962.

The Susan G. Komen Breast Cancer Foundation, the sponsor of Race for the Cure®, seeks to eradicate breast cancer as a life-threatening disease by advocating research, screening, and education. Address: 5005 LBJ Freeway, Suite 370, Dallas, TX 74244. Phone: 972-855-1600 or 800-IM-AWARE for the national breast care help line. Website: http://www.breastcancerinfo.com.

Y-Me National Breast Cancer Organization provides peer counseling, referrals, and written information for breast cancer survivors, patients, family, and friends. Address: 212 West Van Buren, Chicago, IL 60607. Phone: 800-221-2141 (English) or 800-986-9505 (Spanish). Website: http://www.y-me.org/index.html.

Online

Association of Cancer Online Resources (ACOR) at http://www.acor.org provides cancer information and electronic support groups.

Virtual Kid Puberty 101 at http://www.virtualkid.com covers all the changes in your body, including the stages of breast development.

Books

Breasts: Our Most Public Private Parts by Meema Spadola (Wildcat Canyon Press, 1998). Based on a documentary, this book tells people's personal stories about breasts—from adolescents to older women.

Dr. Susan Love's Breast Book by Susan M. Love (Perseus Press, 1995). Comprehensive reference on all things relating to breasts, including screening, diagnosis, treatment, and research.

For more resources and information, see http://www.dealwithit.com

Chapter 2

WHAT'S UP DOWN THERE?

Your sex organs can sometimes seem like mysterious things. Many of them exist inside your body and the ones that don't aren't exactly clearly visible.

But it's crucial to become familiar with what's up down there as you grow and change—for your health, your sexuality, and your overall sense of who you are.

pad cushion pupik bush shrubbery trim pussy
slit hole cunt twat beaver muff box quim
snatch poontang gine vooge flap mohawk vagina
crack cooch coochie fanny jelly roll tail
Y buff puff honeypot vulva hotbox

EXTERNAL REPRODUCTIVE ORGANS

The vulva includes all the outer genitals. It's a good idea to get to know what your own vulva looks like. You can do this by holding a mirror between your legs. Every girl's vulva looks different.

Mons: Also called the mons veneris (mound or mountain of Venus) or mons pubis, it's the soft, slightly raised area over the pubic bone, made up of fatty tissue. Pubic hair often grows here first during puberty.

Urethra: Located between the clitoris and the vaginal opening, the urethra is not a sex organ. It's the tube that carries urine from the bladder to the outside.

Outer lips (labia majora): Unless the legs are spread, the outer lips of the vagina come together and protect the rest of the genitals. They vary in size and shape on different women and become covered with pubic hair during puberty.

HeLLo.

Anus: This little wrinkly hole in your butt is the opening to the rectum, which carries feces out of the body.

Clitoris: The most sensitive spot in the female genitals, the clitoris is a small organ densely packed with extremely sensitive nerve endings, consisting of a head (glans) and body (shaft). Only the glans is directly visible. It is made of tissue that swells during sexual arousal (kind of like an erection in a boy but much less pronounced). The clitoris is the only organ in the body that exists solely for sexual pleasure, and clitoral stimulation is usually necessary to achieve orgasm.

Also see **orgasms** in Sexual Feelings, pp. 76–78.

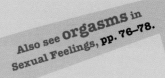

Vaginal opening: This is the opening to your vagina, which is often partially blocked by the hymen. (See the next page for more on the exciting vagina.)

Hymen: A thin piece of skin, the hymen partially blocks the vaginal opening. Hymens come in varying shapes, sizes, and thicknesses, and although most girls are born with one, there are many ways it can be torn or stretched in everyday life. Sexual intercourse can also tear the hymen. So you may still have one, or you may not.

Inner lips (labia minora): The smaller inner lips are hairless and thinner than the outer lips that surround them. There is a lot of variation in shape, size, and color of the inner lips. Some may extend below the outer lips. The inner lips join together at the top to form the hood of the clitoris, and like the clitoris, they are sexually sensitive (they change color when you get sexually excited). A number of other changes happen in your sex organs during sexual arousal.

different looking hymens

See What Is Sex? for more information on **sexual arousal**, pp. 74–75.

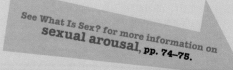

INTERNAL REPRODUCTIVE ORGANS

Cervix: This is the lower part of the uterus.

Vagina: Leading from the uterus (womb) to the outside world, this canal carries menstrual blood and babies. It's about 3 to 5 inches long. When there's nothing inside, the walls of the vagina touch each other. The vagina is very elastic—partly because its walls have many folds, which expand and contract to accommodate whatever it needs to accommodate (a baby, penis, tampon, finger). The vagina is never completely dry. The wetness factor varies according to your cycle, where you are in your development, and sexual arousal. When you get sexually excited, the vagina makes a lot of secretions and feels wet—this provides lubrication for sexual activities. The ever-present secretions also help keep the vagina clean and prevent infection by maintaining the proper pH balance.

The outer third of the vagina has a lot of nerve endings and, as a result, is very sexually sensitive. The inner two-thirds of the vagina don't have as many, so they don't register as much sensation.

Os: This indentation in the center of the cervix is the opening from the uterus to the vagina. It is very tiny, except during childbirth, when it stretches enough to let the baby pass through. The os prevents a large object, like a finger or tampon or penis, from entering the uterus. Menstrual blood flows out through the os, and sperm flows in.

to intestines

Side view

Uterus: The uterus, or womb, is the size and shape of an upside-down pear, unless a woman becomes pregnant. The thick walls of the uterus are very elastic and allow it to grow to many times its original size to accommodate a developing fetus. The lining of the uterus (the endometrium) is what helps nourish a fetus. When there is no fetus in the uterus, the lining is shed monthly—this is menstruation.

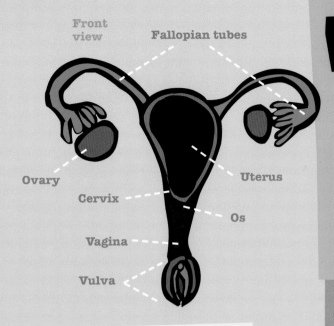

Front view

Fallopian tubes

Ovary

Cervix

Os

Vagina

Vulva

Uterus

Fallopian tubes: These two tubes extend from the top of the uterus in either direction to the ovaries. They are about 4 inches long. Their ends are shaped like fringed tunnels, which surround the ovaries but don't actually attach to them. The fallopian tubes carry the ova (eggs) from the ovary to the uterus each month after ovulation.

Ovaries: About the same size and shape as almonds, the two ovaries house all of the potential eggs in a woman's body. The eggs are stored in little pockets called follicles, and every girl is born with hundreds of thousands of them. During puberty, the pituitary gland produces hormones that travel through the bloodstream to the ovaries, causing the follicles to release one ripe egg per month. This is called ovulation.

OVULATION, MENSTRUATION, AND THE MONTHLY CYCLE

During puberty, girls begin the monthly cycle of ovulation and menstruation, which means they are now able to get pregnant. When this begins is different for every girl. The normal age range for menarche (pronounced "muh-nar-key"; means "getting your first period") is anywhere from 8 to 18 years. Most girls begin to menstruate between the ages of 11 and 14. It takes years before the cycle becomes regular. Menstruation then continues roughly monthly for the next 40 years or so, except during pregnancy and breastfeeding.

Your first period
The best way to predict when you'll start menstruating is to ask female relatives when they started, because a lot of it is hereditary. The rest of your body can also be some indication: the first period usually happens about two years after your breasts start to grow and about one year after you get some pubic hair. It can be frustrating if most of your friends start menstruating before you.

But there are plenty of girls who don't get their first period until their later teens. If you reach 17 and haven't started your period or started to show signs of secondary sexual development (such as breast growth and pubic hair), it's probably a good idea to see a gynecologist.

TICK TOCK

19

Just the facts about
...Periods

Your period is normal as long as it is somewhat regular, whatever the length of your cycle or your period itself.

The length of a cycle is usually 21 to 35 days (28 is average).

The length of each period is 2 to 8 days (4 to 6 days is average), with bleeding stopping and starting throughout.

Cycles change over the course of your life, depending on various things, like stress, age, weight gain or loss, or having a baby.

Women today have more menstrual periods than ever before (400 to 500 in a lifetime). That's because they start menstruating earlier, live longer (because of better nutrition and health care), and have fewer pregnancies.

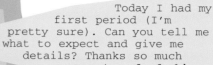

Today I had my first period (I'm pretty sure). Can you tell me what to expect and give me details? Thanks so much guys! - **slamdunkie**

So, you've started your period today. Well, sister, it isn't any grand party. It is gross, uncomfortable, and, in some situations, embarrassing. But, you just wanted advice, so here it is: a) Your period may be very irregular at first, so don't freak if you don't have it again for a couple of months. My best friend had an interval of five months between her first and second periods. b) Pay special attention to your flow at first. It has a tendency to fluctuate constantly and your timing may go a little haywire. I can't think of anything else right now, but, sister, stay strong. Oh, and I forgot to say, congratulations.
- **artista**

Girls, somebody help me out! I just started my first period, but it's brown, not red! I'm not sure if this is normal or what?
- **lilpup**

Most of the time mine is brown and so is a lot of other girls'. It's normal. Every girl is different.
- **pHraNC**

When can you get pregnant?
You can get pregnant anytime there is a ripe egg in your fallopian tube or uterus and there are sperm around to fertilize the egg.

The ripe egg will stay in your fallopian tube for about 3 days after ovulation. And sperm can live 3 to 4 days. So there can be living sperm waiting in the fallopian tubes at the moment of ovulation even if you haven't had sex for 3 days.

It's almost impossible to know exactly when you are going to ovulate, especially because your body sometimes changes on you. Use birth control every time you have sex—it eliminates anxiety and guesswork.

It is possible to get pregnant during your period too—a girl with a shorter cycle could ovulate just 2 or 3 days after her period begins.

Here's what happens every month or so:

WEEK 1

Every month, the pituitary gland in the brain signals the ovaries to produce follicle-stimulating hormone (FSH) and luteinizing hormone (LH), which stimulates at least one follicle to develop a mature **egg**.

As the egg matures, the follicle releases the hormone estrogen, which causes the **lining** of the uterus to grow and thicken.

WEEK 2

OVULATION When it is ripe enough, the **egg** is released from the follicle in the ovary, drawn into the funnel-shaped end of one of the fallopian tubes, and then starts heading for the uterus. It takes the egg a few days to get there. Most women do not notice when they ovulate, but some do feel a slight twinge or a bit of abdominal discomfort.

Around this time, estrogen levels are high, causing your **vaginal discharge** to be copious and watery.

The follicle now releases the hormone progesterone, which nourishes the uterine **lining**.

WEEK 3

After ovulation, as progesterone levels rise, your **vaginal discharge** becomes stickier and scanter.

If sperm is present when the **egg** is traveling down the fallopian tube, fertilization or conception can occur. If it does, the uterine **lining** should be ready to accept and nourish the fertilized egg.

If the **egg** is not fertilized, it disintegrates and flows out the vagina (usually before your period). The follicle decreasingly continues to produce estrogen and progesterone for about 12 days.

WEEK 4

MENSTRUATION As hormone levels drop, the **lining** in the uterus stops being nourished and finally sheds itself—your period. Most of the lining is shed. The bottom stays and is the foundation for the next month's lining.

Once you get your period, the cycle starts all over again.

what's up down there?

Dealing with the flow

Most girls deal with their menstrual flow by using tampons or pads or a combination of the two. As with everything, different girls have different preferences about this, and it's really a matter of finding the method that you are most comfortable with.

However you decide to deal, do not use deodorant tampons or pads—many girls are allergic to the unnecessary chemicals.

tampons

Tampons are internal protection. They are cylindrical objects made out of pressed layers of absorbent cotton, about the length and thickness of a thumb. They have a string attached to one end for easy removal and can come in a paper or plastic applicator, which makes them easier to insert into the vagina. Tampons come in different levels of absorbency (from slim for light flow to super-plus for a very heavy flow). Use the lowest absorbency possible. Cardboard applicators are safer to use than plastic, as there is less chance of scratching your vagina.

Pros: Comfort and convenience! You won't even be aware that you have a tampon in if you've inserted it correctly. Can go swimming during your period with no embarrassment. No mess (as long as you change it often enough).

Cons: Can cause irritation in the vagina, especially if the vagina gets too dry. Small risk of toxic shock syndrome (TSS). (See p. 24.) Some women find that internal protection feels invasive.

The learning curve : Inserting a tampon the first few times can be difficult and uncomfortable. For one thing, you've got to

I'm kinda scared putting in a tampon will hurt too much. Did any of you ever have a problem like this? Sometimes when I try, the tampon won't really go up the hole that much. Am I being immature? Should I just stick it in? Is it supposed to hurt the first time? Please help!
— **nosyparker**

The key is to relax. That's the best thing you can do to make it feel better. Also, insert the tampon at a 30- or 45-degree angle, toward your lower back, not straight. It might hurt a little the 1st time, but like a little pinch. If you're in mortal pain, you have a problem. If after following this advice you're still having the same problems, get your mom, sister, female relative, or friend who already wears tampons to help you—sit in the bathroom with you for a little coaching or something. Believe me, it works!
— **bucketofblood**

find your vaginal opening. For another, you've got to stick something into your vagina, possibly for the first time. Another tricky part is finding the right angle of insertion. Because of the advantages of tampons, the learning curve is usually well worth the trouble. Tampon boxes come with pretty good instructions. So read them and RELAX. It might help to have an experienced tampon user talk you through it. Allow yourself a good amount of time for trial and error. It's a new and unfamiliar routine. It's probably easiest to use tampons with applicators when you're first getting the hang of it.

Are tampons or pads better?
- **pippiL**

there is no answer to your question. me, i like both, but when i am in public and at parties i like tampons. they last longer and you don't have to worry if your butt looks huge. it all depends on what you are more comfortable with.
- **humbelina**

It all depends on your opinion. Some people like tampons becuz they stay in and don't fall out and you can swim in them most of the time, but others feel uncomfortable with a tampon and like a pad better.
- **RNBlover**

I started with tampons because they allow you to go up to 8 hours worry-free. Some people don't think they are comfortable, but I think you should experiment and find out which you prefer.
- **child-o-mine**

i think tampons are so much better than pads. Why? Cause they are so much easier at school. PADS—bulky and bunchy and not as absorbent, and they leak and they can't be worn as long as a tampon. TAMPONS—no odor, as easy to put in as take out, they feel like they're not even there, and they can stay in for about 8 hrs. It's all up to you.
- **dawLparts**

pads

Pads are external protection. They stick to your underwear with adhesive, and lock in the blood as it flows out. They come in all shapes and sizes—thin, thick, with and without "wings."

Pros: No risk of TSS or vaginal irritation from tampons. No tampon insertion learning curve. Some women find that a pad allows for a more natural flow out of the body. Pads keep the wearer consious of the physical experience she is going through.

Cons: Need to be changed every 3 or 4 hours. Can get smelly. Can't be flushed down the toilet—must be wrapped in toilet paper and thrown in garbage. Can make you feel like you're wearing diapers.

alternative protection

There are a few other methods of period protection that might appeal to the environmentally-minded girl. One is a natural sponge (available in health food stores), which you dampen and insert with your fingers, pull out every few hours, wash out with water, and reinsert. If it develops an odor, you soak it in a weak vinegar solution. When it starts to disintegrate, throw it away.

A relatively new product is a soft, disposable "menstrual cup," which can be inserted and left in for as long as 12 hours, less on heavy days. This can be worn during sexual intercourse.

Toxic Shock Syndrome

Tampons are totally safe if you use them correctly. Toxic shock syndrome (TSS) is a rare and sometimes fatal bacterial illness that is usually associated with super-absorbent tampons that are not changed often enough. Although the incidence of TSS is small (about 5 to 10 out of 100,000 menstruating women using tampons), it's important to know its symptoms: sudden fever of 102 degrees or higher; nausea, vomiting, and severe diarrhea; headache or dizziness; sore throat; muscle aches; and a sunburn-like rash or peeling skin (most common on the hands and feet).

If you have any of these symptoms during your period, remove your tampon and see a doctor right away. If you catch TSS early, it can be cured with antibiotics.

Take these precautions to avoid TSS:
- Change your tampons frequently, at least every 4 hours.
- Use the least absorbent one you can.
- Don't sleep while wearing a tampon.
- Use cardboard applicators.
- Wash your hands before and after inserting a tampon.
- Never insert a tampon that has come unwrapped.
- Only use tampons when you're menstruating!

PMS

PMS (premenstrual syndrome) is the term for a bunch of different symptoms that women experience in the days leading up to their periods. Women's experiences of this vary widely. Some women don't experience any difference at all; others just get cramps; others have a combination of highly irritating symptoms. There is no agreed-upon biological cause for PMS, but one thing to know is that hormone levels are lowest during this time. To alleviate symptoms, exercise regularly and limit salt, sugar, caffeine, and alcohol. Eat a balanced diet with lots of vegetables and carbohydrates.

Many premenstrual symptoms can continue during your period.

Depression, tension, and moodiness: Getting more upset than usual about things or getting upset about things you'd otherwise ignore. Vitamin B and calcium help some people with these symptoms.

Bloating: The sodium in salt causes water retention, especially in the stomach and breasts.

For more information on treating breakouts, see **pp. 37–38.**

Fatigue and headache: Rest and over-the-counter pain relievers containing ibuprofen (Motrin, Advil, Panadol) can often help.

Acne: The usual treatments can help hormone-related outbreaks.

Breast tenderness: Breasts may swell and feel sore during your period.

Cramps and backache: Prostaglandins, the hormonelike substances that trigger labor pains, also cause menstrual cramps. They stimulate the uterine muscles to contract and help the body expel menstrual fluid. These contractions can range from mild to intense and can sometimes also be felt all the way around to the back, causing backache. Prostaglandin production (and therefore menstrual cramps) can be blocked by taking ibuprofen, preferably just before the cramping starts, since it's more effective at preventing than curing the pain once it has already started. Stress also stimulates prostaglandin production, so stress-busting exercise, relaxation and deep breathing techniques, and yoga can all be effective. Exercise is good because it releases the body's own natural painkillers, endorphins.

Some natural remedies that work for some but not all women include raspberry leaf tea, cramp bark tea, vitamin B6, vitamin E, calcium supplements, and evening primrose oil (an herbal supplement). Soaking in a warm bath or applying heat to the stomach or lower back can help get you through the tough parts.

It's important to pay attention to yourself and get used to your own cycle so you know what's going on with you. If you do experience any kind of PMS, try out different methods of dealing with it and remember what works. Pay attention to symptoms that recur from month to month. If things get really severe for you in the week leading up to your period and nothing seems to help, see a doctor who is experienced in treating PMS.

the wide world of periods

Here are some of the rituals that have marked menstruation throughout the ages and throughout the world:

In Ghana, the Asante tribe puts a newly menstruating girl underneath a special ceremonial umbrella and sings and dances to her.

The Oglala Sioux in the western United States had an elaborate ritual to celebrate a girl's first period. First, her family built her a special tepee, where she could retreat and reflect on the profundity of her new fertile and womanly status. A holy man conducted a ritual of purification, burning sweet grass, smoking a pipe, and chanting and praying over a painted buffalo skull. The girl was then fed buffalo meat and the family feasted.

Many cultures expect a menstruating woman to isolate herself on the premise that she is unclean and may contaminate others. Some native people in Hawaii, Guyana and Mali make use of "menstrual huts," special structures where women retreat during their periods. A Hindu woman must abstain from worship and cooking and must distance herself from the members of her family during her period. In Zoroastrianism, an ancient religion still practiced by some people in India, women are considered impure while menstruating and need to go through a ritual of purification.

Orthodox Jewish women are also considered impure during their periods, and their husbands are forbidden to have sex with them during this time. Seven days after their period ends, the women are required to take a ritual bath, the mikvah, which makes them ready to resume sexual activity. Among some Orthodox Jewish immigrants at the turn of the century, a girl's first period was accompanied by a slap across the face from her mother, to signify and alert her to the future travails of being a woman.

what's up down there?

Historical and Cultural Views of PMS

For a long time, premenstrual complaints were considered a sign of emotional weakness in women or figments of their imaginations. Sigmund Freud said the discomfort was the result of women crying into their wombs because they weren't pregnant.

PMS burst into the national consciousness in the early 1980s when it was invoked as a defense in several notorious criminal cases in the United States and Britain. In one case a woman claimed she beat her 4-year-old child to death in a rage brought on by PMS.

In 1987 PMS was classified as a psychiatric disorder, a designation that has been criticized by feminists and others as stigmatizing women. If women are thought to be unstable and out of control each month for a week, they could theoretically be barred from certain jobs.

Today, PMS is increasingly recognized as a condition with biological roots.

Menstrual problems

There are certain irregular period symptoms you should take seriously. Most of the time, nothing will really be wrong. A woman's cycle changes over the course of her life. But better safe than sorry, so if you are suffering from any of the following, see your doctor.

Heavy bleeding: You soak through a tampon or pad every hour for a day or more.

Prolonged bleeding: Your period doesn't show signs of slowing down or stopping after a week. (If blood just trickles out at past a week, that's not a problem.)

Irregular cycles: Your cycles are less than 21 days or more than 35 days for three consecutive cycles—although it's common to menstruate irregularly for the first year or so.

Spotting: A day or two of light bleeding that is not during your period. Some women spot regularly around ovulation.

Severe cramping (dysmenorrhea): Your cramps are so strong that they're debilitating, or you're having cramps at times other than the three days before and during your period.

Absence of periods: You haven't gotten your period by the time you're 17 (primary amenorrhea), or you have gotten your period, but it has stopped and you have missed more than three periods (secondary amenorrhea). If your cycles are regular and you are having sex and have missed one period, you should take a home pregnancy test and see a doctor if it's positive.

For information on pregnancy tests, see **p. 123.**

COMMON CROTCH CONCERNS

Although the following conditions are normal, everyday parts of being female, if anything is bothering you, don't hesitate to talk to your doctor about your concerns.

Vaginal odor

Vaginal odor should be pretty inoffensive and is a natural part of having a vagina. Sweat and oil glands in your vulva become more active during puberty, making the whole area moister and more aromatic. The odor changes according to where you are in your cycle, among other factors.

The fact that sex organs have a smell is part of their specific function. There are pheromones (sex attractors) in the vaginal fluid that actually arouse sexual interest. It's not necessary or desirable to mask your odor with douches or vaginal sprays. Keeping yourself clean and changing your underwear (cotton underwear is especially good) daily should be good enough.

If you do notice a particularly pungent odor, you may have an infection. Look for other symptoms of infection, like abnormal discharge, and call your doctor if you suspect a problem.

Does anyone have a, um...weird smell from their vagina? — **hopey**

Sure there's a bit of an odor, but it's perfectly normal to have. — **viceversa**

Urinary tract infection (UTI)

Symptoms: May have blood in urine; painful burning urination; frequent urgent need to urinate.

Treatment: Oral antibiotics.

To prevent: Drink lots of water every day, and try unsweetened cranberry juice. Urinate frequently (don't try to hold it in), and empty your bladder completely each time. Urinate before and after sexual intercourse. And always wipe from front to back.

Douching

Douching is cleaning out the vagina with a solution of water and vinegar or a commercial douche preparation. The solution is put into a special bag or bottle and squeezed into the vagina through a bulb.

There's no need to douche. It only temporarily masks the odor and may even increase cancer rates. Not only is the vagina self-cleaning, but its normal acidic balance can be thrown off by douching. Douching can also introduce foreign organisms into the vagina that can cause infection.

what's up down there?

I'm 13 years old, and for the past few months I've found yellowish or clearish stuff in my panties. It's pretty disgusting. Sometimes it's almost like a gel. It's embarrassing whenever I put my clothes in the laundry because I know my mom sees it—she has to. But she hasn't said anything about it. Anyway, it's really putrid, and I want to know why it's happening. I have heard that it means that I am starting my period soon, but I am pretty small and not very far into "development."
What does it mean?

— **emptyglass**

Relax! This is normal! It's called vaginal discharge. I have been getting it for a while and b4 I was pretty well developed! I've had that discharge for like 2 years and still haven't gotten my period. Don't worry!

— **sPacecowgurl**

Are there any signs that DO mean there's a problem, just to be safe? — **teeenie**

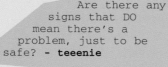

There is normal and abnormal discharge. If your discharge is smelly, thick, cottage cheese-like, or itchy, you might have a problem like a yeast infection. You should call your doctor if you see any of the signs I mentioned. Otherwise everything should be normal.

— **ladyliberty**

Vaginal discharge

The vagina cleans itself out with secretions that eventually end up in your underwear. Vaginal discharge is made up of mucus, bacteria, and discarded cells. You'll probably start noticing this discharge a year or two before your first period.

Normal vaginal discharge is wet, clear to milky white in color and is not itchy or irritating. It may turn light yellow and crusty on your underwear after it is exposed to the air. Discharge changes in amount and texture over the course of the month due to fluctuating hormone levels. Sexual excitement also causes a major increase in vaginal secretions.

As long as your discharge remains colorless and basically odorless, it is nothing to worry about. But there are some abnormal discharges caused by vaginal infections (vaginitis).

For information about STDs, see Protection, **pp. 103–19.**

Vaginitis

Discharge is abnormal if it is itchy or burning, has a foul odor, is mixed with blood (nonmenstrual), or is a different color from your normal discharge. If any of these symptoms occur, see your doctor.

The following chart can give you an idea of some possible causes of your symptoms. This is meant for informational purposes only, not for diagnosis. Only a health care professional can diagnose and treat vaginitis.

YOUR PANTIES

Infection	Looks Like	Feels Like	Treatment
Gardenerella	Thick, creamy grayish-white discharge; foul, fishy odor	Usually non-irritating	Antibiotics (prescribed by a doctor)
Yeast Infection (Candida)	Thick, odorless white discharge; may be lumpy like cottage cheese.	Itching, painful urination	Anti-fungal inserted into vagina, but ask a doctor (don't self-medicate)
Trichomoniasis	Frothy, greenish-yellow, foul-smelling discharge	Itching; painful urination; inflammation of vulva; sometimes lower abdominal pain	Oral antibiotics or topical ones (applied to the skin)

what's up down there?

WHAT TO EXPECT FROM A VISIT TO THE GYNECOLOGIST

Like anything else, your sexual apparatus requires some care to ensure good health. Gynecologists are the doctors who have generously devoted their lives to the maintenance of female crotches. Sometimes they also deliver babies, in which case they are obstetricians as well (ob/gyn).

You should have your first internal exam when you're 18 or when you start to think seriously about having sex, whichever comes first. You should also try to schedule it for a day sometime in the middle of your cycle, when you will not be menstruating or on the verge.

If your doctor is a man, a female nurse probably will stay in the room during the exam. If a nurse doesn't stay, don't be embarrassed to ask for one. The doctor will first talk to you about your menstrual cycle and ask if you have any questions or concerns. This is the time to bring up birth control, if you are (or plan to soon be) sexually active.

Most doctors won't tell your parents or anyone else what goes on during your exam (unless you want them to know). The right to confidentiality in matters of birth control has been the subject of some controversy in Congress in the last couple of years, but no state has yet passed a law requiring parental notification for birth control. Some states leave it up to the discretion of the doctor, so you might want to make sure that you and your doctor are on the same page when it comes to informing your parents.

After you talk, the doctor will examine your breasts and show you how to do a monthly self-exam (to check for lumps).

Next, you'll have to rest your feet in the stirrups (metal U-shapes) with your legs spread. This allows the doctor the right vantage point to see what needs to be seen. The physician sees dozens of vulvas a day and is completely unfazed by them.

Next is the fabulous speculum experience. The speculum is a metal or plastic instrument that looks sort of like tongs and is designed to hold the walls of the vagina apart so the doctor can look inside. Having a speculum put in can be uncomfortable, especially if you are tense. Deep, even breaths will relax your muscles.

The doctor will look into your vagina to make sure everything looks healthy and normal, checking for redness and inflammation of the vaginal walls (signs of infection); for cuts, tears, or cysts in the cervix; and for unusual discharge.

Next comes the Pap smear. The doctor will insert a swab that looks like a large Q-tip into your vagina and rub it across your cervix to sample some cells. This sounds painful, but whatever discomfort you experience is minor and very momentary. The cell sample is analyzed to check for cancer or a pre-cancerous condition of the cervix. You can get an abnormal Pap result from a minor infection.

Cervical cancer is very curable if it is caught in the early stages. That's why it's so important to make sure you **have a Pap smear every year**. Some doctors recommend having them every 6 months if you take birth control pills, have genital herpes, or have numerous sex partners. If you are sexually active, the doctor will also take a sample of cells to check for gonorrhea.

After the speculum is removed, the doctor will perform a bimanual vaginal exam, checking your internal organs with his or her hands. The doctor inserts one or two fingers into your vagina while putting his or her other hand on your lower abdomen. By feeling around and pressing with both hands, the doctor can assess the size, shape, and position of your uterus, ovaries, and fallopian tubes and check for swelling or growths. This might feel weird, but it shouldn't hurt. If you feel pain, tell the doctor.

Sometimes a rectal exam is also performed. The physician will insert a finger into your rectum to feel the internal organs from a different angle.

Then you are all done. If you're getting birth control, now is the time to learn how to use it.

If at any point you feel rushed, are not encouraged to ask questions, or are otherwise treated disrespectfully, find another doctor. It's your body, and you need to find someone you are comfortable with to help you take care of it.

National Organizations

The American College of Obstetricians and Gynecologists (ACOG) has free information on every imaginable gynecological condition and concern. Address: 409 12th Street, SW, Washington, D.C. 20024-2188. Phone: 202-638-5577. Website: http://www.acog.com; or e-mail specific questions about adolescent health to: adolhth@acog.org.

American Medical Women's Association (AMWA) provides information on all aspects of women's health. Address: 801 North Fairfax St., Suite 400, Alexandria, VA 22314. Phone: 703-838-0500. Website: http://www.amwa-doc.org.

Planned Parenthood Federation of America, 810 Seventh Avenue, New York, NY 10019. Phone: 212-541-7800 or 800-230-PLAN to locate a Planned Parenthood in your area. Website: http://www.teenwire.com (Planned Parenthood's candid site for teenagers) or www.igc.apc.org/ppfa.

Online

Body Matters at http://www.bodymatters.com, sponsored by Tampax, helps you understand your body throughout your reproductive years.

Health Index at http://www.healthindex.org provides information about a variety of health conditions, including symptoms and treatments. It also provides links to the sites of major medical organizations.

The **Go Ask Alice** website at http://www.goaskalice.columbia.edu answers a multitude of questions about health, dating, sexuality, drug use, depression, and more.

Museum of Menstruation (MUM) at http://www.mum.org offers a tour of this unique museum in Maryland, open from 1994 to 1998 and currently looking for a new location.

The Red Spot at http://www.onewoman.com/redspot is all about periods.

Virtual Kid Puberty 101 at http://www.virtualkid.com answers your questions about all the changes in your body.

Books

Cunt: A Declaration of Independence by Inga Muscio (Seal Press). A provocative analysis of women's relationships to their bodies.

Finding Our Way: The Teen Girls' Survival Guide by Allison Abner and Linda Villarosa (Harperperennial). A candid take on body image, physical changes, birth control, relationships with friends, and more.

Go Ask Alice: A Guide to Good Physical, Sexual, and Emotional Health by Columbia University's Health Education Program (Henry Holt). Based on the website, the book answers questions about the whole range of health, sexuality, and emotional well-being concerns.

Our Bodies, Ourselves for the New Century: A Book by and for Women by Boston Women's Health Book Collective (Touchstone Books). The classic book on women's health and awareness, recently updated to include online resources and discussions of AIDS.

Changing Bodies, Changing Lives: A Book for Teens on Sex and Relationships by Ruth Bell (Times Books). A superb book covering all aspects of teen sexuality, relationships, and coping with life.

The Period Book: Everything You Don't Want to Ask (But Need to Know) by Karen Gravelle and Jennifer Gravelle (Walker & Co.). Illustrated with cartoons, this aunt-niece team tackles touchy issues about menstruation.

The Planned Parenthood Women's Health Encyclopedia (Crown). Alphabetical entries on all aspects of women's health, with resources throughout.

The Vagina Monologues by Eve Ensler (Dutton). Adapted from the award-winning one-woman show, giving voice to a chorus of vaginal perspectives.

Woman to Woman by Yvonne S. Thornton, M.D. (Dutton). All about women's bodies, written anecdotally by a gynecologist.

Women's Bodies, Women's Wisdom by Christiane Northrup (Bantam Doubleday Dell). Feminist discussion of women's physical and emotional concerns and their treatments, including holistic approaches.

For more resources and information, see http://www.dealwithit.com

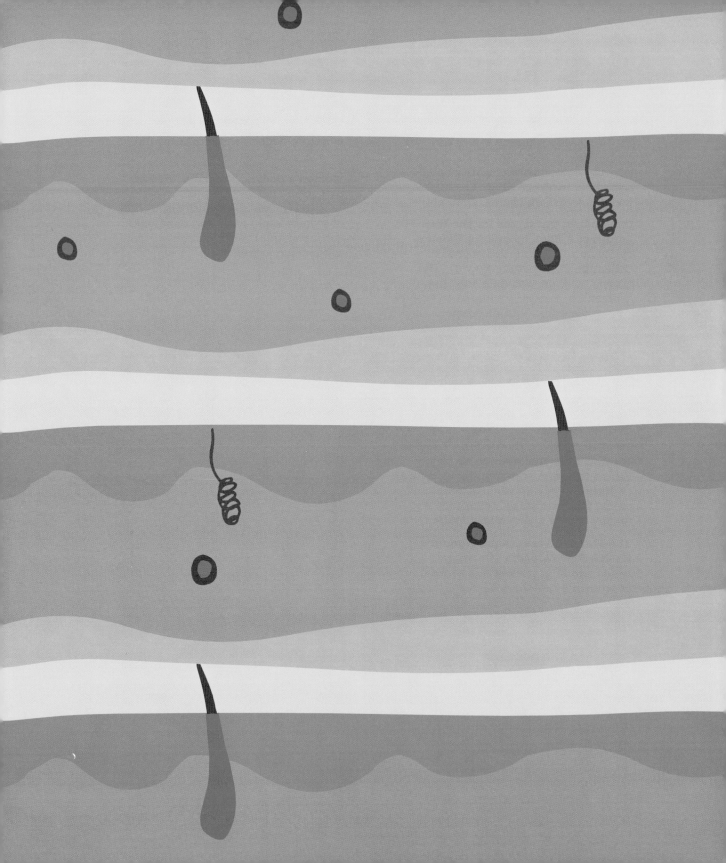

Chapter 3

SKiN

Your skin is your largest organ, covering your entire body. Like other body parts, hormones play a role in how your skin changes during adolescence. This can present some irritating problems.

SOME COMMON SKIN CONDITIONS

Pimples can appear anywhere on the body, but unfortunately tend to congregate mostly on the face, back, and chest.

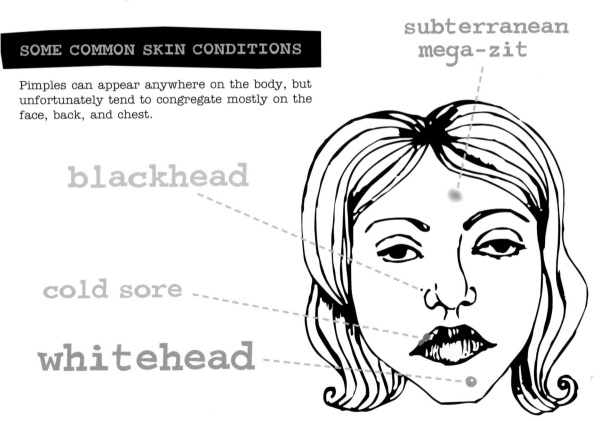

subterranean mega-zit

blackhead

cold sore

whitehead

Zits

The pores of your skin contain sebaceous (pronounced "se-bay-shis") glands, which make sebum (pronounced "see-bum"), an oil for your hair and skin. Usually, the right amount of sebum is made and everything is fine. But sometimes a pore gets clogged up with too much sebum and dead skin cells. Then it ruptures and becomes inflamed and you get a whitehead, blackhead, or pimple.

This is likely to happen when you're a teenager because of the normal influx of androgens, generally considered male sex hormones. (Testosterone is an androgen.) As your body changes and matures, these hormones, produced in a woman's ovaries and adrenal glands, stimulate oil production. The overactive oil-producing glands tend to be concentrated in what is known as the T-zone, which runs across the forehead and down the nose and chin—prime zit territory. There is also an abundance of oil glands in the chest and back, where zits may also appear.

You may notice that you tend to break out more at certain times in your menstrual cycle. In particular, breakouts often tend to occur in response to the increased level of the hormone progesterone, which your body produces after ovulation and before menstruation. Anxiety and stress can also spur breakouts because they cause the adrenal glands to make more androgens.

> My cheeks are nothing but these big red zits that just seem to keep recurring. It's so depressing. I feel like some big medical experiment.
> **— buttknocker**

> I know what you mean—I feel so awful and self-conscious, thanks to my overactive oil glands making these awful spots. Since eighth grade I have never had a day without at least four zits on my face. I can't stand it.
> **— Tetriz**

> This is gross, but does anyone get zits on their behinds? I do, but I hardly ever get them on my face! They hurt too! Is it weird?
> **— spiderleg**

> The other day I was messing with my nose and I squeezed a blackhead and some hard clear junk came out. What was it in my blackhead? Was it okay to pop it?
> **— longface**

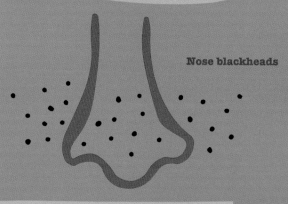

Nose blackheads

Blackheads, whiteheads, and pimples

If a pore gets clogged up but stays open, the top surface can get dark and then you have a blackhead. If a pore gets clogged up and closes and begins bulging from the skin, then you have a pimple. If bacteria gets into a pore, it can infect the oil gland, which produces redness and that gross whitish yellowish pus—the whitehead.

Don't touch, squeeze, pick at, or pop your zits. Squeezing or popping pimples can force the oil and bacteria into the deeper skin layers, which can cause cysts. You can make pimples worse by poking at them or opening them up. Picking at pimples can leave small but permanent scars on your face.

ZIT REMEDIES

> I have a whole bunch of little pimples on my cheeks, and my friend and I both use the same product for our skin. At first her skin was clear for about a year and then her cheeks broke out really badly. I have been using it for a year now too, and I'm scared my skin will get like hers. **- permia**

> I have tried many products that my friends say have worked for them, and have found that different things are going to work for different people. I mean, not everyone has the same acne or the same type of skin...so maybe your skin will be okay.
> **- underthewire**

Basic prevention

Heredity is the number one cause of acne. If your parents and siblings had a lot of pimples, it is likely that you will too. While there's not much you can do about your genetic makeup, there are various treatments you can use for more or less serious pimple problems.

It's important to keep your face clean, especially if you are prone to getting pimples. Bacteria and a lot of dead skin cells lying around can exacerbate the situation. Cleaning the problem areas of your skin should be done gently: use mild, preferably liquid, cleaners rather than soaps, harsh detergents, astringents, or, worst of all, abrasive exfoliants. No scrubs! Scrubbing, even with a washcloth, can actually create acne.

Different kinds of skin require different kinds of care. What works to get rid of a zit on one person's face will not necessarily work for another. People with dry skin need to avoid drying it out further (with astringents or benzoyl peroxide, for example), since it can become red and irritated more easily. With combination skin, which is usually oily in the T-zone (forehead, nose, and chin), and dry everywhere else, you'll need to treat different parts of your face with special care.

Over-the-counter stuff

Benzoyl peroxide is the old standby in treating acne, and it is an ingredient in many over-the-counter medications. It kills bacteria, slows the production of oil, and is a peeling and drying agent. It helps the body loosen the plugs in clogged pores and follicles and slough off the dead cells.

Alpha-hydroxy acids (AHAs), also found in over-the-counter creams, are good for mild acne and fine facial lines. These acids are derived from milk, sugarcane, and other fruits that are thought to be skin-softening.

Dermatologist-prescribed drugs

If washing and applying over-the-counter salves don't make a dent, see a dermatologist. The doctor may suggest antibiotics or the more radical drug Accutane. Each of these has side affects. If you have any kind of adverse reaction from a drug, call the doctor for advice.

Retin-A is a cream available by prescription only. It contains a derivative of vitamin A, which is actually the oldest skin-care vitamin. It works by accelerating the turnover of skin, slowing the buildup of debris in the pores, and boosting the production of elastins in the skin. Not only is it effective in treating pimples, it also seems to erase fine lines, freckles, and blotches. The downside is that it can leave the skin more sensitive to the sun and, if overused, can cause irritation, scaling, and peeling.

Accutane is an oral medication prescribed for severe cases of acne. It contains a powerful synthetic vitamin A derivative that sharply reduces oil production. The downside is that it is very drying and can leave the lips, nose, and eyes rather parched. It should be used in conjunction with a good moisturizer. Also, very important, do not use it if you are pregnant or think you might be. Doctors will prescribe the pill along with Accutane to ensure that you don't get pregnant while taking it because Accutane has been associated with birth defects.

Natural remedies

There are tons of alternative or "natural" remedies for skin problems out there. Different things work for different people.

Many people put masks on their faces (made of clay, fruits, vegetables, mayon-

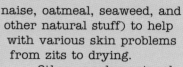

naise, oatmeal, seaweed, and other natural stuff) to help with various skin problems from zits to drying.

Other popular natural skin remedies include: steaming your face (holding it over a bowl of boiling water) to open and unclog pores; or applying vitamin E to reduce the effects of scarring.

Food and skin

Some people believe that eating chocolate and greasy foods makes your skin break out. More doctors than not say that what you eat has nothing to do with your skin. Still, as always, paying attention to yourself is a good idea. If you notice any patterns to your breakouts, take them seriously. If you always get pimples after you eat a certain thing, stop eating it and see what happens.

One of the best things you can do for your skin is to drink lots and lots of water. It flushes out impurities and helps keep the skin hydrated in a healthy way.

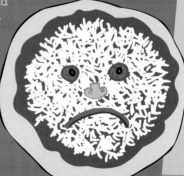

Cold sores and the herpes virus

Cold sores or fever blisters are caused by a strain of the herpes virus (herpes simplex I), which is a close cousin to the virus that causes genital herpes (herpes simplex II). Like many viruses, the one that causes cold sores is contagious. It enters the body through the skin and mucous membranes (the nose and mouth—where most breakouts usually occur). Some people are more susceptible to cold sores than others. Being run-down and sick makes people more vulnerable to all viruses, including this one. Since cold sores are contagious, it's best to avoid mouth contact with people when you have one, or when they do. You also shouldn't share lipstick or a toothbrush, and should consider getting rid of any lipstick you do use during a flareup, or at the very least, cutting off the tip.

For more information on genital herpes, see STDs, p. 112.

The herpes virus never leaves your body once it's there, and many people get cold sores on their mouths periodically throughout their lives. Flareups are often provoked by stress, sickness, or sun exposure (using sunblock around your nose and mouth can help prevent breakouts). Untreated, cold sores usually go away within a week or two.

There are various over-the-counter creams that can help with the symptoms of cold sores, and some that claim to help prevent them. Natural medicine practitioners also suggest taking lysine supplements. (Lysine is an amino acid that isn't produced by the body—supplements are available in most drug stores or health food shops.) If cold sores are a big source of angst for you (and they are for many sufferers), you can talk to your doctor about prescription medication that can be taken orally to lessen your outbreaks.

STRETCH MARKS

During puberty, stretch marks can appear where growth has been quite sudden and pronounced, mostly hips and breasts, sometimes stomachs. Stretch marks start out as purplish lines where the skin has lost some of its elasticity. Some women get stretch marks on their bellies after pregnancy. Also, people who drop a lot of weight in a relatively short time may get them.

Some people find it helpful to rub Vitamin E or almond oil on their stretch marks. There are also special creams with cocoa butter, made for reducing stretch marks from pregnancy. Stretch marks don't generally altogether disappear, but with time, they fade to shimmery, silvery lines.

Stretch marks come and go with weight gain and loss and some eventually will fade while others won't.

I think I'm sort of average weight, but I have stretch marks all over: On my inner thigh I have marks running about 1/3 of the way down to my knee. I also have them on my hips and a little on my chest. I'm embarrassed to wear swimsuits. In fact, last summer every time I went swimming I wore a T-shirt over my swimsuit.
— **mewmew**

I know how you feel. I have stretch marks on my butt, thighs, and boobs. I have mine because I went thru my growth spurt at a young age and my skin couldn't keep up with my bones.
— **criebaby**

Don't be afraid to wear a bathing suit! No one will even notice. My friend has some stretch marks and she wears a bathing suit all summer. — **cHirp**

Don't sweat it. The same thing happened to me. It will take some time, but your stretch marks will almost disappear. You won't really see them because they are light!
— **gunshy**

skin

future wrinkled person

SUN PROTECTION

There isn't much doubt anymore that long-term excessive exposure to the sun and frequent tans and sunburns are a terrible idea. They age the skin prematurely and have played a major role in the increased incidence of skin cancer worldwide.

Each year, the sun is solely responsible for one million new cases of skin cancer. Most are not life-threatening, but many are disfiguring. Most people's damaging sun exposure occurs before the age of 20.

For any outdoor activities, use a "broad spectrum" sunscreen, meaning one that protects against both kinds of ultraviolet radiation from the sun (UVAs and UVBs), with a sun protection factor (SPF) of at least 15. It's good to apply it 20 minutes before going outside, and to reapply every few hours, even on cloudy days.

Everyone needs to learn about sun protection from an early age and practice it religiously.

People with really fair skin should take additional measures, like wearing tightly woven clothing, wide-brimmed hats, staying in the shade, and avoiding peak sun hours between 10 a.m. and 4 p.m. Although people with fair skin are most vulnerable to sunburns, people with all skin colors are susceptible to skin cancer and should practice sun protection.

B.O.

Sweat is the body's way of cleansing and cooling itself naturally. Androgens stimulate sweat and oil glands in the armpits, back, hands, feet, and vulva. Hormone levels are highest right before your period, causing more sweat. Odor often accompanies sweat, since bacteria grow in warm, wet places.

Dealing with B.O.

Keeping clean helps to keep bacteria and odor away.

Clothes and underwear made of natural fibers (cotton, wool, silk) absorb and ventilate wetness better than clothes made of other materials and so keep you drier.

And then you have the choice of using a deodorant or antiperspirant.

Deodorants partially cover up the smell but do not stop the sweating.

Antiperspirants actually stop perspiration before it starts, due to the chemical aluminum chlorohydrate.

There have been studies that suggest that the aluminum may soak through the skin into the bloodstream and cause harm, though nothing conclusive has come of these studies. Some people are allergic to aluminum chlorohydrate. If you start itching, switch to a deodorant only.

Though certain antiperspirants and deodorants are supposed to be specifically for men or women, this gender-based deodorizing is strictly a marketing ploy.

One of my friends has horrible body odor. She is really nice and I really like being her friend. But her smell just grosses me out. When she walks down the hall, people go "who smells?" I feel bad for her. But should I tell her? - **sosagirl**

Girl, you need to tell your friend that she has body odor. If you don't, someone else will, and they might not be as gentle as you would.
- **smoonie**

Maybe it's best if you don't tell her, as she might get seriously offended. Instead, try to make her smell wonderful by buying some products and saying "This smells really nice. Do you wanna try it?" Maybe you should also try to hint about the smell, but don't tell her directly.
- **myaimistrue**

For information on vaginal odor, see **p. 27**.

RESOURCES

National Organizations

American Academy of Dermatology (AAD), 930 North Meacham Rd., Schaumburg, IL 60173-4965. Phone: 888-462-3376. Website: http://www.aad.org.

Online

Acne-Net at http://www.derminfo-net.com/acnenet provides information about treatment for acne.

Health Index (http://www.healthindex.org) provides information about a variety of health conditions, including symptoms and treatments. It also provides links to the sites of major medical organizations.

The Mayo Clinic sponsors a website (http://www.mayohealth.org/mayo/library/htm/tocskinc.htm) that answers common skin care questions.

Memorial Sloan-Kettering Cancer Center (www.mskcc.org/document/WICSKIN.htm) is a good resource for skin cancer.

The Skin Cancer Education Foundation at http://www.scdefderm.com educates people about the dangers of skin cancer.

The Skin Cancer Foundation at http://www.scfa.edu.au provides useful information about caring for your skin.

The Skin Cancer Zone at http://www.skin-cancer.com is devoted to providing information about skin cancer.

Books

Healthy Skin: The Facts by Rona M. MacKie (Oxford University Press) explains how to keep your skin healthy.

Overcoming Acne by Alvin Silverstein (William Morrow). Skin solutions for teens.

Skin Wise: A Guide to Healthy Skin for Women by Annette Callan (Oxford University Press) covers skin care, emphasizing women's skin.

A Woman Doctor's Guide to Skin Care by Wilma F. Bergfeld and Shelagh A. R. Maseline (Hyperion) discusses skin care for women of all ages.

For more resources and information, see http://www.dealwithit.com

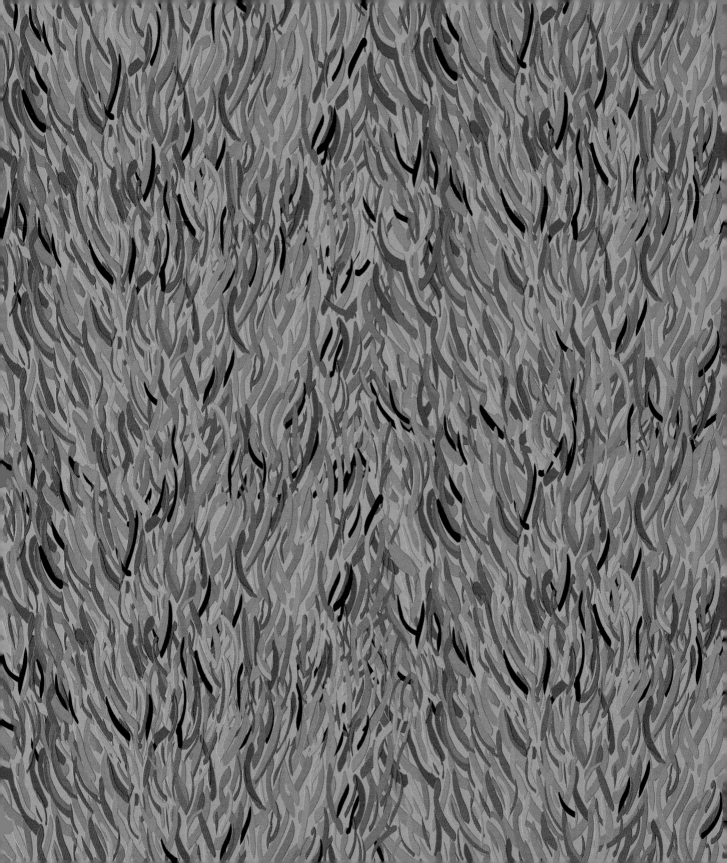

Chapter 4

HAIR, HAIR, how do your gardens grow?

Everybody has body hair. We're all born with a certain amount of it—head hair, eyebrows, peach fuzz, etc. During puberty, coarser, usually darker hair appears in new places: the crotch, underarms, upper lip, legs, arms, and various other embarrassing areas. You name it, and it can grow hair. Specifically, it's the androgen hormones that cause the new growth. Boys have much greater quantities of androgen, which is why they generally get hairier than girls.

Places new hair will appear:

crotch

legs   underarms

Places where hair may appear:

upper lip

nipples   toes

arms   chin

butt   back

43

Growing hair and dealing with it are a lifelong process. Depending on hormonal changes, certain medications (like the birth control pill), and the environment, new hair can continue to pop up in new places throughout life. Color, visibility, and quantity of body hair are largely a matter of heredity and ancestry. For instance, women from the Mediterranean countries Greece, Italy, and Spain often have the most visible hair.

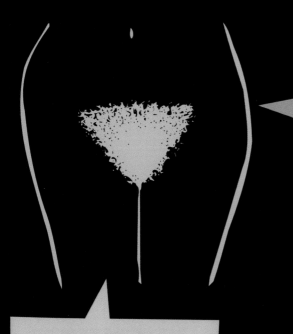

Underarm hair

Usually some time after pubic hair has appeared and boobs have started growing, underarm hair begins to appear. Armpit hair fills in gradually.

Pubic hair

Pubic hair develops at relatively the same time as your period starts and your boobs appear, give or take some months. No matter when it arrives— before or after boobs and periods— pubic hair generally grows in stages, thinner and more centralized at first and eventually forming a bushy tri-angle. Every girl has her own growth pattern. For some girls, pubic hair extends down to the upper thighs; oth-ers stop at the bend of the leg, etc. The reason for pubic hair, from an evolu-tionary perspective, is to protect this now more sensitive area of the body from dirt and other irritations.

Leg hair

Leg hair and, in some cases, arm hair can change and get darker and thicker dur-ing puberty.

The technical name for the area that pubic hair covers is **mons**, Latin for "mound," since it sticks out a little when viewed from the side.

in other places

...g adolescence, hair can sprout and
...n over the lip, on the nipple of the
...t, on toe knuckles, on the chin, and
...here else you can imagine.

> I get
> thick black hairs
> that sometimes grow on my
> nipples. Does anybody else?
> — fun-fun

> I'm a little
> hairy...but in all the
> wrong places. I mean how many
> salons are going to appreciate me
> walking in and saying "Hi, could
> you wax my asscrack?"
> Not too many.
> — hirsute

> I have a
> very hairy back.
> Does anyone think that's
> nasty cuz sometimes I get embar-
> rassed about it? — zipo

Just the facts about ...Hair

Humans have two kinds of hair:

Vellus hair: the soft, downy,
light hair that covers our body

Terminal hair: the kind that's
on our head, eyebrows,
armpits, groin, legs

Hair grows in cycles. The average life span of a head hair is
2 to 7 years. The average life
span of an upper lip hair is
4 to 5 months. Americans
spend between $2 billion and
$5 billion on hair removal per
year. Hair removal isn't just
for women. One estimate is
20 percent of men have some
unwanted hair removed, usually
from their backs.

Women and razors

Women did not start shaving until the
safety razor was invented in the early
1900s, and the Gillette company began to
advertise the supposed sanitary benefits
of shaving your armpits. Women began
shaving their legs during World War II,
when a shortage of silk stockings forced
women to go bare-legged more.

> Does shaving your legs really
> make the hair grow faster,
> thicker, and darker?
> — kateryna

Some girls with coarser body hair do
experience a thicker growth as a result
of hairs splitting from frequent shaving.
Shaving may also alter the texture—hair
grows in stubbly, not soft. Waxing, on
the other hand, may eventually lead to
thinner regrowth.

HAIRY STRATEGIES

Whether you shave it or clip it or tweeze it or wax it or bleach it or chemically annihilate it or just let it be, body hair just keeps on growing. What you decide to do with your own body hair is completely up to you. Everyone has her own unique hairy situation and everyone develops her own strategies for dealing with it.

I'm 13, almost 14, and haven't started shaving yet. I think I have to when I turn 14. It's kind of embarrassing, so I always wear pants-even in the summer. I'm sort of shy about the issue, so I haven't asked my mom to show me how. How do I ask her?
— **lidsville**

Just tell your mom that you think you are ready to start shaving. Some people shave, and some don't. There is no real reason to start shaving just because you are 14.
— **thewatcher**

I say I'm making a statement by not shaving. But it's just that I'm a little too lazy for all of that work. — **SadYgirL**

I haven't shaved a thing in years. My boyfriend loves the hair and I have always liked not having to shave. I don't have a problem going out with sleeveless tops or shorts or skirts. I do get a few strange looks but mostly people are curious to know which country I am from or if I am a feminist or a hippie. I am American, I am not a feminist or hippie and I don't shave.
— **kameleon**

I pluck the annoying little hairs that grow on my nose and I use Nair to get rid of my mustache!
— **pluckee**

I shave my bikini line, pits, legs (oh, how I love the feeling of waking up to legs that were freshly shaved the night before!), and once I actually shaved the top of my big toes. I also have hair around my belly-button, and I was once told that I was "Happy go Lucky" cause of it, who knew? — **squeeky**

I have the worst pubic hair...it's so untamable. It always crawls out from under my bathing suit. Some people saw me swimming and now they call me Bush Woman. It's humiliating. I use depilatory on my bikini line or, if I shave, razor burn from hell! - **paps**

46

I have naturally hairy eyebrows and I've been plucking them for about 4 years. Finally, I had had enough. I now go to the electrologist, and it's been great! Sure it's a bit painful at some times, but after all of my sessions are over, I'll never have to pluck again!
— **TheGirlinPurple**

I HAVE THE BLACKEST HAIR IN THE WORLD!!! If I didn't shave all the time people would mistake me for Chewbacca! My arms are hairier than my boyfriend's. I tried to bleach my arm hair one time but it didn't work. I trim my pubes, but I have to be really careful to make sure no one walks in on me while I'm doing it! I pluck the hairs around my belly button and watch the ones around my nipples, because I don't want my boyfriend to get stabbed, you know. I am a total hair removal addict.
— **sincerely**

I have hairy legs and forearms. I used to shave my forearms, and then I realized that it was just another part of me I should learn to love. And it still amazes me to have people point it out to me, like in all of my 17 years I hadn't noticed. At any rate, I pluck my underarms and shave my legs, but I usually get little red bumps everywhere a razor touches skin. — **Emulsifier**

My mother doesn't think I am too young to shave—she thinks it's not right for African Americans to shave their legs, and she thinks I am influenced by the media to shave. I am 14 in the 9th grade. How do I get my mom to think shaving isn't just for Caucasian people?
— **Hawaii50**

Maybe you could tell your mom that this is a decision that you are making because if you shaved you would feel better about yourself. You could tell her it isn't because you want to be different from her, but you like how it looks and how it feels.
— **overtheedge**

Ingrown hair

Every once in a while, sometimes as a result of frequent shaving or some other hair removal process, a hair takes root where there is no follicle and no skin pore to let it out. Since the hair can't come out of the skin, it continues to grow under the skin. Sometimes, these ingrown hairs can get infected, start hurting, and require treatment by a doctor with an antibiotic or by lancing.

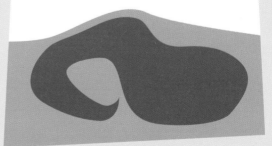

hair

HAIR REMOVAL TECHNIQUES

Because hair removal has become so important to so many American women, whole industries have sprung up around it, and new methods, products, and technologies, like laser treatments, are being invented and refined constantly. If you choose to remove your hair, you have many options:

TWEEZING/PLUCKING

What it is: Pulling hair out one by one with a pair of tweezers.

Frequency: As needed. Once you tweeze a hair, it's gone for a good month, but others grow nearby.

Cost: If you do it yourself, nothing, once you've bought the tweezers. $

Pain: Hurts for a second or two, especially in sensitive areas.

Pros: You do it yourself (you control cost, the extent, and whether to continue to do it).

Cons: It can hurt at the time. It's only temporary.

TRIMMING

What it is: Using scissors to cut unwanted hair (like pubic hair that hangs out of your bathing suit).

Frequency: As needed.

Cost: Nothing, once you have the scissors. $

Pain: None.

Pros: You do it yourself, and it doesn't hurt.

Cons: Though it reduces the length of the hair, it doesn't remove it from sight.

DEPILATORY

What it is: A cream or gel that you put on the area where you want hair removed. It burns, melts, and otherwise damages the hair roots. Then you wash the stuff and the hair off.

Frequency: Lasts a couple of weeks to a month.

Cost: Not prohibitive. Buy a reputable product at your drugstore. $$

Pain: Can burn or irritate sensitive areas. (Always follow the directions carefully, and use only on the recommended parts of the body.)

Pros: You do it yourself and the result is a very smooth, hairless area that lasts longer than shaving.

Cons: It can burn or leave the skin area red if the skin is sensitive. It smells bad, even the stuff labeled "fresh scent."

SHAVING

What it is: Using a razor to cut off hair right at the skin.

Frequency: Daily to weekly depending on how fast the hair grows. (Can be done less often in winter.)

Cost: Just the cost of razors and cream or soap. $$

Pain: None, if you don't cut yourself. But can cause some irritation.

Pros: You do it yourself anytime.

Cons: Once you start shaving, hair comes back nubby and potentially thicker. Can cause ingrown hairs (see p. 47) in the crotch area. Razor burns, shaving nicks, and other razor mishaps can also cause discomfort.

BLEACHING

What it is: Chemically lightening the color of hair. Usually used only for facial hair.

Frequency: Depends on how fast your hair grows; usually lasts about a month. Repeat when hair becomes two-tone.

Cost: Slightly more than depilatories. Buy a name brand. $$

Pain: Can cause some irritation in sensitive areas. Might be wise to test it on some less visible area first.

Pros: Doesn't involve removing the hair, so you don't have to deal with how the hair will come back (no stubble—just dark).

Cons: It is a chemical, so the skin may get irritated. It doesn't remove the hair, so if there is a lot of it, even if it is blond, it may be visible. May actually make hair more visible against dark skin.

WAXING

What it is: Spreading heated wax over the area where you want hair removed, letting it dry, then pulling it off— hair, roots, and all. The most common wax job is a bikini wax, especially as bathing suits get more revealing.

Frequency: Lasts 4 to 6 weeks.

Cost: If you do it at home, not much more than depilatories or bleaching, but having it done by a pro costs almost the price of a haircut at a beauty salon. $$ – $$$$

Pain: Sort of like ripping an adhesive bandage off a large area of skin. Some redness and irritation can follow (kinda painful—think about a bikini wax. ouch).

Pros: Removes hair for up to a month or more.

Cons: Ripping hair out by its roots with hot wax is very painful. Having it professionally done can be expensive. Ingrown hair from hair yanked awkwardly.

ELEC- TROLYSIS

What it is: Technically, it's when a qualified practitioner inserts a filament, or long thin needle, into each individual hair follicle and zaps it with an electric current. This is the only permanent, or nearly permanent, method of hair removal. Used mostly for facial hair.

Frequency: To remove, say, a mustache, usually requires weekly visits for a few months (because new hair grows all the time); then you can taper off with touch-up visits.

Cost: Expensive. Probably several hundred dollars for a mustache; less if you're just having a few stray whiskers removed. $$$$$

Pain: No picnic, but not as bad as a bad day at the dentist. Helps to take ibuprofen or another pain reliever about a half hour before. There are also creams such as emla that you can rub on your skin to temporarily numb the area.

Pros: Hair removal is eventually permanent.

Cons: Each session is very expensive, the treatment is fairly painful, and you need to find a good practitioner in order for the work to be permanent and to avoid slip-ups that can cause scarring.

LASER HAIR REMOVAL

What it is: Invented in 1995, laser hair removal involves waxing first to remove hair, then rubbing a carbon-based lotion on the skin, then passing a laser over the area. Follicles are damaged, but not the skin. It is said to work best for people with light skin and dark hair.

Frequency: Results are not permanent, but they are long-term.

Cost: Very expensive. Price varies according to the area being treated, but most treatments will cost at least a thousand dollars. $$$$$$

Pain: Less painful than electrolysis, except to the wallet.

Pros: Near-permanent hair removal.

Cons: Thousands of dollars so you won't grow hair. An inexperienced technician may burn your skin.

Chapter 5

body image

Your body is where you live. It is inseparable from who you are, and how you feel
about it definitely affects how you feel about yourself. Bodies
come in different shapes, sizes, and abilities, all of which can
affect your body image.

Some portion of your attitude about your body comes from
what you put into it and how you use it. But being healthy is
only one part of the picture.

Most people are concerned with the way they
look. It isn't exactly news that our society places a
certain stress (to put it mildly) on beauty, and that
women are most often the focus of that stress.

For information on health
and nutrition, see **pp. 58–61.**

Despite the microscopic range of types of
women celebrated as beautiful by the media, beauty in the
real world is a million different things in this country—and even
more when you look at beauty ideals in other countries and cultures. The sooner you figure this out, the sooner you can figure
out what makes you feel best about your own body and beauty.

There are so many different kinds of

body image

BODY IMAGE ISSUES

I am 5'1" and 128 pounds! Is that fat? Is that normal?
- **littlevera**

There is no "normal" weight for any height. You have to consider bone structure. One person can have less body fat than another and weigh more. Also, muscle weighs more than fat. Weight is just a number; don't let it take over your life!
- **factorygirl**

Weight

Weight is probably the greatest obsession of our body-obsessed culture. Girls especially have a lot of anxiety about how much they weigh, how much they eat, and the general shape of their bodies. Sometimes this anxiety, when mixed with other emotional and psychological problems, can escalate into a full-fledged eating disorder. Even when it doesn't, it can be debilitating or, at the very least, a waste of energy. Eating well and exercising are the best ways to ensure that your body weight is healthiest for you.

See Eating Disorders, p. 184.

The diet business

A huge U.S. industry has been built around the public hysteria about weight loss. Whether it's on exercise classes, diet books, pills, or weight-loss programs, millions of dollars are spent every year by people who want an answer to their weight "problem."

People keep wasting their money in this way even though the failure rate of dieting is somewhere between 95 and 98 percent. Within just a few years, nearly everyone who loses weight dieting goes back to their former weight or higher. In fact, diets may be contributing to the country's increasing rate of obesity.

There are physical as well as psychological reasons for this. For one, denying yourself food makes you think about it all the more and almost automatically produces cravings. At any rate, most bodies seem to have a natural weight that they more or less cling to and return to when all the dieting is done. There may be little you can do to change that.

i hate being so skinny. a lot of people think that NOBODY's body type is naturally skinny...and they claim that i have some kind of eating disorder. but i don't!!! - **jigsaw**

I hate it when you're feeling pretty good and then someone has to say, "I'm so fat!" Then everyone else joins in and says stuff like "You're not fat at all! I'm the fatty!" It makes everyone else start thinking about how they look, and it turns into a big mess. If you want to feel good about yourself, STOP saying stuff like that! - **Holisticgurl**

Get people to stop saying things like that this way: When they say, "I'm so fat," just look at them and say, "If you say so..."
- **zipo**

I really AM fat, and I am not like those girls who think that they are, when their body fat count is like...nonexistent. I NEED to lose weight. It makes me sick to go into a mall where I don't fit into MOST of the clothes there. Instead, I have to go somewhere for Plus Sized Women. No one knows how much it sucks.
- **snipper**

I know some girls who will just sit there and say, "I'm really fat so I'm going to starve myself." I think people say it for attention, 'cause they know how everyone is going to react. Why would you tell someone that you are fat if you wanted them to agree with you? - **starpwer**

52

Height

Height is another area that can make girls feel self-conscious, especially if they are at either extreme end of the spectrum.

I'm 5'9" at 14 years old and I hate it. I'm not even like a giant or anything, but I feel like one. I can't buy normal (or even tall!) women's jeans—I have to buy men's! Shirts never fit me right—I have broad shoulders and my body is too long. I would kill to be shorter than I am.
- **atallone**

I have lots of gurlfriends who are really tall (try 6 feet!), and though at 14 (we're 18 or 19 now) they felt like giants, now they feel comfortable with themselves as they are and even wear high heels quite often. Feel good about yourself, gurl—you're special, you stand out from the crowd!
- **gunshy**

I am REALLY short for my age (the doctor said I was in the bottom 7 percent for height when I got my physical at the beginning of the year), and I know there is nothing I can do about it. But I was wondering if there's anything that would help me fit in better. I have friends, but I feel so childish compared to them. Does anyone know a way to look taller and older?
- **XSalien**

I'm 17 and I'm only 5'2". Even for an Asian, I'm short. I look like I'm 13 or 14—I know how you're feeling. But there's nothing wrong with being small. A lot of people want a younger appearance. I mean, when you're 50, you could look 40. How about that? I know it's not so hot now, but it will get better.
- **sQuidee**

Body parts

And then there are specific body parts which girls obsess about. Body parts come in all shapes and sizes, and it can seem like yours are never quite right.

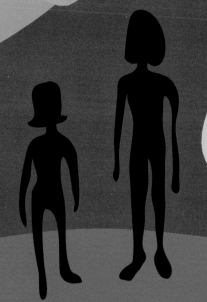

I wanna try out for the swim team. But I'm worried that I'll look fat in a swimsuit because I have fat thighs.
- **phanatic**

Don't let the appearance of your thighs stop you from getting involved in a sport. Think about it, all girls have things that they don't like about themselves—chances are they'll be worried about how THEY look and won't even notice your thighs.
- **shiMMyD**

BEAUTY IMAGE

The very concept of a beauty ideal is exclusive, oppressive, and obnoxious. But it is undeniably part of our culture and unlikely to evaporate anytime soon. One of the sometimes fascinating, sometimes problematic joys of "becoming a woman" is learning how to reconcile your body image with the ideals of the rest of the world. To do that, it can be helpful to understand how beauty ideals are created and to get a little historical perspective.

A history of beauty ideals

Although the skinny look has been naggingly persistent for most of the recent past, other generations were subjected to entirely different beauty ideals. These standards were probably no easier to deal with for the women who didn't measure up (or down) to them. It's interesting to look back and see how things change, even if the essential problem stays the same.

Ancient representations of women, such as the famous statue Venus of Willendorf, focused on women's fertility.

Round = fertile, baby!

All the better to assert superhuman powers with.

Statues of Greek and Roman goddesses, such as Nike of Samothrace, were sculpted with strong, sturdy bodies—

My body does not exist for it is shameful.

My organs are squashed and I can't breathe— but, boy, am I fashionable!

I'm not fat, I'm Rubenesque.

In the Middle Ages, religion governed aesthetics and the body was all but ignored.

In Renaissance paintings, women were generally voluptuous. The artist Peter Paul Rubens was particularly famous for his fleshy female nudes.

Plump continued to be fashionable until the beginning of the twentieth century, when the thin thing began to seep into the aesthetic consciousness.

First, there were corsets, minimizing the waist to create the fashionable hourglass figure.

You're so straight up and down you don't even look like a woman.

That's the point, Mom.

In the 1920s young women played down their curves, trying to achieve a more androgynous look that fit their aim of equality between the sexes.

This more masculine line continued through the '30s and early '40s, when women began to work (many, for the first time), replacing the male workforce that had gone off to fight World War II. Rosie the Riveter became a feminine role model.

By the late '40s and '50s, the hourglass figure had returned, with Marilyn Monroe as its ultimate embodiment. The family was proclaimed a more important goal for women than work, and the curvaceous physique celebrated "feminine" virtues like childbearing hips and full, pointy breasts.

The '60s brought a rebellion against the image of woman as sex object or homemaker. Androgyny returned with the super-skinny ideal of Twiggy (a famous British model).

In the '70s ideal bodies were long and lean, capped with glorious heads of flowing hair. (Think Charlie's Angels.)

Okay, I can meet you, but only for 10 minutes because I have a personal trainer session at 7 and a very important dinner party at 8 SHARP.

In the '80s exercise and body improvement became an obsession. The ideal body was thoroughly aerobicized and controlled, part of a generally control-crazed climate.

I always wanted to look like Barbie.

Probably the greatest "revolution" in body image in the '90s was the explosion of plastic surgery. Suddenly, it was scientifically possible to BUY the body of your dreams. The results can sometimes be scary.

body image

The Image-Making Machine

The media is a powerful vehicle for showing people what beauty is. The people we see on TV, in the movies and magazines, are often famous partly because they are considered nice to look at. More often than not, these people tend to fall within fairly tight boundaries of appearance—and a girl who doesn't slip seamlessly into that super-narrow space might consider her body and her beauty less than "ideal."

Whether it makes any sense or not, resisting the urge to compare yourself to a picture in a magazine is not easy. But before you torture yourself in this fashion, there are a few things you should remember about the making of that picture.

1

Before photo shoot

Magazine decides what they want the shoot to look and feel like to the reader (mood and attitude). People involved: creative director, art director.

Depending on this stuff, the model is chosen by face, body, ability to convey image, and attitude. People involved: model editor, art director, fashion editor, photographer.

Clothing is selected. People involved: fashion editor, stylist, art director.

2

At the shoot

Any or all of the following adjustments may be made to the clothing to make it fit better: pinning in back, cutting, boobs taped into place (to improve cleavage or position).
People involved: stylist.

Makeup is applied. This can range from color applications to covering bruises, zits, and other skin imperfections to false eyelashes, extended liplines, reshaped eyebrows, and nose contouring.
People involved: makeup artist.

Hair is styled. This may involve extensions, wigs, hairspray, gel, cream, mousse, temporary dye, permanent dye, pomade glaze.
People involved: hair stylist.

And so on.

3

After photo shoot

The film (several rolls of it) is developed. The most flattering photo is selected out of dozens of takes. Any "imperfections" are then "corrected"—thighs slimmed, wrinkles smoothed, face or body parts magnified or reduced (giving the model larger eyes and a smaller waist, for example).
People involved: photo editor, photo retoucher.

In the end it takes a staff of at least ten people to produce the image you see in a magazine.

THE BODY AS EXPRESSION

Expressing yourself through your body can be empowering and gratifying (not to mention really fun). It is exciting to have control over what people see when they look at you.

The palette of possibilities is huge: clothes, hair, makeup, and body adornment (piercing, tattoos) to, at the extreme end of the scale, body modification through surgery. Some changes are temporary, others will be with you for your whole life. It is obviously important to take these factors into account when deciding whether to do something to your body.

When you use your power to transform yourself, it's important to remember that the changes you make might not be perceived the same way by everyone, and certain people may have negative responses. Personal style has historically been a source of some conflict between teenagers and various authority figures. You have to decide whether the change you want to make is worth the trouble it may cause you.

As with all other aspects of yourself, your beauty image is a work in progress and will change, evolve, and fluctuate over time.

TATTOOS ARE PERMANENT

RESOURCES

Online

About-Face at http://www.about-face.org is committed to changing the image of the ideal female body type.

Smash! at http://www.dandyweb.com/smash/smash.html is a strong advocate of positive body images for women of any dress size, age, religion, or other classification.

Books

Adios, Barbie! by Ophira Edut and Rebecca Walker (Seal Press). Irreverent essays about body image.

Beyond Beauty by Jane Pratt et al. (Clarkson Potter). Celebrity teens and real girls talk about their relationships to their beauty image.

The Body Project by Joan Jacobs Brumberg (Vintage). Discusses how women have reacted to their maturation over time.

Hope in a Jar: The Making of America's Beauty Culture by Kathy Lee Peiss (Owl Books). Well-researched, fascinating window into 100 years of American beauty.

Real Gorgeous: The Truth about Body and Beauty by Kaz Cooke (Norton). Challenges the beauty, fashion, and diet industry in a funny and reassuring way.

For more resources and information, see http://www.dealwithit.com

body image

Special Section

Taking Care of Yourself

If your body is not healthy, it can be hard to feel good about how you look. Similarly, you'll look better when your body is being taken care of.

What you need for good health is basic:

* good nutrition
* proper exercise
* the right amount of sleep and rest

If you shortchange any of these things, it can lead to health problems in both the short and the long term. A well-rested, well-nourished body can more easily fight off germs and illness.

NUTRITION BASICS

We all need a certain amount of food every day. At a minimum, your body needs to consume 1,200 calories a day. The ideal amount to consume is 2,000 to 2,500 calories, especially when combined with an active lifestyle (where you're actually moving around during the day). But calories are not the only thing to think about. Where the calories come from is equally important.

Three basic principles to keep in mind for good nutrition are:

balance variety moderation

Healthy eating habits

Developing healthy eating habits early in life offers short- and long-term health benefits, including increased energy, defense against disease, and much better prospects for life-long weight control.

Eat breakfast. Just about every nutritionist recommends eating a good breakfast to get the blood sugar level up. Fruit and whole grain cereals and toast are particularly good foods to eat in the morning, as they give the body both fiber and complex carbohydrates to work off of for the next few hours.

Don't skip meals. It can lead to overeating the next meal. Nutritionists suggest it might be healthier to eat more and smaller meals, every day, giving the body a constant and more efficient source of fuel, and also increasing the chances of eating a variety of foods. The largest meal probably should not come at the end of the day, but more toward the middle. At night, it's best to eat light, but not to go to bed hungry, which can inhibit sleep.

Eat fruits and vegetables. Eating three to five daily servings of fruits and vegetables cuts the risk of a dozen different cancers, as well as the risk of heart attack and stroke, and the incidence of adult blindness and obesity.

Eat plenty of iron. Since anemia can be a problem for menstruating girls, iron is particularly important. Good sources include broccoli, potatoes, kidney beans, red meat, eggs, and whole or enriched grains. Also be sure to get vitamin C, contained in citrus fruits and juices, berries and tomatoes, and cabbage—it aids in iron absorption.

Drink water. Eight glasses a day is ideal. You need lots of water because so much of your body (60 percent) is actually made up of water. Water carries nutrients throughout the body, rids your body of wastes, and lubricates joints—just to name a few of its essential functions. In addition to drinking plain water, you can get your daily dosage from seltzer, fruit juices, and herbal teas (caffeinated teas actually eliminate water from your body). Depending on the quality of the local water supply, you may opt for filtered or bottled water.

The five food groups

To maintain good overall health, eat food from five essential food groups everyday:

Carbohydrates
Examples: Bread, rice, pasta.
How much: 6 to 11 servings per day. (A serving is relatively small—one slice of bread or a half-cup of rice.)

Vegetables
Examples: Green leafy vegetables like spinach, collards, and other greens. Orange and root vegetables like carrots and yams. Other vegetables like broccoli, cauliflower, the squash family, beans, and eggplant.
How much: 3 to 5 servings per day. (A serving is about a half-cup.) Note: Within this category, as well as others, there is tremendous variety. It's good to eat lots of different vegetables—including green, yellow, orange, and purple ones, all of which are rich in different vitamins and minerals.

Fruits
Examples: Apples, pears, oranges, grapes, melons, fruit juices, dried fruits.
How much: 2 to 4 servings per day. (A serving consists of a piece of fruit, or melon wedge, or three-quarters of a cup of juice.)

Dairy
Examples: Milk, yogurt, cheese.
How much: 3 or more servings per day. (A cup of milk is a serving.)

Protein
Examples: Meat, poultry, fish, dry beans, eggs, nuts.
How much: 2 to 3 servings per day. (A serving consists of 1.5 to 3 ounces of meat.)

Empty calories

Nutritionists recommend eating fats, oils, and sugar sparingly. These foods are highly caloric and not very nutritious.
Examples: Butter, cooking oil, candy, and sugar and other sweeteners. (Some fats and oils and sugars are contained in other basic food categories. For example, both meat and dairy have fat, and fruit contains fructose, a kind of sugar.)

The more processed food is, the more likely it is to have an excess of sugar and fat. Processed foods include packaged cookies and cakes—anything that's treated in an unnatural way to extend its shelf life. Check out the list of ingredients on your packaged food sometime. There's sugar in everything.

Many people have noticed that when they eat a lot of sugar, they get a brief high or buzz, after which their energy plummets. Eating a lot of fatty food makes people feel sluggish and eventually clogs up arteries and other vital passageways in the body.

Vegetarianism

People opt to be vegetarians for a variety of reasons: to avoid the additives, pesticides, and contaminants in meat; to reduce chances of heart disease and other cancers; to avoid killing or benefiting from the killing of animals; and to eat more cheaply. If you choose a vegetarian diet, it's important to educate yourself so that you're getting enough nutrients.

There are many types of vegetarian diets, but the two most common are

* **lacto-ovo**—includes eggs and milk products but not meat
* **vegan**—avoids all forms of animal products

There is often a concern that lacto-ovo vegetarians will not get enough protein in their diets without eating meat, poultry, or fish. But there are numerous other sources of protein, including eggs, cheese, beans, nuts, and soy products like tofu. It is also possible to combine certain vegetable proteins in order to make a complete protein. For example, rice combined with a variety of beans is greater than the sum of its parts in terms of providing the body with a complete and very efficient protein.

Vegan vegetarians may be prone to deficiencies of several nutrients, particularly vitamins D and B-12, calcium, iron, zinc, and perhaps other trace elements. Like all essential nutrients, these vitamins and minerals are required to maintain proper growth.

For information on a healthy vegetarian diet, or vegetarian recipes, see Resources, pp. 64–65.

Psychological aspects of eating

The mental aspect of eating may also get in the way of good nutrition. If a person has obsessive eating patterns or an eating disorder, she or he is much less likely to be concerned with the nutritional aspects of eating.

It is important also to listen to your body, since it often will indicate what it needs more of by craving certain foods. You might crave a burger if you haven't had enough protein, or some orange juice if you're low on vitamin C.

See Healthy Eating and Eating Disorders, pp. 58–59, 184–91.

I keep telling my mom that I'm a vegetarian, but she still fixes her usual all-meat dinners. She thinks it's a phase, that I am just doing it to lose weight and always says "You won't be able to not eat meat" or some other rude comment. It hurts because I want her to back me up on this decision.
— **Vegghead**

Sit down with your mom (when you're not eating) and tell her that you are serious about being a vegetarian and that you would appreciate it if she could help out with making non-meat meals. My parents used to bug me in the beginning, but after a while it wasn't an issue. They even started buying vegetarian meals and all sorts of food I could eat. Also try making a vegetarian meal for your family once a week to show them you mean business.
— **bugBUTT**

Vitamins and Minerals

A well-balanced diet should provide all the vitamins a body needs, but some people opt to take supplements. There are times, such as if you are pregnant or nursing, when no matter how well you're eating, it may be beneficial to take vitamins. Habits like smoking, doing drugs, and drinking alcohol or a lot of caffeinated beverages (coffee, tea, or colas) deplete the body's store of certain vitamins.

The following chart highlights the most important vitamins and minerals, explaining why you need them and which foods contain them.

	WHAT IT DOES	SOURCES
Vitamin A	Prevents infection; helps eyes adjust to light and darkness; helps maintain skin and tissues such as those inside the mouth, lungs, bones, and teeth.	Milk, egg yolks, cheese, liver, and dark green leafy, yellow, or orange fruits and vegetables.
B vitamins, including thiamine, riboflavin, niacin, folic acid, choline	Help metabolism, steady nerves, aid digestion, improve energy and alertness, boost immune system.	Whole-grain breads and cereals, wheat germ, green vegetables, legumes (beans), nuts, seeds, chicken, lean pork, liver, eggs, potatoes, fish.
Vitamin C	Helps maintain healthy cells and bones, boosts immunity and healing, aids in iron absorption.	Citrus fruits, bell peppers, berries, melons, tomatoes, broccoli, cauliflower, green leafy vegetables.
Vitamin D	Helps calcium absorption, which is vital to strong bones and teeth.	Sunlight, fortified milk, fish, egg yolks.
Vitamin E	Preserves other vitamins. Good for membranes.	Vegetable oils, wheat germ, egg yolks, legumes, corn, almonds.
Iron	Helps maintain blood's ability to carry oxygen from lungs to rest of body. A shortage of iron leads to anemia and weakness.	Dried fruit, blackstrap molasses, spinach and other green leafy vegetables, liver, egg yolks, sardines, whole-grain bread.
Calcium	Builds strong bones and teeth, aids blood clotting.	Dairy foods (milk), leafy greens, broccoli, molasses, artichokes, salmon, tofu (soybean curd), legumes (peas and beans), seeds, nuts, calcium-enriched grain products, lime-processed tortillas.
Potassium	Maintains healthy nerves and muscles (particularly important for people who exercise heavily).	Bananas, potatoes, legumes (peas and beans), meat and poultry, milk.
Sodium	Helps regulate and maintain fluid content of the body (especially important for heavy exercisers who lose a lot of fluid through sweating).	Salt.
Magnesium	Aids metabolism.	Seafood, nuts, whole grains, leafy greens.

EXERCISE

Exercise has a number of benefits. It's fun, it enhances energy, and it keeps your body fit and healthy. Exercise protects the body from heart disease, hypertension, osteoporosis (brittle bones), and colon

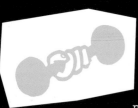

cancer. It also wards off depression and can reduce PMS and menstrual cramps, as well as increase confidence and energy.

It's important to make regular activity a part of your everyday life. One good idea is to seize opportunities for activity whenever they present themselves. Try walking short distances quickly rather than automatically hopping into a car. Take the stairs instead of an elevator.

The Centers for Disease Control recommends at least 30 minutes of moderately intense activity every day. The most efficient exercise in terms of burning calories and boosting energy is challenging but not utterly exhausting. Start with moderate exercise and build up the intensity, so you don't burn yourself out in the beginning.

The three basic kinds of exercise

Stretching: Improves flexibility and range of motion; raises heart rate slightly. Before stretching, always warm your body up with moderate activity, such as jumping jacks or jogging in place. This increases your body temperature and makes your body more supple and amenable to stretching. When stretching, try not to bounce, which can lead to muscle tears and injury. To avoid injury, you should feel tension in the area being stretched but not pain.

Aerobic exercise: Good for cardiovascular fitness, the heart, the lungs, and the respiratory system. Any kind of exercise that temporarily increases the heart rate is aerobic exercise, including running, walking, swimming, or dancing.

Strength and muscle-building exercise: Builds muscle mass and strength and bulk. The most efficient way to accomplish this is by weight lifting. For strength training to do any good, you need to lift weights at least twice a week. It's a good idea to get someone who knows what he or she is doing to give you some pointers on weight lifting to start out.

See Resources for more information on exercise, pp. 64–65.

DEALING WITH STRESS

Life is full of stresses, large and small. Constant stress or tension that is stored in the body makes it hard to relax, interferes with sleep, and can result in indigestion, high blood pressure, angry emotional outbursts, and depression. Everyone can benefit from techniques for avoiding and reducing stress.

Certainly, exercise, diversions, laughter and having fun can reduce stress, and keep things in perspective. Every girl has her own methods of making herself feel good.

Figure out what works for you and set aside time for those experiences.

People also use a variety of relaxation techniques.

Meditation: Studies show that meditation lowers both stress and blood pressure. The object of meditation is to quiet your mind, letting your thoughts come and go as they please, and to live in the moment.

To meditate, begin by sitting straight and comfortably on the floor. Breathe comfortably through your nose. Avoid keeping track of time. Keep your focus on the moment. If you find your attention wandering, bring it back to the moment. Some people break a train of stressful thoughts by focusing on a simple word, sound, or prayer.

Deep breathing: This technique involves focusing on your breath through a variety of breathing exercises, including deep inhalations, holding your breath for longer than usual, and exhaling longer. It's hard to think about much else when you are thinking about controlling your breathing.

Progressive muscle relaxation: Get into a comfortable position, probably lying on your back, and notice where the tension is in your body. Then try to relax that area. The jaw, mouth, and tongue frequently hold a lot of tension. Shoulders and necks do too. Another way to go about relaxing each area of the body is to start at your toes, relax them, then work your way up through your feet, ankles, knees, and so on, all the way to the top of your head. Try this also if you're wound up and can't get to sleep.

Imagery and visualization: Imagine being in a pleasant place, looking at the mountains, the ocean, a desert—whatever place you enjoy most. Just concentrate on all the sights, sounds, smells, and sensations.

Yoga: The practice of yoga has many benefits, both physical and psychological. It is simultaneously exercise, leaving the body energized, fit, and strong; a stretching and strengthening of muscles; and relaxation and meditation, focusing the mind. It can be therapeutic for ailments like asthma, stomach troubles, headaches, and weakness, plus it gives you a very good workout. It's a great way to cope with stress.

There are several different kinds of yoga. Some provide more rigorous workouts than others. In all, you assume different postures, or series of postures, which help align the body and strengthen it.

Aromatherapy: Aromatherapy is an ancient approach to healing and health maintenance that uses fragrances to balance the body by influencing physical, psychological, and spiritual levels. A few drops of essential oil, plant fragrances distilled and condensed down to their essence, may be placed in a bath or inhaled on a tissue. Or the oils might be used to scent a room or along with a massage.

Some even believe that these essences have antibiotic and antiviral qualities. Some people believe it relieves PMS, stress, moderate anxiety and depression, sleep problems, digestive problems, backaches and similar pains, and infections, although there is not much hard scientific evidence to prove these benefits.

Getting enough sleep

Teenagers need to sleep more than other people because they are undergoing an intense growth spurt. Not getting enough sleep can cause all sorts of problems:

* inability to focus and concentrate
* mental lapses
* clumsiness
* poor judgment
* emotional upheaval
* bad skin

Sleep restores the body and the brain. With sleep, as with other things, it's good to have a regular routine. The body has its daily rhythms (called circadian rhythms), which are linked to light and darkness, and craves going to sleep and waking at approximately the same time every day. It's best to sleep regularly all week. If you deprive yourself and try to make up for lost sleep on weekends, sleeping in until noon or so, it's just harder to go to sleep the next night.

Napping is another way to make up for lost sleep, although some say naps are best kept short (around 20 minutes). Beyond that, the body falls into deeper sleep, which can make you groggy when you wake and may interfere with your night's sleep.

RESOURCES

Health and nutrition—National Organizations

The American Dietetic Association. Call their hotline at 800-366-1655 and a registered dietitian will answer any question you may have.

Health and nutrition—Online

On the Teen Scene at http://www.fda.gov/oc/opacom/kids/html/7teens.htm, sponsored by the U.S. Food and Drug Administration (FDA), includes articles covering important health information for teenagers.

For Teens at KidsHealth.org at http://www.kidshealth.org/teen/index.html discusses teenagers' concerns about food, health, sex, and sports.

The American Medical Association's site on Adolescent Health can be found at http://www.ama-assn.org/insight/h_focus/adl_hlth/teen/teen.htm.

Girl Power! by the Department of Health and Human Services at http://www.health.org/gpower/girlarea/index.htm includes games, health info, your own web page, and book ideas.

Health Index (http://www.healthindex.org) provides information about a variety of health conditions, including symptoms and treatments. It also provides links to the sites of major medical organizations.

Health and nutrition—Books

The Complete Book of Fitness by the Editors of Fitness magazine (Three Rivers Press). A comprehensive guide to cardio training, strength training, diet and nutrition, and wellness.

The Complete Guide to Health and Nutrition by Gary Null (Doubleday). A popular approach to detailed, essential information about health and nutrition and vitamins and minerals.

The New Our Bodies, Ourselves by the Boston Women's Health Book Collective (Simon & Schuster). The classic women's health resource.

Women's Bodies, Women's Wisdom by Christiane Northrup (Bantam). A holistic guide to women's wellness.

Other considerations

There are a number of reasons why people may have extra issues to consider in taking care of themselves. Certain medical conditions may require dietary adjustments, regular medication, or changes in routine. These changes can range from being merely inconvenient to completely life-altering, and can impact everything

For more on body image, see pp. 50-57.

from your body image to your psychological health to your physical well-being. Whatever your situation, it is a good idea to find out as much about it as possible. Chronic conditions (diabetes, scoliosis, multiple sclerosis, certain mental illnesses, etc.) can require great patience and adaptability. In these circumstances, especially, it is important to feel positive about and comfortable with your health care professionals.

Vegetarianism—Online

http://www.peta.com has tons of information on protecting animals and living a vegetarian lifestyle.

Vegetarianism—Books

Almost Vegetarian by Diana Shaw (Clarkson Potter). Good recipes for vegetarians or for people transitioning to vegetarianism.

Diet for a Small Planet by Frances Moore Lappe (Ballantine). This bestselling book promoting vegetarianism explains everything you need to know about eating well.

A Teen's Guide to Going Vegetarian by Judy Krizmanic (Puffin) An excellent guide for beginning or younger vegetarians. The book covers both diet and activism.

Yoga—Books and videos

The American Yoga Association's Beginners Manual by Alice Christensen (Fireside).

Beginning Yoga by Vijayendra Pratap (Charles E. Tuttle).

Breath, Mind, and Consciousness by Harish Johari (Inner Traditions).

Basic Yoga video by the American Yoga Association.

Living Yoga: A.M./P.M. video.

Aromatherapy—Online

Ancient Healing Art website at http://www.halcyon.com/kway/home.htm provides information and sells essential oils and aromatherapy products.

Aromatherapy—Books

The Complete Illustrated Guide to Aromatherapy by Julia Lawless (Element). Explains how to use aromatherapy for cosmetic and medicinal purposes.

For more resources and information, see http://www.dealwithit.com

PART 2

sexuality

Sexuality is ambiguous, amorphous, and powerful.

It means different things to different people—something that can be difficult to remember when you're being bombarded with media images and ideas trying to tell you what sex or sexy is. Sexuality extends well beyond the act of doing "it," fooling around, touching, making out, kissing....It includes all the things that make you feel sexy, sensual, comfortable or just generally in the mood.

Sexuality is everywhere. Learning to understand it, channel it, and deal with it safely and smartly is a lifelong process that can be complicated, difficult, and incredibly exciting.

Chapter 1

Sexual Feelings

The way you feel about your sexuality is influenced by many different factors. For more on this, see Attitudes Toward Sex, **p. 92.**

VAGUE FEELINGS OF ATTRACTION

It's not easy for most people to pinpoint the exact moment when they first notice their sexual feelings. Often it happens gradually.

Sometimes the early roots of sexual feelings aren't even connected to people. Some girls just get a sense of something new happening. It may be some kind of physical sensation or an emotional twinge, or a combination of both.

These vague feelings may be difficult to connect to the definition of sex you've learned. It can be much easier to recognize your early sexual feelings when they come in the form of a crush.

If girls start having sexual feelings before their bodies begin to develop, or vice versa, it can be hard to deal with the difference between the way your body looks and the way you feel.

The five senses and the chemistry of desire

You perceive the physical world through your five senses. All of these come into play in the grand scheme of sexual arousal. Your brain interprets the signals that your senses take in. When we see or otherwise sense something we find attractive, the information is sent to the brain's limbic system, which processes that information and sends messages to various parts of the body, telling them to respond sexually.

Sexual attraction is a very unique, personal sensation. What turns you on doesn't necessarily turn on anybody else. Sometimes there may be a direct mental connection between what the senses take in and previous sexual experiences. Often, the link is a mystery. Different girls find different sensations sexy...

sight

i like the sight of really strong hands and long fingers...

environmental phenomena like lightning or other interesting lighting effects in nature...

staring at someone over a long distance, like across the room...

anyone who's androgynous looking...

the sight of really soft looking lips...

it's kind of cheesy, but i like mountains, high mountains...

touch

being gently kissed on my ear...

the feel of someone's biceps...

i'm totally into the back tickle...

i like lying in the hot sun...

on a really cold morning, i love the feel of a hot, hot shower...

taste

the taste of saltwater on somebody's body...

i like the taste of those kind of fruity lip glosses...

i really like the taste of persimmons when they're perfectly ripe

i like the taste of metal...

i definitely get off on really hot mustard...

70

smell

i like the smell of **chlorine** on people's skin...

the smell of those **pine green** air fresheners that hang from people's rear-view mirrors...

the smell of **suede**...

a bouquet of freesia... that's my favorite flower...

sound

i like a deep voice...

silence turns me on...

the sound of **rain** falling...

the sound of a loud **city outside** when it's quiet inside...

i like to hear somebody who i like, making other people **laugh**...

See the steps of sexual arousal, pp. 74–75.

Getting turned on

Feelings can create a response in your body whether you want them to or not. Boys get erections. Girls get wet (bodies produce vaginal lubrication). Sometimes all it takes is the thought or touch of someone or something you like.

The body responds to arousal in many other ways, too. Hormones called androgens and estrogens create lots of physical changes in the body, and regulate the sex drive in both men and women. While men have more androgens (such as testosterone) and women have more estrogens, both sexes have some of each. It's the androgens that are responsible for the sex drive. Estrogen, on the other hand, helps the body get ready for sexual intercourse by lubricating the vagina and keeping it elastic.

Your sex drive can be affected when the levels of these hormones change. If your menstrual cycle is regular, you may notice that you are more interested in sex at certain times of the month. Just before ovulation, for example, the ovaries produce a small amount of testosterone, which is like a foot on the gas pedal of your sex drive. This is one of the body's ways of encouraging a woman to have sex at a time when she's likely to get pregnant. Later in your cycle, when the hormone progesterone is higher, the sex drive is sometimes reduced.

Pheromones

Some people think smell is a particularly powerful aspect of "chemistry" between people. Pheromones, human scent signals, are produced by glands in the armpits and genital, anal, and nipple areas. In fact, one theory about pubic and underarm hair is that they evolved to distribute these chemicals.

In the animal world, pheromones play an important role in reproduction by indicating to males that a female is in her fertile stage.

In humans, researchers suspect that pheromones may control or at least influence sexual activity and compatibility. If so, they operate on a totally unconscious level. Their presence is detected by a special organ in the nose called the vomeronasal organ (VNO).

Pheromones are also thought to be responsible for the way that women's menstrual cycles tend to synchronize with one another when they live communally, as in dormitories.

sexual feelings

MASTURBATION

playing with yourself jerking off whacking off
petting the bunny spanking the monkey
jacking off jilling off buttering the biscuit

So you get turned on. What do you do about it? Some people do nothing and wait for the feeling to go away. Others take the sexual energy they feel and apply it to other things (sublimation). Other people touch themselves. Actually, many people do. Masturbation, or self-stimulation, is probably the primary sexual activity of the human race, and it's safe to assume that more people masturbate than participate in any other kind of sex.

Guys may be more up-front about this activity than girls are, but anyone who says girls don't masturbate is lying. Girls masturbate; they just may not talk about it much. They do it standing, sitting, or lying down. They use their fingers outside. They put their fingers inside. Some rub themselves against a pillow. Some do it in the bathtub with the shower nozzle or water from the faucet. Some look at books or movies or magazines while they do it. Others fantasize. Some don't think about much of anything except how they feel.

Masturbation is a way of figuring out what feels good to you. It's a helpful way to get acquainted with your body and to learn how you respond to things. In a way, everyone is her own first and most efficient sex partner. Knowing what you like and being able to communicate it is part of being a good lover to someone else.

With masturbation, there's no risk, no pressure. It is the ultimate safe sex. You can't get pregnant or catch any diseases, and since it is done alone, there's no embarrassment or performance anxiety.

72

If you have a removable showerhead, turn it on to jet mode and spray the water onto your clit. It feels really good.
— flicka

IT DOESN'T WORK FOR ME!!! I've tried simply rubbing my clit, using a vibrator, and putting fingers in my vagina ...nothing works. It feels okay, but I never orgasm.
— venter

The only problem I've had is that it can get a little boring because you're always doing the same thing. One of the best things to do is to rub your clit with an ice cube. It lubricates you so that you can stick your finger in easier. It feels great to rub, tickle, and/or hump. **— bugbutt**

Lie down and put your hands or a blanket or something between your legs, squeeze, & rock back & forth.
— BiBal

I feel really embarrassed about saying this stuff, but when I masturbate, I'm usually thinking of my boyfriend or some other guy. It feels strange, but it feels great afterward. **— TRIX**

A good way to masturbate is to rub your clit with your finger. You can apply pressure if you want, and rub in a circle as fast or as slow as you want. I think it usually works best if you do it fast & hard, but it feels really good no matter what.
— wilmaf

Masturbation myths

There are millions of stories about bad things that can happen to you if you masturbate. Not one of them is true.

Assuming you're not spending all of your time masturbating, and you don't masturbate in public spaces, there is hardly any danger to it at all. In fact, it could even keep you healthier if it prevents you from having sex with the wrong person and sooner than you are ready for it emotionally.

One slight danger with masturbation is infection if you masturbate with something unclean. Also, you may irritate your sex organs by rubbing too hard for too long. If that happens, stop, and the irritation should go away. If you experience pain or discomfort that lasts more than a few days, something else may be going on, and it makes sense to see a doctor. (It's unlikely that masturbation has done any harm.)

Another myth about masturbation is that people do it only when they are not in a sexual relationship with somebody. Masturbation, alone or with a partner, often continues in the context of good and healthy sexual relationships. Actually, it can be a great tool for showing someone what you like. Many people get turned on by watching other people touch themselves. Masturbating together is a fairly popular activity among couples who have sex on a regular basis.

None of this means that if you don't masturbate, there's something wrong with you. Some people don't start masturbating until much later in life. Some don't masturbate until they become sexually active or are in a close relationship. Others never really get into it at all. As far as touching yourself goes, whatever feels good to you is the right thing to do.

sexual feelings

SEXUAL AROUSAL—WHAT'S GOING ON

Although it's the most natural thing in the world, sexual arousal is a fairly complex process. Its stages are not automatic. Just because you start the ball rolling, so to speak, doesn't mean you're going to glide through to step 4 without a glitch. It takes a steady stream of excitement and stimulation to move from one step to another.

Step 1: The first part is really mental. You have to be receptive to getting turned on. To be aroused sexually, quite simply, you have to be interested in sex. You have to be thinking about it, curious about it, and generally wanting it in some way.

Step 2: Once you're mentally aroused, your brain sends a signal that makes your blood pressure and heart rate go up, increasing the blood flow to your genitals (called engorgement) and increasing the sensitivity of your skin, all over.

Step 4: Otherwise known as the plateau phase, it's not about flattening out, but about reaching a more intense level of excitement and kind of riding there for a while. Muscle tension increases. The heart and breathing rates keep going up, making the body feel hotter. Some people get something called the "sex flush," a reddening of the skin on the chest. The outer part of the vagina swells and tightens, while the inner part expands.

Step 3: If your sexual interest is still aroused, engorgement continues and vaginal lubrication starts. The inner part of the vagina expands, the labia lips open and enlarge, the clitoris swells and pulls back against the pubic bone. When aroused, the clitoris becomes more sensitive to touch. It pulls back so its head is protected from direct contact. The nipples may also experience engorgement and can swell and become erect.

74

Step 5: If you're lucky, the big "O"—orgasm. It's hard to describe what an orgasm feels like because there are so many varieties. Everyone is different, so everyone experiences pleasure differently. Though more intense, orgasm does not last as long as the other stages of arousal, which can go on anywhere from minutes to hours. Orgasm usually lasts just a few seconds to 10 seconds. It happens when muscle tension and the feeling of pelvic fullness reach their peak and get released, often in a series of involuntary muscle contractions, radiating out from the genitals, uterus, and anus. Some people describe orgasms as a great buildup of tension and tightness, followed by an explosion. On the less intense end of the scale, an orgasm can be like a sigh of relief or a pleasant rush of warm feelings.

For more on Orgasm, see next page.

Step 6: After orgasm comes what is sometimes called the resolution phase. The body returns to its normal state. Blood leaves the genital area, the genitals shrink and return to their original size and position, breathing slows, and blood pressure returns to its usual level.

Even without an orgasm, the body will eventually return to its normal state, but it takes a little longer, and the various parts of the body that were in a state of arousal may ache for a while.

whenever i read something about sex or a book where people have sex or even if i just think about sex, my "down there" area gets all hot and tingling and i can feel a pulsating. is this a tiny orgasm? did you girls ever have this feeling? IF YOU DONT, YOU SHOULD—IT FEELS REALLY GREAT!
 - tiziana

I believe you're feeling aroused, and yes I do get that too.
 - Ovo

I know this question might be a little weird but how do you feel when you get "horny"?
 - orchata

When you get "wet" you are horny. Like, when the mucus comes out of your vagina.
 - wispy

sexual feelings

the big "O" coming getting off getting your rocks off the little death

Although orgasm is used to define a specific physiological process, the fact is that more than just your sex organs are involved in sexual climax. Feeling sexy involves the whole body and the mind as well. It requires relaxation and trust and feeling comfortable with the idea of losing control.

Sexual responsiveness can change with age. Lots of women don't start having orgasms until they are in their twenties and thirties, either because their bodies aren't ready or because they just don't know how. Most women get more comfortable with their sexuality as they age and there is evidence that some women become more orgasmic with age.

Orgasms are undeniably great, but there can be too much emphasis placed on them. If trying to attain an orgasm becomes the be-all and end-all of any sexual activity, it may actually spoil the enjoyment of sex. There should be no pressure to reach orgasm—sex can be fun without it. Not having an orgasm doesn't mean that you or your partner has failed.

Orgasm & the clitoris

For women the primary pleasure center is the clitoris, which is located a good inch or so away from the vagina, at the top of the vulva. Orgasm is most easily attained by manipulating and stimulating the clitoris. But the methods and preferences for clitoral stimulation vary. Some women like direct contact; others find it too uncomfortable. Pressure on the mons area, which can move the clitoris against the pubic bone, feels good to some women, but not all.

For a diagram of the external sexual organs, see **pp. 16–17.**

The act of sexual intercourse—inserting a penis inside a vagina, and moving it in and out—doesn't pay much attention to the clitoris. Only a small percentage of women

For more on different types of sexual activities, see **pp. 84–90.**

I just wanna know what happens when you get an orgasm. I know "it's the best feeling" but I wanna know what it actually feels like, and what happens. Is it good for you? — **robogurl**

No one can describe an orgasm. It's just too hard. All i can say is that it feels REALLY good...like a good back massage after a day's worth of work. It's a shivery, tired feeling. I'm pretty sure it is good for you. — **themostcake**

It's a wave of pleasure that goes over you and your muscles sort of contract really tight—it's a weird sensation. Sometimes it feels as if I'm going to sneeze down there and feels real good, then all of a sudden it is relieved. — **permia**

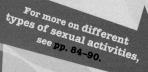

(one estimate is about 30 percent) experience orgasms through intercourse alone. Stimulation of the clitoral area by the woman or her partner during intercourse can lead to orgasm. Orgasm can also be reached through oral sex or manual stimulation. Those sexual activities are considered foreplay to some, but when they lead to orgasm, they can be the main event.

This does not mean that sexual intercourse isn't extremely fun and pleasurable for women, even if it doesn't lead to orgasm. Different positions can be more pleasurable for different women, and some allow for direct stimulation of the clitoris. When the guy is beneath or behind the girl, she and he have more access to the clitoris, making it easier to stimulate it manually.

> Your heartbeat, blood pressure, and breathing are at their HIGHEST point. How an orgasm feels depends upon the amount of stimulation you get, and what is going on in your mind.
> — **GaZella**

> I've been sexually active for about 8 or 9 months, and i've never had an orgasm, but everyone else says it's like a rush, and you know when you get it. It might take a while though, because it does for many people. — **JOfArc**

Multiple orgasm

Generally after an orgasm, the body, satisfied, starts to enter what is called the resolution phase, where everything returns to its prearoused state. The clitoris wants to rest and may be far too sensitive for any further stimulation, which is kind of how a guy's penis feels.

But some women are able to maintain a high level of arousal even after an orgasm and can be elevated pretty quickly to another climax (and possibly another and another). Those who have multiple orgasms say there is a "pyramid effect," each one building on the last in intensity. Also, some say G-spot orgasms (see next page) lend themselves more to multiple orgasm than clitoral ones.

For most people, though, one orgasm at a time is more than enough and most women are perfectly happy without ever experiencing the legendary multiple orgasm.

Orgasm & the vagina: The G-Spot

Some women do have orgasms as a result of vaginal stimulation. Different parts of the vagina are more sensitive than others and can be stimulated through intercourse or other methods. In general, the first couple of inches of the vagina have more nerve endings than deeper inside. The front wall of the vagina also seems to be more sensitive, possibly because it's closer to the clitoris, and possibly because of something known as the G-spot. Most women learn

sexual feelings

their own sensitivities and preferred angles of penetration only by experimenting with a partner.

The G-spot is named after Ernest Grafenberg, a German physician who is credited with discovering it in 1950. In some ways, it's still a mystery. What is known is that there is a place inside the vagina that—for certain women— can create powerful sexual pleasure. Some women swear by it, others have searched endlessly and not been able to find it, and some people (even some doctors) say it does not exist.

It is not usually pictured on anatomy charts, but the area known as the G-spot is approximately 2 inches inside the vagina, behind the pubic bone and next to the urethra. In its unstimulated state, the G-spot is said to be about the size of a dime. Though it's an area and not an organ, when it is stimulated, it grows (much as the sex organs do) to approximately the size of a half-dollar.

When women do find the G-spot and it is rubbed and stimulated, the sensations can be intensely pleasurable, although some women say they don't like it. Probably because of the proximity to the urethra, having the G-spot rubbed can make you feel like you have to pee. This sensation usually goes away after a little while. Fingers can reach the G-spot, and certain positions of intercourse, such as when the woman is on top, lend themselves more to G-spot stimulation.

Female ejaculation: It's well known that guys ejaculate, releasing a fluid (semen, in their case) during orgasm. Some women have been known to ejaculate as well, and they say that these orgasms are even more intense than ones without ejaculation.

The G-spot is often associated with a kind of female orgasm that includes female ejaculation or gushing, a convulsive expelling of some fluid from the vagina. This fluid is said to be thicker than urine and somewhat sticky, and the amount of it really varies. People who are skeptical of the G-spot don't believe this is a special fluid; instead, they say it's probably urine mixed with some vaginal mucus.

Simultaneous orgasm

Simultaneous orgasms during intercourse are more rare than movie mythology would have us believe, due to the fact that most women reach orgasm through clitoral stimulation, something the act of intercourse alone doesn't promote. Stimulating the clitoris during intercourse can increase the possibility. Simultaneous orgasms may be more attainable through oral or manual stimulation.

Why women fake orgasms: They're too tired or afraid of hurting a partner's feelings; they want to please a partner. **Why women shouldn't fake orgasms:** It's completely counterproductive! How will your partner ever figure out what you like if you pretend to be enjoying something when you aren't?

National organizations

Planned Parenthood Federation of America. National headquarters: 810 Seventh Avenue, New York, NY 10019. Phone: 800-230-PLAN. Website: http://www.plannedparenthood.org.

Online

All About Sex at http://www.allabout sex.org is a site dedicated to positive feelings about sexuality.

The Go Ask Alice Web site at http://www.goaskalice.columbia.edu answers a multitude of questions about health, dating, sexuality, drug use, depression, and more.

Sex, Etc. at http://www.sxetc.org is a very strong, well-done newsletter for and by teens about sexuality.

Teenwire at http://www.teenwire.com is Planned Parenthood's candid site for teenagers.

Books

Changing Bodies, Changing Lives: A Book for Teens on Sex and Relationships by Ruth Bell (Times Books). A superb book covering all aspects of teen sexuality, relationships, and coping with life.

The Go Ask Alice Book of Answers: A Guide to Good Physical, Sexual, and Emotional Health by Columbia University's Health Education Program (Owl Books). Based on the website, the book answers questions about the whole range of health, sexuality, and emotional well-being concerns.

Our Bodies, Ourselves for the New Century: A Book by and for Women by Boston Women's Health Book Collective (Touchstone Books). The classic book on women's health and awareness, recently updated to include online resources and discussions of AIDS.

For more resources and information, see http://www.dealwithit.com

sexuality

sexual feelings

Chapter 2

WHAT IS SEX?

SEX IS COMMUNICATION

Sex is people communicating with their bodies. By its very nature, sex requires trust. When you get close to someone and literally put your body in that person's hands, you need to feel safe both physically and emotionally. Regardless of how in sync you and another person may be, there are issues to be discussed. Without trust and communication, sexual experiences can be unsatisfying, disturbing, and potentially even dangerous. With trust and communication, these experiences can be fun, deep, emotional, and thrilling.

Everybody starts **experimenting sexually** at different ages and different rates. Nobody should do anything they aren't comfortable with or ready to do.

My bf and I really like each other.
My only problem is that he hasn't kissed a girl before me and
isn't too good at it, but I have kissed worse. Should I
just tell him he isn't the greatest kisser or will he
get more used to it after a little while? I
don't want to make him mad by telling
him. Yet I hate how he
kisses. Any advice?
— **vulcano**

My ex
was the same
way, so what I did
was just try to force my
way of kissing onto him (if that
makes any sense). You can also say "I
really like it when we kiss like
this," then kiss him that
way. — **hydrochic**

Communicating your boundaries

Before you can communicate your boundaries, you've got to
know what they are and what you're comfortable with....

If you are not comfortable with something going on between you and
someone else, you have the absolute right to stop at any point for any
reason. You determine what your limits are, and those limits must be
respected by your partner—even if your reason for wanting to stop what
you're doing seems totally arbitrary or inconsistent with the way you were
acting previously. If you try to stop or slow the momentum, you should be
listened to—and if you aren't, be more assertive.

You have no responsibility to "finish what you started" or otherwise
take things further than you want to. Some boys may complain that you
are leaving them with a case of "blue balls"—extremely aroused penises
and testicles can ache if they do not release the mounting tension
through an orgasm. But it's not the end of the world, and it's not your
problem. (Female genitals can ache too, for the same reason.)

Respect goes both ways. It may be that you're the one who
wants to escalate things while your partner is hesitant, and you
need to heed the signals as well. Pushing a sexual encounter to
an uncomfortable place for either of you can often lead to bad
feelings afterward.

Communicating your needs

There is no formula for sex. You can't learn the rules and know how to solve the problem of "how to do it." Everyone likes different things, and good communication is crucial for good sex.

One of the most difficult things to do is to communicate with your partner about what you like. You can do this by showing or telling. It can be hard to say things like "That feels good," "Keep doing that," or "A little higher...softer... harder" out loud, but if you don't tell the other person what you want, it will be very difficult to know how to make you feel good.

Whenever I am around my boyfriend all I want to do is make out but he never makes the move. Sometimes it really annoys me. He never really wants to or at least it seems that way, but then other times he does make out with me. It just makes me con- fused. — **Urgh**

If you really want to make out more often, talk to your guy about it. You will only have fun if you're both comfortable.
— **phyllo**

the kind of kisses i don't like are sort of closed mouth and stiff lipped kind of kisses...

one of the best parts about a good kiss is before the first kiss with somebody...in that moment...

i like that moment in kissing when you go from just kissing with your lips to opening your mouth and using tongues...

Kissing

Kissing is sharing, literally (swapping spit) and emotionally.

Kissing can really run the gamut—from the totally nonsexual hello/good-bye kiss to the super-passionate make-out (which can be much more intense than more "advanced" fooling around).

Like everything else, kissing has a variety of meanings, and different girls have different kissing preferences...

i like a kiss on the cheek and how that can be really sometimes even more intimate or nicer than a big sloppy sort of french kiss...

i like being kissed gently, in a lot of ways, like when somebody just kisses you really, really softly...it's really nice...

tongue is good...don't go too crazy with it, ya know...

i like it when people kiss my neck, definitely...

i kind of like it when it's sort of like a conversation and the person that you're kissing responds to you and what you're doing...

i like dry kissing...like the ones you give one after the other, over and over...

kissing peoples' eyelids is really nice too...

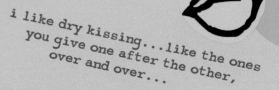

i like kissing in general because it
seems like it's a focal point on
understanding
or reading what's going on between you
and the other person...

how do
you make out
with a guy? what does
it feel like? how do you know
he wants to? do you go slow? do
you close your eyes right away?
do you pull away, or
should he?
— **aquafaery**

Making
out is whatever
comes. If it makes you
feel more comfortable clos-
ing your eyes then do it! I open my
eyes to see if his eyes are open but
then i shut them again...Believe me,
you'll know what a guy wants to do!
But if you don't want to do it, just
say so. The key is, don't let ANY guy
force you to do ANYTHING! don't be
nervous, just relax, and if you're
w/the guy you want to be with it
DOES feel good.
— **madamething**

I'm not really
the heavy make out type person
but I just want to be prepared
for what can happen. how do u
kiss a guy on his neck? i mean
do you suddenly just grab them
and start sucking on them?
does anyone have any suggestions, advice, words of
wisdom or anything?
— **gothamgirl**

It's
sort of like
after you kiss
for a while and you're
just hugging, then your
mouth is right there. It's never
something I plan. — **penny17**

my new
boyfriend is
really experi-
enced (but hasn't
gone all the way). he
has had a lot of grrl-
friends and he knows what
he's doing. i feel nervous
and stupid with him cuz i am
kinda shy about initiating our
make-out sessions. he has a
great body and i think i'm
fat (i'm trying to get into
better shape). i know he
really likes me, but i
feel like i'm not good
enuff for him. i am
inexperienced compared
to him and i'm para-
noid he's going to
think i'm
pathetic.
— **swat**

Performance Anxiety
It can feel very vulnerable to be
physically intimate with someone,
since you are opening up such a personal part of yourself to that person.
There can be a lot of things to worry
about: what your partner will think
about your level of experience, your
lack of knowledge, your body, your
size, your odor, your sex organs, or
your previous sexual encounters. It
is totally natural to be nervous about
your first sexual experiences (and
those that follow too). The more
comfortable you are with your sex
partner, the likelier it is that you
will be able to get over your anxiety
or, at least, be more comfortable
with it. Boys are definitely not
immune to this type of thing and
have their own worries about
their penises and performances.

For more information on guys,
see Boys: A Primer, pp. 158–63.

what is sex?

Touch

Touch is an important part of how human beings, and even many animals, relate to one another. There is a huge range of ways people can be made to feel good by touching, from a supportive pat on the back, to a massage, to directly touching someone's sex organs with the intention of bringing him or her to orgasm.

The line between these different kinds of touching can seem blurry at times. It's generally a good rule of thumb that if you touch (or are touched by) someone in any kind of intimate way—such as with a back rub or long hugs—you should feel comfortable and good about being with that person. If you're not interested in sexual intimacy with someone, you may avoid an uncomfortable situation by communicating your boundaries clearly before allowing that person to intimately touch you.

Everybody likes different things when it comes to being touched. And people have different erogenous zones, areas that are particularly sexually sensitive. Figuring out what feels good for you and the person you are with is a trial and error process that can be helped along a great deal by open communication.

Fingering: Touching a woman's sex organs, either externally (vulva, clitoris) or internally (inserting one or more fingers into the vagina); masturbation on a woman.

My boyfriend wants to finger me, but I am scared because I don't know exactly what it is. I know that his hand goes in my underwear, but does he actually put his finger "inside" me? And how long do guys usually do this? Does it start to hurt after a while?
— **lemonfiend**

Feeling up: Touching breasts and/or nipples with hands

I know what being felt up is...but what exactly happens?
— **willynilly**

It's just what the name implies...the guy literally "feels you up."
— **babar_x**

Most guys love girl's breasts. Since I'm not a guy, I can't give you the exact reason WHY they do, but they do. There's not much that goes on, guys just feel around. There isn't much more to say! — **miro**

it all depends on the guy. i don't think any guy does it the same. it depends on his position, your position, his fingers, etc.
— **celis**

if it's too hard to tell him what you like, just move his hands to where you want to be touched. moan or something to let him know how much you like it. if you keep doing that he'll get the idea.
— **janeygirl**

My boyfriend and I were fooling around and he started to stick my hand down his pants, so I finished it off and went all the way down. The thing is, I have no clue what to do when I get down there. He asked me if I was having troubles but I didn't know what to do. What do I do down there that turns a guy on?
— **cauliflowermary**

Just squeeze and move up and down as steadily as possible. And ask HIM what feels best. I'm sure he'll be more than happy to share.
— **tuFFie**

Just one little tip...be gentle. It's a sensitive area.
— **emasuma**

Hand job: Using hands to stimulate a man's penis (the name hand job generally implies that ejaculation is the goal); masturbation on a man

Usually when I give hand jobs, it's after we've been making out for a while and we're starting to take each other's clothes off. I just kind of GO for it :-) anyways, it seems to drive him crazy no matter what I do. If your boyfriend's like that, I doubt he'll notice you don't have much experience. He'll probably just think you have you own style. — **catballou**

Me and my boyfriend just recently started fooling around. He always gets me off, and I never have a problem with it. But when it comes to me giving him a handjob, he can never get off! It takes me about 40 minutes to actually get somewhere, but in the end he usually just stimulates himself by giving himself a handjob, and then when he is about to go, I just take over. I feel terrible, like I should be doing something. — **thepearl**

Man, you sound exactly like me! Wow! With my ex, no matter what I did, it didn't ever seem to get him off. It was so funny because he would be like "try it a little faster" or "a little tighter might help." Nothing seemed to work and I felt like my arms were going to fall off. He eventually had to stimulate HIMSELF and I think it was a little embarrassing for both of us. — **seaglass**

what is

Sex with your clothes on: Dry humping, going through the motions of sex with some or all your clothes on, preventing genital-to-genital contact

My boyfriend and I have had "dry sex" and I've felt his penis through his pants near/against my vagina. Is there any chance I could get pregnant? — **sisyann**

Dry humping is completely safe, as long as your clothes are still on. You can't get pregnant, and you can't catch anything. — **LaKeisha**

going down on him
giving a blow job
fellatio

Oral sex on a guy: Using the mouth (including lips and tongue) to stimulate a guy's sex organs.

I try to look into my boyfriend's eyes when I'm sucking. It seems to get him off faster. I also lick and suck his balls, but not too hard. If my mouth gets tired I use my hand to jerk him off for a little while until I can suck again. Don't suck too hard—I try to make my mouth feel soft but tight. — **salome**

The first time I ever went down on a guy, I literally sucked on his penis....he ended up with a HUGE hickey and he said it hurt to go pee. With time and experience I learned that when you "suck" on a guy, what you actually do is just kinda put him in your mouth (careful of those teeth) and bob your head up and down sliding your hand up and down his penis at the same time.
— **freethrowqueen**

Concentrate on the head, like little kisses, etc. (that's the most sensitive part). Underneath the shaft is also a good place to concentrate (roll your tongue down the bottom of it). If it's kind of a big one, then don't try to get the whole thing in your mouth, 'cause it might make you gag, which is hardly romantic. Have fun and just go with what seems right. — **Nadine14**

To swallow or not to swallow?

Am I supposed to swallow it when he comes in my mouth? I feel like I'm going to gag.
— **laccee**

I think guys like it better if you swallow, but if it grosses you out, you can sort of move your mouth away and just make sure you cover the head with your hand so he's not squirting all over the place. — **miNimouse**

You shouldn't let your boyfriend make you feel bad just because you don't want to give him a blow job. It's not fair of him to say that you don't love him just cuz you won't give him head. — **greenone**

Oh, it ain't so bad. I wouldn't put it on my cornflakes, but it doesn't taste too heinous! — **BlossomD**

eating out cunnilingus going down

Oral sex on a girl: Using the mouth (including lips and tongue) to stimulate a girl's sex organs

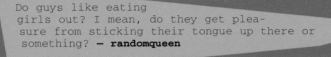

Hey, about how girls get oral sex: You've more than likely heard the term "going down on a girl" or "eating a girl out." Well, in a way it's like fingering a girl—same concept—just using the tongue.

— LilyT

Do guys like eating girls out? I mean, do they get pleasure from sticking their tongue up there or something? **— randomqueen**

Some guys feel that if they make a girl cum, than they have done a good job pleasing her. some guys just like eating girls......my b/f does it to me cuz he loves me and he knows that I like it a lot.

— maybelle

Safe oral sex: The only totally safe way to perform oral sex is with a condom on the penis or by using a "dental dam" on the vagina when a girl is on the receiving end. Condoms even come flavored ("touch o' mint" is standard) for this purpose. It is important to note that a guy doesn't have to come in your mouth during a blow job in order for fluid to be transmitted. Something called pre-ejaculate or pre-cum comes out of the penis before the sperm, and it carries all of the potential diseases the sperm carries.

For more information on the prevention of pregnancy and STDs, see pp. 103–19.

69 is simultaneous oral sex (people talk about it more than they do it)

Girls having sex with girls
Girls having sex with girls can engage in any or all of the activities mentioned here except for the ones that require a penis.

See How do two girls have sex? and Safer sex between girls, **p. 138.**

Cleanliness and oral sex:
There is nothing inherently unclean about vaginas or penises as long as they are washed regularly. And there is no need to feel self-conscious about your vaginal taste and mild odor. If someone makes you feel awkward or bad about it, you might want to think twice about having sex with that person.

Vaginal fluids are meant to be aphrodisiacs. That's why people get off on going down on girls: the smell, the taste, all of it combined is very stimulating.

When you start to do it, do you think, "Did he wash it?"
— SportyQ

sexuality

hiding the salami shtupping pOking screwing
laying knockin'boots making love sexual intercourse
fUcking doing it doing the nasty bumping uglies

Vaginal sex: Penis in vagina.
This is generally thought to be the only kind of sex that can
result in pregnancy (though it is possible to get pregnant if a
man ejaculates close to your vagina). For this reason, it's often
what people think of when they think of "sex." In fact, penis-
vagina penetration is just one part of sex, and not necessarily
the best part, either. That said, vaginal intercourse is, to some
people, the ultimate act of love that a man and woman can
engage in and as close as two people can get.

Sexual positioning
It is possible to have sexual intercourse in many different
positions. You are really limited only by your body's flexibility and your
own imagination. Probably the three most popular positions are:

Vaginal intercourse
poses high risks for
both getting diseases
and pregnancy. Anal
sex poses high risk for
disease. Learn how to
protect yourself.

See Protecting Yourself, for detailed
information on safer sex, pp. 103–19.

boy on top
(also called
missionary position)

girl on top

boy behind girl
(known as doggie style)

Lubrication: For
the movements of sex to
go smoothly, it is important
that the vagina be well lubricated.
Bodies provide their own lubrication, but sometimes not enough. If
you find yourself feeling uncomfortable during penetration, you could
try a commercial lubricant from a
drugstore. Water-based lubricants
are the only kind that work
with condoms.

Anal sex: Penetration of the anus by a
penis (or other stuff, such as fingers).
There are lots of nerve endings in and
around the anus, and many people find that
stimulation of this area can be pleasurable.
It can also, however, be very painful. Any
experimentation in this area should
involve substantial lubrication and
should be treated as highly risky sex.
The tissues inside the rectum are very
susceptible to damage and the subsequent
bleeding can transmit diseases.

SEX IS PLAY

For many people, sex involves more than just the basic activities described in the preceding pages. Sex is supposed to be fun and many adults consider it to be a kind of "play" (not without risks, obviously). If you are in a trusting relationship, there is a world of possibility.

Toys

Some people like using objects for sexual stimulation, whether they are specifically designed for that use or not. Thousands of different kinds of sex toys are available. (Sales are often restricted to people over 18.) Some common sex toys:

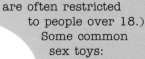

Dildos are objects designed for penetration and often, but not always, resemble a penis.

Vibrators, either electric or battery-operated, produce vibrations, which many people find pleasurable. Some vibrators are designed for penetration, others for external use.

Anything, as long as it's clean, unbreakable, and has no sharp edges, is fair game as a sex toy. In a larger sense, sex toys include everything people use to enhance sex—flowers, feathers, food, oils, whatever gives you pleasure.

> Body Massagers are little gadgets that serve about the same purpose that vibrators do...they vibrate. You cannot insert it, but it massages your clit. You may even have one at home which your parents use to alleviate their aching backs...or do they really?
> — **Marlys**

Fantasies

Many people fantasize about various sexual situations. They may pretend to be someone else (role playing) for a little while and even dress up to help fortify the fantasy.

Some people are turned on by the idea of sex as a power relationship. Tying each other up (bondage) is one way to do that. Sadomasochism (S&M), in which one partner deliberately inflicts pain on the other, is also a kind of power role-playing.

These games can be fun to experiment with—if they happen within the context of a healthy, adult relationship. But they can also be dangerous, psychologically and physically. People have different ideas about what's okay, so it is crucial to understand both partners' feelings, desires, and boundaries before even dabbling in this kind of play.

Multiple partners

Three-way sex is called a threesome or a ménage à trois. An orgy or group sex refers to sex with more than three participants. When multiple people are involved in sexual activities, it can stop being about an emotional connection and become more of a physical interaction. Sometimes it can be a way of same-sex experimentation without the intimacy of a one-on-one experience.

Emotionally, multiple-person sex can be pretty intense. It is important to consider the feelings involved and the risks, which increase when there are more people to potentially communicate diseases.

what is sex?

ATTITUDES TOWARD SEX

Because sex means so many different things to different people, it inspires very strong opinions and emotions. Everyone's opinions are affected by other peoples' attitudes, family background, religious beliefs, the media, cultural attitudes and laws, and personal experiences.

The decisions you make about sex should be your own, but it's important to have a sense of perspective about the attitudes of others so you can have a clear idea about what is actually important to you.

Genital mutilation

In some traditional cultures, mostly in Africa and Southeast Asia, the horrifying practice of female genital mutilation is practiced on girls to ensure that they never experience sexual pleasure. This procedure involves the scarring or removal of a girl's external genitals (clitoris and labia). There has been worldwide outcry against this practice, but like many deeply ingrained traditions, it is dying hard. Women living in these societies who don't get cut are shunned as outcasts.

People who have very strict religious upbringings tend to have different and far more modest notions about sex than those who don't. The notion that sex is primarily for the purposes of procreation rather than pleasure—automatically discounting masturbation, premarital sex, and bi- or homosexuality, among other things—is a strong thread in many religions.

Women who are raised in strict religious households can develop intense feelings of shame around their sexuality, which can inhibit sexual pleasure and turn a healthy, enjoyable aspect of life into a minefield of negative emotions.

The double standard

The idea that boys are supposed to get as much action as possible but girls are supposed to be virgins until they are married is unfair and outdated. Yet remnants of this attitude persist. Girls sometimes feel that admitting or acting on their desires will make people think they are slutty or overly sexual. It's hard for some people to see that women are healthy, sexual beings who don't have to choose between being "good girls" or "bad girls," virgins or whores.

Family attitudes about sex

Our earliest impressions about sex and intimacy come from our parents and the way they express affection and love to each other. Some parents are extremely open about the fact that they have a sex life and sexual urges, while others are very uncomfortable and uptight about it and may convey a sense of disapproval when you start to have such feelings. You can't help but be affected by your parents' attitudes toward sex, and if they view it as something that is wrong or bad, you may have to contend with those feelings in yourself.

Sex and the media

Sex, in one way or another, is a big part of what we see and hear in the media. Sex is used to sell everything from beer and cars to cosmetics, clothing, music, movies, and more. The images we see in the media help to define how some people think about what turns them on. This can be annoying if you think about how idealized a lot of these images are. There is no woman on earth who is as flawless in real life as the retouched photos in most magazines.

Porn

In addition to the presence of sex in the media in general, a whole industry is devoted exclusively to producing media that are explicitly about sex and sexuality. Videos, movies, websites, books, magazines, and other publications whose primary purpose is to cause sexual excitement are commonly referred to as pornography (porn) and/or erotica.

The thing to remember about pornography is that it is specifically created as fantasy. Whether the fantasy is about how sexy someone looks or a person's willingness to have sex in a particular way, nothing matters in porn but sex. In the real world, this is obviously not the case.

Why is so much porn geared toward guys only? There has been a long-running debate over the idea that girls and guys get turned on by different kinds of things. One theory is that guys respond more to visual stimuli, whereas girls tend to be more aroused by ideas or words. However, there are many women who disagree with this theory. And porn is increasingly being made by and for women.

Erotica, which refers to depictions of sex in fine art and literature, as well as in some magazines and movies, has classier connotations than pornography, which is the commercialized, mass production of sexual images. However, one person's pornography is another's erotica. Even the Supreme Court has had trouble defining pornography, with Justice Potter Stewart writing in 1964 that he couldn't define it, but he knew it when he saw it.

Sex and the law

Somewhat bizarrely, even today some states have laws on the books that prohibit oral and anal sex, and these acts are considered "crimes against nature" even when they are performed between consenting adults. Although the term "sodomy" originally referred to anal intercourse only, at some point the definition was broadened to include oral/genital contact as well. Even if the sodomy laws of certain states seem obsolete, the Supreme Court affirmed states' rights to have such laws in 1986.

For information on sex crimes, see pp. 147–57.

Prostitution, or sex for money, is the world's oldest profession. Although practiced widely, it is illegal everywhere in the United States, except in the state of Nevada. There has long been a debate about the decriminalization of prostitution. Some find it morally wrong, and view sex workers as exploited victims. Others see it as an economic transaction between two consenting adults.

sexuality

what is sex?

Chapter 3

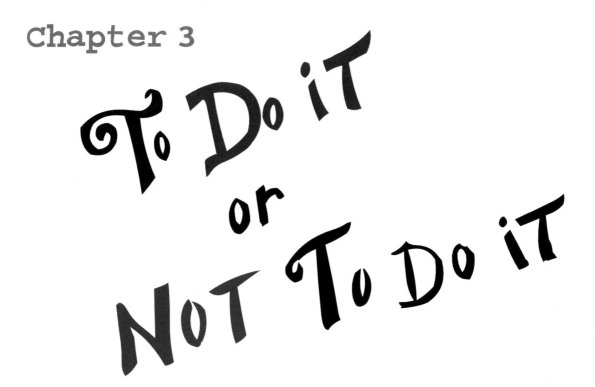

To Do it

or

Not To Do it

Everyone has different beliefs and levels of experience, and nobody should ever feel pressured to have sex or to get more sexual experience.

Sexual intercourse is only one part of sexual intimacy, though it is a huge, loaded part. Virgin or not, the real issue is to be comfortable with your decision every time you participate in sexual intimacy, whether you are deciding to make out, give or receive oral sex, have intercourse, or anything else. Each time is a new choice, and your actions always deserve thought and attention.

In all areas, communication between the people involved is extremely important. But even before there can be good communication, you need to know in your head what you WANT and what is right, safe, and appropriate for you at any time in your life. Do what you are comfortable with and do it safely!

TO LOSE IT OR NOT TO LOSE IT

When someone is trying to decide whether to have sexual intercourse for the first time, there are many factors to consider. The issue of whether to "lose your virginity" can be huge, or it can be one aspect of a larger view of your sexuality, depending on your ideas and beliefs. Virginity has many social and cultural implications, but in the end it means something different and personal to each girl in a given situation.

It is a good idea to think about what "losing your virginity" means to you and to try to understand what you want for yourself. If you are clear about this with yourself, it will be much easier to be clear with your partner.

Many teenage girls say they started having sex involuntarily or with great reluctance, and only after succumbing to pressure from their partners. In one study, 60 percent of the women who had sex before they were 15 said they had not really wanted to. The reasons people cite for having sex when they don't really want to include not knowing how to say "no," being under the influence of drugs or alcohol, not wanting to hurt someone's feelings, and peer pressure. The longer people waited, the more likely they were to feel in control and embrace their first sexual experience as positive.

Just the facts about . . .virginity

A 1998 study by the Kaiser Family Foundation and YM magazine of 650 teenagers from 13 to 18 determined:

Among 17-year-olds, 51 percent of girls have had sexual intercourse.

Among 16-year-olds, 40 percent of girls have had sexual intercourse.

Among 13- and 14-year-olds, boys and girls,13 percent have had sexual intercourse.

Among teenagers who are sexually experienced, the average age of first sexual intercourse is 15. Nearly half said they were pressured before they were ready.

Uncertainty

No one can tell you whether you're ready for sex. You're the only one who knows whether you can handle the responsibility.

If you are uncertain about whether to have sex, pay attention to your own concerns. Don't have sex unless you know for sure that you want to. And when you do, do it safely.

I'm 18 and I'm still a virgin. I don't think there's anything wrong with that, 'cause I've always wanted my first time to be special 'n stuff...but recently I've been more than obsessed with sex. I don't have a boyfriend, but I KNOW I could do it with one of my guy friends (we're pretty close buddies). I really think I wanna have sex, but I'm afraid I'll regret it later.
– theprocrastinator

 My boyfriend is not a virgin but I am. He said he would wait for me. Should I have sex with him or should I wait? **– MADEIRA**

So like the day before my 18th birthday I can't, but the day after I can? Marriage? Nah. So I guess the age for losing my virginity is the age when I'd be willing to take care of a baby 24-7.
— **Quinney**

To me, sex isn't about waiting for your spouse, it's about waiting for the guy YOU CHOOSE to have sex with. — **cpcake**

I have been dating my boyfriend for over a year and we have never had sex. There have been times when we have gotten close, but we fought our way through it. We are definitely waiting till we get married. — **EarlofGray**

PARTNER pressure

It can be uncomfortable and unpleasant to feel pressure from your partner to have sex, or to appear experienced. Teenage girls with older boyfriends may feel this pressure more acutely.

There also can be physical pressure from your partner in the moment. If you feel that someone is pressuring you into something you don't want to do, make your feelings known in a clear way and make sure things stop. It may feel awkward and embarrassing, but it can feel even worse if you do not speak up.

Communication and trust are essential to sex between two people. If you feel that you can't trust your partner, take that feeling very seriously.

I kinda told my boyfriend that I'm not a virgin when really I am, and I'm wondering if I should tell him I am or just let it go.
— **digitalhead**

Under the influence
People can make bad decisions about sex when they are drunk or stoned and their common sense is impaired. Sex is a great and powerful thing, but it is no fun to wake up wondering what you did last night and who you did it with. Nor is it any fun to have a sense of regret about any of your actions.

See the **Altered states** for more info, **pp. 200–213.**

A couple of weeks ago I was making out with my B-friend (now my ex) and he asked me to have sex and I said "no." And he got all pissed off. The reason I said "no" is 'cause I didn't want to and 'cause I was afraid it would hurt. — **garp**

PEER Pressure

There can be a lot of pressure from your friends to either "lose your virginity" or "keep" it.

> I have different beliefs than some of my friends on sex. I respect my friends' beliefs, but they don't really respect mine. One friend is always saying, "Why wouldn't you? It's not a big deal."
> — **DarbEE**

> My friend recently lost her virginity, and I feel like I am SOOOO behind! I am afraid that I'll sleep with the next guy who comes along, even if I really don't like him that much. — **t2sday**

> My friends don't really agree with my decision to give up my virginity with my b/f cuz they said it was too early. — **trinket**

> Listen, gurl, I don't know how old you are, but there really isn't such a thing as being "far behind." Your friend lost her virginity—so what? If she loved the guy and was sure that the time was right, good for her. If she just did it as a spur of the moment thing, or so SHE wouldn't be "behind," then I feel bad for her. — **harmonious**

> Teenagers don't get enough credit for being mature. They always talk about how we cave at the slightest bit of peer pressure, but that is just not true. Some of us know when it's right. If it isn't, we won't do it.
> — **phyllo**

Reputation

Your sex life is your own business, but people will invariably form opinions about it. If you don't feel good about the circumstances under which you've had sex, you may be more susceptible to worrying about what other people think. Unfortunately, the idea that "good girls" don't experiment sexually before marriage still persists.

> About a month ago I started dating this guy who was 3 years older than I am and when he asked me if I was a virgin I said "no" because I didn't want him to think I was a loser. I slept with him the first night I met him and then he broke up with me a week later, but now he thinks I'm a slut! — **Gilda**

THE FIRST TIME

There can be a lot of expectation and emphasis placed on the first time, and it can be difficult for any experience to measure up to that kind of pressure. There is no correct way to have sexual intercourse—it's about what works for the two people involved. You may have to stop and start many times (over the course of one night or several days). To make the first time the best it can be, it's important to be completely comfortable with your decision and with your partner—and to be safe.

Doing it safely

If you do decide that you want to be sexually active, you must learn how to protect yourself, both from pregnancy and from sexually transmitted diseases!

Making the decision to be sexually active means taking on the responsibility for your sexual health. Part of this responsibility is talking to your partner about safer sex, birth control, and attitudes about pregnancy and abortion, since no birth control is 100 percent effective.

If you haven't done so before, you should see a gynecologist for a pelvic/vaginal exam.

The pain factor

There may be some discomfort the first time you have intercourse. Much of it depends on how unstretched your hymen is. Also, if you are tense and anxious, the vagina may be both drier and tighter. As a woman becomes more aroused and relaxed, her vaginal entrance will become looser and more lubricated, which can make the experience less painful. The more you trust and are comfortable with your partner, the more relaxed you'll be. You may want to try a lubricant such as K-Y Jelly or Aqualube or use a lubricated condom to lessen the pain. If your hymen hasn't been broken before, there may be some bleeding.

> For me it hurt bad the first time, and I can't speak for everybody, but I don't think sex feels that great for girls their first time. I was close to crying!
> — **ortiz**

> I'd suggest that you request he performs oral sex on you first. This lubricates things up so it goes in easier. And bring your own condoms around with you—the lubricated kind. Remember, tell your boyfriend if you want him to stop (because you feel pain or for any other reason).
> — **sneakykate**

> If gurls hurt having sex for the first time, does it hurt guys too if a gurl is "tight"?
> — **faedra**

> Guys don't hurt when they lose their virginity—all they feel is the pressure on the penis (which is where the pleasure comes from). We feel pain because our organs are being stretched to new sizes, dealing with a new, uncomfortable thing inside.
> — **cHirp**

use cOndoms!

For information on safer sex, see pp. 103–19.

to do it or not to do it

sexuality

Emotions

Sexual activity or intercourse adds its own unpredictable emotional impact to the mix of emotions already floating around in any relationship.

> It's hard for me to let go of him because I lost my virginity to him.
> — **desdemono**

> I lost my virginity recently and I've been feeling/acting so strange. I feel happy/depressed/confused, despite the fact that I am confident with the decision I made.
> — **Gales**

> Since my bf and I had sex, I feel much closer to him. But now I am totally overprotective. We were both virgins. Now I always worry about him doing it with another girl. I know he wouldn't do it, but I can't help thinking about it and I get mad at him a lot easier.
> — **schmetterling**

the wide world of virginity rituals

Bizarre virginity rituals have been common in history and all over the world. In ancient Greece, for example, an aristocratic young girl who had reached marrying age would have her hymen pierced by the stone penis of the Greek god Priapus. The symbol of male virility and fertility, Priapus was represented as a strange little gnomelike man with a huge erect penis. The piercing of the young girl's hymen was meant to ensure her readiness for marriage as well as her future fertility. In ancient Rome, a wooden statue of Liber, the Roman counterpart of Priapus, was used to perform the ceremony.

Among some African peoples, until as recently as the nineteenth century, a king would be offended if he was offered a virgin bride. Deflowerment was considered potentially too much messy work, beneath the dignity of a king, better performed by the tribe's holy man or with a dildo.

Another tradition of deflowering virgins was used by the Sumerians in Mesopotamia in 3000 B.C.E. Called the "Right of First Night," it took place on a couple's wedding night, when the groom would allow his bride to have sex first with his master, king, or high priest as a form of homage. The Chinese, Kurds, and various Muslims all practiced some form of the Right of First Night, which continued into the 1700s in Europe. In later years and in different societies, the Right of First Night became a form of oppression and rape by the ruling classes, as when it was practiced by slave owners in the American South on their slaves' daughters.

Although now sexual and women's liberation have made these rituals and beliefs obsolete, there are still some cultures that view women as property and therefore cling to the belief that a woman's virginity is sacred. In parts of Turkey, virginity tests are still performed on young girls. The practice was questioned in the 1990s when five girls ages 12 to 16 attempted suicide by taking rat poison and jumping into a deep water tank to avoid being tested. Even after the outcry, the government defended the practice for girls who are wards of the state.

And in Thailand's child sex trade, a high premium is placed on virgins (who are thought to be AIDS-free), which has meant that younger and younger girls are coerced and forced into becoming prostitutes.

The hymen and virginity

Although virgin technically means any person who has not had sexual intercourse, guy or girl, it has traditionally referred mostly to girls. That is because, for much of human history, there was thought to be an observable physical indicator of a woman's virginity—the hymen, the thin membrane near the entrance of the vagina that can break and bleed the first time a woman has intercourse. People used to place a lot more importance on the hymen than they do today. The hymen was considered the symbol of a woman's purity, and a woman who could not prove her purity, generally with a bloodied bedsheet on her wedding night, was considered "fallen," "damaged," "tarnished," and "dirty." Worse still, she was worthless on the marriage market. This was partly because in patrilineal societies (where property is passed from father to son), the husband wanted an absolute guarantee that any child his wife produced was his biological heir.

In the Western world, the hymen retained its importance until the 1920s, when comparatively liberated young women became more open about sex and this new attitude filtered through to the rest of society. Now, it is common knowledge that girls are born with hymens of such a variety of shapes and sizes that some will break and bleed upon first penetration and some will not. Also, many girls lead such active lives, from horseback riding to biking to gymnastics, that even those who are born with noticeable hymens may not make it to their teens with the hymen still intact. Finally, the use of tampons and even a pelvic examination by a doctor can alter the state of a hymen, removing it from the virginity equation.

RESOURCES

National Organizations

Planned Parenthood, 810 Seventh Avenue, New York, NY 10019. Phone: 800-230-PLAN. Website: http://www.plannedparenthood.org.

True Love Waits encourages abstinence until marriage. Phone: 800-LUV-WAIT.

Online

National Campaign to Prevent Teen Pregnancy at http://www.teenpregnancy.org provides information on preventing teen pregnancy.

Sex, Etc. at http://www.sxetc.org is a newsletter by teens about sexuality.

Teen Advice Online at http://www.teenadviceonline.org answers teenager's questions about all range of subjects.

Teenwire at http://www.teenwire.com is Planned Parenthood's candid site for teenagers.

Books

Changing Bodies, Changing Lives by Ruth Bell (Times Books).

Go Ask Alice by Columbia University's Health Education Program (Henry Holt).

For more resources and information, see http://www.dealwithit.com

I just lost my virginity 2 days ago. It was extremely painful and I bled a ton. Now the pain has gone away but I'm still bleeding a little. Is this abnormal? Now that I've gone thru "pain of entry," it won't be nearly as bad next time, right?
- **FaythFul**

It is pretty normal for there to be more blood for a while, so I don't think you need to worry about that. And yes, it will be less painful the next time.
- **edgy**

to do it or not to do it

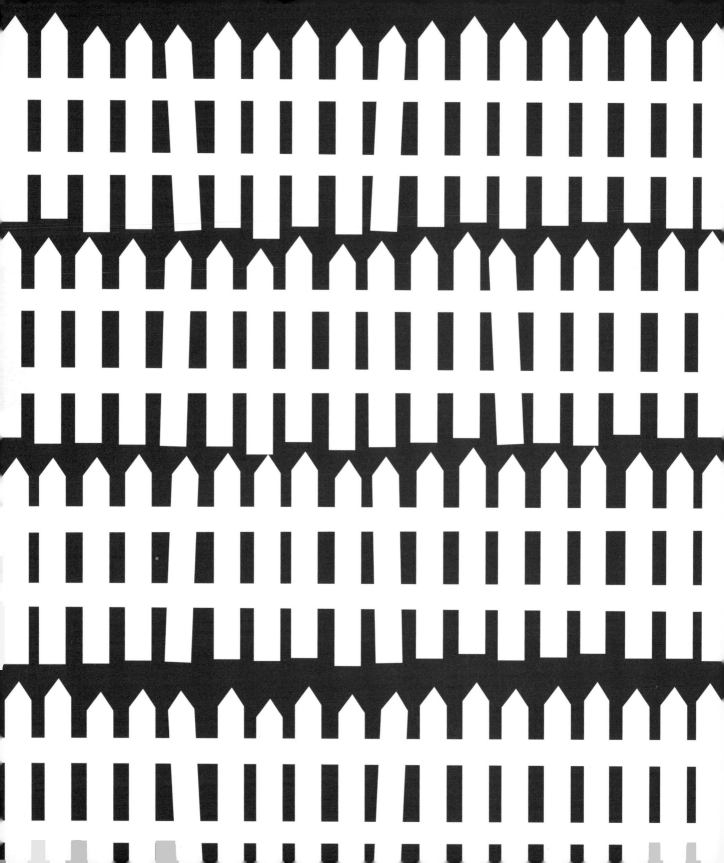

Chapter 4

PROTECTION

If you decide you are ready to have sex or if you're having sex already, there are two huge things to think about —>

safer sex: protection from sexually transmitted diseases (STDs)

and

birth control: protection from getting pregnant

If you are not ready to think about this stuff, you are not ready to have sex.

If you are having sex and not protecting yourself on either or both of these fronts, you are treating yourself and your sex partner with a huge amount of disrespect and putting both of you at risk.

Girls having sex with girls don't need to worry about birth control, but they most definitely need to worry about STDs!

There are precautions to take on both fronts, and it's important to understand the options, the risks, and the potential consequences of your behavior.

Just the facts about . . .
teenagers and protection

The Centers for Disease Control (CDC) estimates that:

By the twelfth grade, two-thirds of teenagers have already had sex, and a quarter of them have had four or more partners.

More than half of these teenagers reported that they did not use a condom the last time they had sex.

The average teenager is sexually active for up to a year before using methods of birth control and STD protection. (The earlier teenagers become sexually active, the more likely they are to be irresponsible about STD prevention and birth control.)

Every year, one million teenage girls become pregnant in the United States.

Three million teenagers (one-tenth of all adolescents and about a quarter of those who are sexually active) get an STD every year.

The earlier you start having sex and the more partners you have sex with, the greater your chances of contracting an STD, particularly genital warts and herpes, which are very widespread (at least one in four Americans has one or the other). As many as one-third of sexually active teenagers have chlamydia. One in five Americans over the age of 12 has genital herpes, and adolescents make up between one-quarter and one-half of those with genital herpes. Between 20 and 40 percent of college students have an STD.

for information on specific STDs, see the STD Chart, p. 112–13

Effectiveness of Different Birth Control Methods

Birth Control Method	Effectiveness against STDs	Effectiveness against Pregnancy
Condom	High. Except for abstinence, this is the best protection against STDs.	86–98% (male latex condom) 79–95% (female condom)
Diaphragm with spermicide	Low. Spermicide may protect against chlamydia and gonorrhea.	80–94%
Cervical cap with spermicide	Low. Spermicide may protect against chlamydia and gonorrhea.	80–90% (for women who haven't had a child) 60–80% (for women who have had a child)
Spermicide alone	Low. May protect against chlamydia and gonorrhea.	72–94%
Birth control pill	None	95–99.9%
Depo-Provera	None	99.7%
Norplant	None	99.9%
IUD (intrauterine device)	None	97.4–99.2%
Surgical sterilization	None	Above 99%
Sponge	None	64–94%

104

Note: The percentages above range from "typical use" to that which is always consistent and correct.

As you can see, condoms are the only method effective against both STDs and pregnancy. And no birth control method (except abstinence) is 100 percent effective against pregnancy. If you have sex, no matter which birth control method you use, there is a chance you will get pregnant. Given this, it is important to think hard about what you might do if you became pregnant accidentally and whether you want to put yourself at risk for this.

See also Getting Pregnant, p. 121–31.

STD prevention is not only about using barrier methods. It's also about communicating with your partner, knowing your partner's history, and understanding the risks involved with different kinds of sexual activity.

For more about communicating with your partner see, pp. 81–83.

Abstinence is 100 percent effective in preventing both STDs and pregnancy, but it's not always a practical option.

CONDOMS

use cOndoms!

To be as safe as possible, use condoms during any sex with any man. If a guy says he won't use a condom, then don't have sex with him. Using condoms is easier than dealing with an STD.

The male condom

What it is: A thin latex covering that fits over the erect penis. There are also animal-skin condoms, but they are not as effective against viruses like HIV, so they are not recommended.

How it works: Provides a barrier to the sperm that come out of the penis during male orgasm. Some condoms have a reservoir tip at the end to catch sperm and make breakage less likely. Some condoms come with spermicide (sperm-killer), usually nonoxynol-9.

Effectiveness against pregnancy: Average is 86 percent against pregnancy. Careful use can improve that number. Using it in combination with spermicide can be very effective.

Effectiveness against STDs: The KING of disease prevention, especially when combined with spermicide.

When effective: As soon as you put it on properly.

Side effects: Some people are allergic to latex and to nonoxynol-9 spermicide, which comes with many condoms.

Available: Widely, at drug and convenience stores. No excuse not to have some.

Cost: About $1 apiece; less if you buy in bulk.

Benefits: Cheap and easy to get. Can prolong erection.

Disadvantages: Must interrupt sex to put it on. Some guys complain that they can't feel as much with it on. Less effective against pregnancy than other methods when used alone. Condoms can break or slip. Guys must pull out right after orgasm, while still erect, to make sure the condom stays on, so there's not much time to savor the moment afterward.

Common mistakes: Condoms are regulated and inspected by the Food and Drug Administration (FDA), so the failure rate usually results from improper usage, tearing one accidentally, putting it on after intercourse has begun, and/or failure to withdraw while the penis is still erect.

How to put on a condom: After your partner is erect and before his penis goes anywhere near your vagina, open the package carefully with your fingers, without a sharp implement, so as not to tear the condom. Note: If you prefer, you can open the condom package (leaving the condom inside the wrapper) before you begin fooling around so it takes less time to

sexuality

put it on when you and your partner are aroused.

Pinch the tip to squeeze out the air and create a little space for the sperm to go.

Put the stiff ring around the head of the penis and unroll down to the base of the penis.

Add water-based lubricant or spermicide if desired. Do not used oil-based lubricants such as petroleum jelly (these can weaken the latex).

How to take off a condom: Immediately after ejaculation, while the penis is still hard, the guy should withdraw his penis while holding the open end of the condom to seal in juices. Slide the condom off and throw it away.

CONDOMS

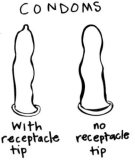

With receptacle tip

no receptacle tip

Storing condoms: Take care to store them in a dry place that's not too hot. Replace them if it's past the expiration date printed on all FDA-approved condom packages.

Different kinds of condoms

Condoms come in different shapes, colors, and flavors. These days, there is an incredible variety of condoms on the market to suit every preference.

Contoured Condoms: Instead of being just straight, uniform cylinders, these are designed to grip the head of the penis either more firmly or more loosely.

Ribbed Condoms: These have a ridged texture in concentric rings. They are marketed as being more pleasurable for the woman, although many say they don't notice the difference.

Reservoir-Tip Condoms: With their built-in sperm-receptacle area, these are less likely to break, making them a good choice.

Testicle-Cover Condoms: As the name suggests, they cover not just the shaft of the penis, but the balls as well, for an extra measure of safety, both in terms of birth control (they stay on better) and STD prevention (by further reducing skin contact).

Black Condoms: These are designed with darker skin tones in mind.

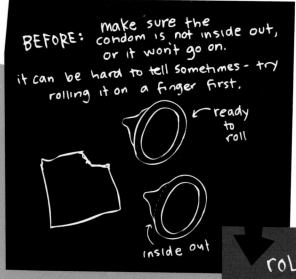

BEFORE: make sure the condom is not inside out, or it won't go on.

it can be hard to tell sometimes - try rolling it on a finger first.

ready to roll

inside out

putting on a condom

roll the CONDOM ON.

Leave extra room at tip

roll all the way DOWN

OK

Colored Condoms: Purely aesthetic—if the idea of having sex with a blue penis turns you on, go for it.

X-Large Condoms: Although condoms are a one-size-fits-all item, some well-endowed guys may find regulars too constricting and should give these a try. But for a condom to work effectively, its fit at the base of the penis must be snug. Using a condom that is too loose could decrease its effectiveness.

Flavored and Novelty Condoms: Chocolate-flavored, mint-flavored, you name it. The main thing is to make sure the condom does the job you need it for, so read the packages of novelty condoms carefully.

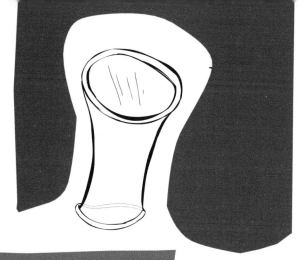

The female condom

What it is: Polyurethane sleeve that fits into the vagina with rings on both ends.

How it works: Blocks semen, viruses, and skin contact.

Effectiveness against pregnancy: 75 to 95 percent, depending on how well it's used.

Effectiveness against STDs: It covers more surface area than a male condom.

When effective: As soon as you get it in place.

Side effects: None.

Available: At drugstores.

Cost: About $2.50 each.

Benefits: Great protection against STDs; and can be inserted in advance of sex to maintain the mood.

Disadvantages: Can be ungainly and a bit odd to use. It is reported to squeak.

Common mistakes: Not to be used along with a male condom—they pull each other off.

Condoms and oral sex

Opinions vary on the necessity of using condoms or another barrier method when giving or receiving oral sex. Herpes definitely can be transmitted from genitals to the mouth and vice versa during unprotected oral sex. There are few clear cases of HIV transmission during oral sex.

You can lower your risk by making sure your gums, lips, mouth, and throat are healthy, as well as by not letting men come in your mouth and by not performing cunnilingus on menstruating women. Some sex educators recommend not brushing or flossing for up to 2 hours after giving unprotected oral sex. To be even more safe, use a condom on a man and a dental dam, a cut-open condom, a Glyde® dam, or non-microwavable plastic kitchen wrap on a woman when giving oral sex.

Slippage and breakage: Condoms can slip or break during sex. If this happens, stop and put on a new condom.

If you only realize this after sex, and you think you are at a fertile point in your cycle and definitely don't want to get pregnant, **see emergency contraception, p. 123.**

WHAT IS SAFER SEX?

When it comes to protection from sexually transmitted diseases, the only truly safe sex is no sex at all (or sex with yourself only).

See Masturbation, pp. 72–73.

Any sex with another person introduces an element of risk. If you choose to have sex anyway, the idea is to keep the risk level as low as possible. One way to do this is to always use barrier protection.

Use condoms! If you are not using condoms with a guy for intercourse, you are not practicing safer sex.

If you are sleeping with girls, you obviously don't need condoms unless you're sharing sex toys. But you do need barrier protection. STDs can be transmitted through vaginal fluid too (although not as easily). The chances of disease transmission of AIDS and hepatitis B are increased if you have even tiny cuts on your mouth or hands through which germs can enter your bloodstream. Dental dams, cut-open condoms, Glyde® dams, and plastic wrap, the kind used in the kitchen, can be used during cunnilingus to cover the vaginal area. For sex involving fingers, latex gloves and individual finger coverings called finger cots can be used.

Is it ever safe not to use barrier protection?

STDs are not only transmitted through sperm and vaginal fluid. They can be transmitted skin to skin and saliva to saliva, as well as blood to blood. In fact, most STDs are transmitted when someone with an STD-infected penis or vagina directly touches another person's genitals, which is skin-to-skin transmission, not bodily fluid transmission. This is why male or female condoms are not 100 percent effective against diseases like herpes and HPV. They can't cover every inch of a person's genitals.

Safer sex is also

- understanding your own sexual history
- getting yourself tested for STDs at least every year if you are sexually active
- understanding your sex partner's sexual history
- understanding the relative risk of different sexual activities
- understanding the different diseases and how they are passed along

For more information on the symptoms and transmission of STDs, see pp. 112–13.

use cOndoms!

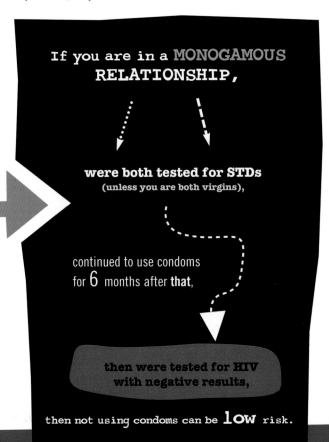

If you are in a **MONOGAMOUS RELATIONSHIP,**

were both tested for STDs
(unless you are both virgins),

continued to use condoms for **6** months after **that,**

then were tested for HIV with negative results,

then not using condoms can be **low** risk.

Understanding your own sexual history

Have you had unsafe sex with anyone who may have had unsafe sex with anyone else? Think about any sexual activity you have had and think about all the people you've had it with. If the answer is yes, get tested for STDs! Go to a doctor. Taking cultures for laboratory analysis is the only way to definitely diagnose many STDs. In fact, the CDC recommends that those who are sexually active (in non-monogamous relationships) get tested for STDs every six months.

Understanding your partner's sexual history

Up to one out of three sexually active teens are infected with an STD. Not everyone who has one knows he or she has the STD. So asking your partner if he or she is "clean" isn't really a preventive act, although it's probably not a bad first step in broaching the subject. It can definitely be awkward to get into this kind of discussion with someone you haven't slept with yet, but it is SO important. Basically, you are trying to figure out the answers to the same things you asked yourself:

Has this person engaged in unsafe sex?

How many partners has this person had?

Did he or she practice safer sex with previous partners?

How many of them were with strangers? drug addicts?

Did he or she have sex with multiple partners?

If so, has he or she been tested for STDs, and how long ago?

You should always use barrier protection with a sex partner until you are totally confident that both of you are STD-free!

If you think you have an STD

Some symptoms of STDs are pretty common and that can be confusing. Burning sensations when you pee can be a sign of a urinary tract infection or chlamydia. Gross smelling discharge and vaginal itchiness can indicate any number of things. Generally, any unexplained growth or sore is a sign that something is wrong and should be checked. The potentially confusing nature of the symptoms is the reason why it's really important to familiarize yourself with your vagina, know your own odors and the way things normally look and feel. Be attentive to any changes, and if you do notice anything suspicious, don't self-diagnose. Go to a doctor.

Try not to feel awkward about bringing up fears of an STD with your doctor—they are used to it. Testing for certain STDs like chlamydia and gonorrhea is very simple and routine for gynecologists, who are also bound by rules of confidentiality and won't tell anyone (including your parents) about your consultation. Many cities and most college campuses have clinics where testing for STDs is free or very cheap.

If you have been tested and already know you have an STD, it really is your responsibility to tell any past and potential sex partners about your condition. Your past partners should be checked out by a doctor and treated, if necessary.

It may not be easy to tell potential partners about the STD, but it is necessary and respectful to let them know before things go too far. Presumably, you would want the same consideration of your sexual health! Condoms and other barrier methods are good, but not 100 percent effective in preventing transmission of these conditions, and people deserve to know what they are getting into by having sex with you. The more you know about your STD and the way it's transmitted, the easier it will be for you to communicate to other people.

Understanding risky behavior

Different sexual activities pose different levels of risk. It's important to understand what risks are connected with which activities so you can make informed decisions about what you want to do. You may decide to delay some activities that carry the most risk. You should decide to practice most activities with extreme caution!

And don't forget those activities that carry extremely low or no risk and are fun too: masturbating, hugging, dry kissing, dry humping, massaging.

	What you can get	Cut the risk by
Very low risk French kissing	Colds and flus, hepatitis B.	Hepatitis B vaccine. Not making out with people who are sick.
Low risk mutual masturbation	Nothing if there are no cuts on hands or lesions on genitals. If you do have cuts or lesions on your hands and engage in this with someone who has HIV, you're at risk if infected sperm or vaginal fluid enters your bloodstream.	Using latex or plastic kitchen wrap.
Risky oral sex on a man	Herpes, HIV, hepatitis B, gonorrhea, syphilis, warts.	Using a condom (flavored or not).
oral sex on a woman	Herpes, HIV (less risky than oral sex on a man, but still possible), hepatitis B, gonorrhea, syphilis, warts.	Using a female condom, dental dam, cut-open condom, Glyde® dam, or plastic kitchen wrap.
High risk vaginal intercourse	Herpes, HIV, hepatitis B, gonorrhea, syphilis, chlamydia, warts. Also pregnant.	Using a condom (male or female) and spermicide.
anal sex	Herpes, HIV, hepatitis B, gonorrhea, syphilis, chlamydia, warts.	Using a condom and spermicide.

UNDERSTANDING STDS

Although STDs (other than AIDS) generally won't kill you, some of them, if left untreated and undetected, can leave you infertile, which is bad enough. Here's a rundown of the most common STDs. Bear in mind that some STDs share symptoms (like itchy genitals, burning, difficult urination, and foul-smelling discharge) with other "crotch concerns," including urinary tract infections, yeast infections, bacterial vaginosis, and trichomoniasis—infections that can also result from sex.

See also **Common Crotch Concerns, p. 27.**

STDs are a pain in the butt, but if treated and managed properly, they probably won't kill you. The exception is the human immuno-deficiency virus (HIV) and the disease it causes, AIDS. HIV is a viral infection that lives in the blood and breaks down the immune system of the body. The potential for contracting HIV has upped the ante immeasurably for sexual encounters and has led to the unfortunate truth that sex without precaution can cost you your life.

HIV can be transmitted by bodily fluids, blood, semen, vaginal fluid, and breast milk. Vomit, mucus, sweat, tears, and saliva don't carry enough virus to cause infection. It is impossible to get HIV through casual contact.

The virus itself does not kill, but rather it is the virus's effect on the body's immune system that leaves it vulnerable to a whole host of opportunistic infections, some of which lead to death.

Women make up 42 percent of the population that is living with AIDS, and most contracted it through heterosexual sex. Their numbers are rising in comparison to men. During vaginal sex, women are more vulnerable to HIV transmission because vaginal walls present a larger and more penetrable surface than the penis does. Also, sperm carries a higher concentration of the virus than vaginal fluid does. Although much safer, unprotected oral sex also poses a threat, since it is not uncommon for people to have small cuts in the mouth through which the virus can enter the bloodstream. Women can also pass on the virus to their children in utero or through breast milk.

AIDS is scary, but it is also preventable. It just makes the practice of safer sex—condom use combined with a spermicide (which kills not only sperm but the viruses inside it)—a life-and-death matter.

Getting tested:

Anyone who has any suspicions about exposure to HIV should get tested. The test is a blood test, which detects whether there are HIV antibodies in the blood. If confidentiality is a concern, there are clinics that do anonymous testing. Your doctor can advise you on how to keep the results confidential as well. Since the virus can be in the blood for 6 months before giving rise to detectable antibodies, two tests, 6 months apart, are recommended.

SEXUALLY TRANSMITTED VAGINITIS

A common form of vaginitis, trichomoniasis, or "trich," is one of the most prevalent STDs, infecting up to five million Americans each year—both men and women. The infection is not always—but frequently—transmitted through vaginal sex with an infected person. Symptoms, though they aren't always noticeable, can include frothy, green or gray, smelly discharge (sometimes with spotting) from the penis or vagina; itching in and around the vagina; swelling in the groin; and frequent urination, often along with pain and burning. Using condoms is a good way to prevent trichomoniasis, and spermicides also offer some protection.

Although it may go away by itself, it is important to treat trich with antibiotics. Left untreated, it can increase the risk of acquiring or transmitting HIV. And pregnant women infected with trichomoniasis are at risk for premature births and low-birth weight babies.

	Gonorrhea	Crabs	Genital Herpes
What it is	A bacterial infection, also known as "the clap."	Lice (little whitish bugs) in the pubic area that feed off blood. May also live in armpits and hair.	There are two strains of the herpes virus. Herpes simplex I may appear as cold sores or fever blisters around the mouth in the aftermath of a cold or when you are rundown. It's extremely common. Herpes simplex II usually appears on the genitals or buttocks and can appear orally as well. This kind of herpes is characterized by painful, itchy, blisterlike sores anywhere in the genital region. What's confusing, though, is that oral herpes can appear on the genitals and cause similar symptoms to genital herpes and vice versa. The herpes virus occupies nerve centers at the base of the spinal column and lives there permanently. People with this virus have sporadic outbreaks; some have very few after the initial (usually the most severe) outbreak. Some have them more frequently. Outbreaks can be triggered by fatigue and stress, among other factors.
How you get it	Vaginal, anal or oral sex.	Through close contact with a person who has it. Sharing underwear, clothes, bedsheets, and blankets. Pets can also carry these bugs.	Usually through oral, genital, or anal contact with an active herpes sore. When the sore is active, it is said to be shedding. You can also get it through skin-to-skin contact. Vaginal fluid and sperm can also carry it from the sore to another location.
Symptoms	More obvious for men than women, who may not show any symptoms. Men have extreme pain in urination and discharge from the penis. Women can have discharge and swollen, tender labia. Sore throat from unprotected oral sex.	Mild to severe itching. Possibly little specks of blood in underwear from bites. If you look closely, you can see them.	The first time, usually one or more blisterlike sores appear in the genital region. These may break, ooze, and itch, but they dry up in 7–14 days. Sometimes the outbreak is preceded by flu-like symptoms (headaches, body aches, fever, and fatigue) and difficulty urinating. Symptoms can appear up to several months after exposure. Subsequent outbreaks are usually milder and can be mistaken for other things that cause genital itching. Outbreaks can also happen without any visible symptoms.
Prevention	Avoid intercourse until the person is cured. Condom and spermicide reduce risk, but not entirely.	Avoid close contact with someone who is infected.	Always use condoms, since there is some risk of transmission even between outbreaks when sores are not visible. Female condoms cover more genital surface than male ones.
Treatment	Antibiotics.	Over-the-counter medicine. Wash all clothes worn recently, anywhere the bugs might live. These creatures can be very tough to get rid of, and you may need to repeat the shampoo treatment a few times.	Topical ointments can reduce the discomfort of a herpes outbreak, reduce itching, and speed the drying-up process. Sitz baths and anesthetic creams may also help reduce discomfort. Some prescription oral antiviral medications can reduce the severity and frequency of outbreaks. Eating right and getting plenty of sleep also help.
Long-term implications	Untreated gonorrhea can lead to pelvic inflammatory disease (PID) and sterility. It can also lead to male sterility.	None	Once you get herpes, you'll need to manage it carefully throughout your life. Outbreaks will decrease in severity and frequency over time. Wash your hands frequently when you have outbreaks, particularly avoiding touching your eyes and face after contact with a sore. Herpes in the eyes is extremely serious and can lead to blindness. The other serious long-term implication is in childbirth. Vaginal delivery during a primary herpes outbreak poses a serious danger to the baby, which is why a baby may be delivered by C-section during a primary herpes outbreak.

Genital Warts and Human Papillomavirus (HPV)	Chlamydia	Hepatitis B	Syphilis
Very common sexually transmitted viruses. Some can cause genital warts. A few can cause cervical, penile, vaginal, and vulvar cancer.	A bacterial infection in the genitals.	A virus that causes liver damage.	A bacterial STD that gets into the bloodstream and causes sores and rashes.
Skin-to-skin contact. Vaginal, anal, or oral sex with someone who has the virus.	Skin-to-skin contact. Anal or vaginal contact.	Transmitted by all bodily fluids, including saliva. You can catch it by kissing an infected person. Any sexual activity—oral, anal, or vaginal. Sharing dirty needles, razors, toothbrushes, nail clippers, and unclean implements for body piercing and tattooing.	Oral, anal, or vaginal sex. Possibly kissing, since sores can appear on the mouth.
Usually painless, sometimes itchy warts appear anywhere in the genital region, externally or internally. They have a different appearance depending on where they are: harder and whiter or browner on the outer genitals, softer and pinker inside the vaginal canal or on the cervix. They may appear individually or in clusters.	Very often there are no symptoms or they go unnoticed—a burning sensation when peeing, change in texture and smell of discharge, itchy genitals, possibly abdominal pain.	Rashes, jaundice, fatigue, nausea, vomiting, body aches, abdominal aches, loss of appetite. Some people, however, don't have any symptoms.	Appears in several stages and need to be paid attention to because the disease must be halted as soon as possible. First a sore appears where contact was made; the sore becomes oozy and eventually dries up. (The oozy stage is the most infectious.) Untreated, the bacteria can live on and then appear as a rash, fever, and headache. If that clears up on its own, the disease can become latent, and the person becomes a carrier. In the final stage, the mind, heart, bones, and organs are affected.
Barrier methods, such as condoms and diaphragms, help reduce the risk, but since it's transmitted skin to skin, you can still get it. Lots of people have HPV and don't know it.	Make sure you and your partner are screened. Use condoms (male or female) when having anal or vaginal sex to reduce risk.	There's a vaccine for this, given in a series of three shots. Hepatitis B is highly contagious, so you need to avoid intimate contact with people who have it. Barrier methods can reduce risk during intercourse, but you're still at risk if you kiss the person.	
Once a doctor has diagnosed warts, they can be frozen, burned, lasered, or just plain cut off. The body's immune system seems to clear the virus from the body, permanently or for a long time. Take-home topical medications are also available.	Easily treated with antibiotics if diagnosed early. Increasingly, the trend among gynecologists is toward routine screening for chlamydia.		Barrier methods reduce risk. Of course, people should make sure they are cured before resuming sexual activity with anyone.
		Shots of immune globulin help strengthen the immune system to fight symptoms.	Antibiotics.
Some untreated warts can just keep growing, possibly breaking and bleeding if they are irritated. Some strains of the virus (HPV) are also linked with cervical cancer, as well as precancerous conditions of the cervix, although the number of such cases is relatively small. The Pap smear is a reliable way of detecting precancerous conditions that can lead to cervical cancer, which are far easier to treat and cure in earlier stages. Every woman needs regular Pap smears, usually once a year. Those who have many sex partners may need tests as frequently as once every 6 months.	Undiagnosed and untreated, it can cause further damage in urinary tract and reproductive organs leading to pelvic inflammatory disease (PID) in women and sterility in women and men as well as disabling reactive arthritis in men.	If you take very good care of yourself, with rest, a good diet, and no alcohol, and you seek medical help, this disease can run its course. It is, however, chronic and can recur. Untreated and unmanaged, it can lead to liver damage and death.	Untreated syphilis can lead to degeneration of vital organs, brain damage, and death.

Apart from abstinence, the basic categories of birth control are:

Hormonal methods that a woman takes internally, through shots, pills, or implants.

Barrier methods include condoms, diaphragms, cervical caps, and female condoms.

Spermicides, a type of barrier method, come in creams, foams, and suppositories. These are more effective when used in conjunction with another barrier method. Used alone, you shoot it into your vagina with a kind of syringe or insert the suppository an hour to 10 minutes before sex.

An IUD, or intrauterine device, is inserted into the uterus by a gynecologist or health practitioner. T-shaped and made of some combination of copper, plastic, and progesterone, it usually prevents fertilization and can also make the uterus inhospitable to a fertilized egg. These were very popular in the 1960s and 1970s, but less so now, since they have been linked to pelvic inflammatory disease (PID) in women who are at risk for STDs. In women who have no children, insertion may be more painful. They are safe to use in monogamous relationships, but are not a great choice for teenagers.

Permanent birth control is not reversible and therefore not that popular among teenagers. For a woman, permanent birth control means tubal sterilization, or getting your tubes blocked through surgery. A small portion of each fallopian tube is usually removed, and the ends are sealed. Without a continuous tube, an egg and sperm cannot meet. Tubal sterilization does not, however, interfere with menstrual periods.

See also When you can get pregnant, p. 122.

Then there are a couple of birth control methods that are not advised for teens and are completely ineffective against STDs:

The rhythm method—the attempt to time sexual intercourse for when the woman is not in the fertile part of her cycle. This is unreliable because sperm can live in your body for up to seven days, and a woman may ovulate when the sperm are waiting in the fallopian tubes. Also, not everyone is perfectly attuned to when she is ovulating, and many menstrual cycles are less than regular.

Early withdrawal, or coitus interruptus—when a man pulls out before coming. This may fail to work because there is a small amount of pre-ejaculate fluid that can contain sperm. It also sometimes doesn't work because the guy fails to pull out in time, despite his intention to do so.

Here's a rundown of birth control options that are effective **(Remember: None of the hormonal methods prevents disease.)**:

Hormonal Methods

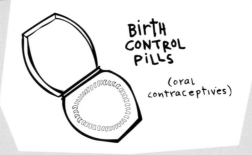

BIRTH CONTROL PILLS

(oral contraceptives)

What it is: Pill containing hormones that you take daily.
How it works: The "pill" essentially works by fooling the body into thinking it is already pregnant. It comes in two forms and a variety of dosages. One form combines the synthetic hormones estrogen

and progestin (synthetic progesterone), and it suppresses ovulation. No egg means nothing to fertilize. The second—slightly less effective—form is progestin only, and this type can prevent ovulation but usually thickens cervical mucus, making it hard for the sperm to swim up the fallopian tubes and meet an egg. It also makes the uterus inhospitable to a fertilized egg.

Effectiveness against pregnancy: 95 to 99.9 percent, when taken every day.

Effectiveness against STDs: There is less risk of PID, an infection that is caused by STDs.

When effective: Immediately effective if started on the first day of your period. Use a back-up method for one week if you start at another time.

Side effects: Especially in the first 3 months: possible nausea and midcycle bleeding, headaches, bloating, weight gain, breast tenderness, depression, changes in sexual desire. If these symptoms persist, ask your doctor to prescribe a different pill. Stop taking the pill if you experience any of the following symptoms: severe headache, swelling and pain in legs, dizziness, numbness, blurred vision, slurred speech. The pill is inadvisable for smokers especially if they are over the age of 35.

Available: Only with a prescription.

Cost: $20 to $30 per month, plus doctor visits.

Benefits: Extremely effective birth control. Possibly lighter and more regular periods with less cramping. Reduces PMS, osteoporosis, and chances of ovarian and endometrial cancer.

Disadvantages: You have to take it every day, no fail. Does not prevent disease.

Common mistakes: Forgetting to take the pill or thinking you should take a break from it.

DEPO-PROVERA

What it is: A progestin-only hormone shot administered every 3 months.

How it works: Suppresses FSH (follicle-stimulating hormone), disrupting the production of an egg and the menstrual cycle.

Effectiveness against pregnancy: 99.9 percent.

Effectiveness against STDs: None.

When effective: Starting 1 week after the shot.

Side effects: Can have some of the same side effects as the progestin-only pill, including acne, breast tenderness, depression, weight gain, vaginal dryness, and changes in sex drive. The most common side effect is irregular bleeding—which may include irregular intervals between periods, longer menstrual flow, spotting between periods, or no bleeding for months at a time. Although it has not been proven, some scientists believe that prolonged use of Depo-Provera may decrease bone mass in young women under the age of 15 or 16.

Available: Through a doctor.

Cost: About $120 per year.

Benefits: Effective birth control that is less of a hassle and more private than the pill.

Disadvantages: Shots every 3 months. Can take up to 18 months to restore normal ovulation. Does not prevent disease.

Common mistakes: Forgetting to get the shot.

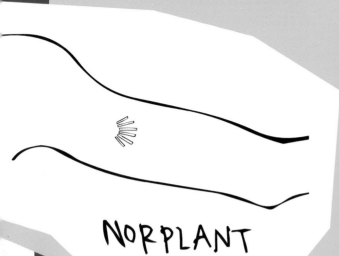

NORPLANT

What it is: Six match-sized hormone-filled capsules surgically inserted into the upper arm.

How it works: Time-releases the hormone, which inhibits ovulation and sperm mobility over the course of 5 years.

Effectiveness against pregnancy: 99.99 percent.

Effectiveness against STDs: None.

When effective: One week after insertion.

Side effects: The most common side effect is irregular bleeding, which may include irregular intervals between periods, longer menstrual flow, spotting between periods, or no bleeding for months at a time. Some weight gain, breast tenderness, and decreased bone density.

Available: Through a doctor.

Cost: Several hundred dollars for 5 years of protection.

Benefits: Hassle-free protection for the long-haul. Lighter periods, less cramping, decreased anemia.

Disadvantages: Surgery to put in and take out can be uncomfortable, and can result in scarring. Hard to reverse if you decide you want to get pregnant. Does not prevent disease.

Common mistakes: Women forget to have Norplant removed after five years.

See also Condoms, p. 105.

Barrier Methods

DIAPHRAGM

What it is: Soft rubber disk or bowl that fits over the cervix.

How it works: Blocks sperm's passage through the cervical opening.

Effectiveness against pregnancy: With spermicide, 80 to 95 percent.

Effectiveness against STDs: Minimal. Spermicide can kill some germs.

When effective: Insert up to 1 to 2 hours before intercourse and reapply spermicide for each act of intercourse.

Side effects: Possible irritation to men and women from spermicide. Very slight chance of toxic shock syndrome if left in for too long—it should be removed 8 hours after intercourse.

For more on TSS, see p. 24.

Available: You have to get fitted by a doctor.

Cost: About $20, plus doctor visit.

Benefits: You can put it in early, up to several hours before intercourse, so it doesn't interrupt the mood. May protect against cervical cancer

Disadvantages: Can be slightly tricky to insert, before you get good at it. You have to be refitted periodically, and you should check it for holes by holding it up to light and looking for pinholes. You have to leave it in for 8 hours after intercourse. Urinary tract infections (UTIs) are more common with its use.

Common mistakes: Not reapplying spermicide. Improper insertion (which is very uncomfortable).

CERVICAL CAP

What it is: A snugger-fitting diaphragm that forms a tight seal over the cervix.

How it works: Blocks sperm's passage through cervical opening.

Effectiveness against pregnancy: For women who have not given birth, nearly the same as a diaphragm: 80 to 91 percent if well fitted and used properly with spermicide. For women who have given birth, howevever, effectiveness falls to 60 to 80 percent.

Effectiveness against STDs: Negligible. Spermicide can kill some germs.

When effective: Can be inserted a day ahead of time, or just before, and left in for 2 days total. You must reapply spermicide for each new act of intercourse.

Side effects: Spermicide may irritate men and women. Very slight danger of toxic shock syndrome if left in for more than 48 hours. Can cause unpleasant vaginal odor or discharge.

Available: Must be fitted by a doctor.

Cost: About $30, plus doctor visit.

Benefits: Can be worn comfortably for 2 days.

Disadvantages: Can be hard to insert and remove, and many women can't use it, because it only comes in four sizes.

Common mistakes: Failure to add new spermicide.

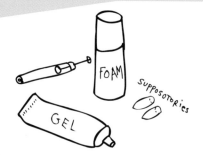

SPERMICIDE

This is not a very effective barrier method, but it is often used in conjunction with barrier methods as a back-up.

What it is: Jelly, foam, cream, or suppositories, squirted or inserted into vagina.

How it works: Contains chemicals that make it impossible for sperm to move.

Effectiveness against pregnancy: About 74 to 94 percent effective—and even better with the use of condom or diaphragm.

Effectiveness against STDs: Limited unless combined with a condom.

When effective: Insert at least 10 minutes before intercourse. Protection may last up to an hour. Leave in for 6 to 8 hours after.

Side effects: Some people are sensitive to some brands. Switching brands may be helpful.

Available: At drugstores.

Cost: $6 to $10 for a tube or suppositories.

Benefits: Some disease protection, but better with a condom.

Disadvantages: Tastes horrible and is messy.

Common mistakes: Failing to insert more spermicide for each act of intercourse.

SPONGE

What it is: A doughnut-shaped, disposable, polyurethane sponge permeated with nonoxynol-9. It is removed by pulling a small loop.

How it works: Blocks sperm's passage through cervical opening. Immobilizes sperm with spermicide. Traps and absorbs semen in sponge.

Effectiveness against pregnancy: 85–90 percent.

Effectiveness against STDs: Negligible.

When effective: Insert anytime before sex for 24 hours of protection. Leave in for 6–8 hours after sex.

Side effects: Spermicide can irritate men and women. Slight danger of toxic shock syndrome if left in for over 30 hours.

Available: At drugstores in packs of six.

Cost: About $2 each.

Benefits: Repeat sex over 24 hours does not require reapplication of spermicide like the diaphragm and cervical cap.

Disadvantages: Relatively high failure rate. Can be difficult to remove (sponge can turn over, making the ribbon hard to grasp).

Common mistakes: Removing too soon.

RESOURCES

National Organizations

CDC (Centers for Disease Control and Prevention), 1600 Clifton Road NE, Atlanta, GA 30333. Phone (STD hotline): 800-227-8922. Website: http://www.cdc.gov.

The Female Health Company makes and sells the female condom. Phone: 800-274-6601 (for samples and information) or 800-635-0844 (to buy). Website: http://www.femalehealth.com.

Home Access provides home AIDS tests and counseling. Phone: 800-HIV-TEST.

National Campaign to Prevent Teen Pregnancy provides information on preventing teen pregnancy. Address: 2100 M Street NW, Suite 300, Washington, DC, 20037. Phone: 202-261-5655. Website: http://www.teenpregnancy.org.

National AIDS Hotline provides information regarding HIV and AIDS and referrals, confidentially and anonymously. Phone: 800-342-AIDS.

National STD Hotline: 800-227-8922

National Herpes Hotline: 800-227-8922

The Norplant Foundation, P.O. Box 25223, Alexandria, VA 22313-5223. Phone: 800-760-9030.

Planned Parenthood, 810 Seventh Avenue, New York, NY 10019. Phone: 212-541-7800 (national office) or 800-230-PLAN (for the Planned Parenthood health center nearest you). Website: http://www.plannedparenthood.org.

Society for Human Sexuality, 1122 East Pike Street #1276, Seattle, WA 98122-3934. Phone: 206-781-5396.

Teens and AIDS Hotline: 800-440-TEEN.

Online

The AIDS Education and Trust at http://www.avert.org has an informative youth section.

All About Sex at http://www.allaboutsex.org is a site dedicated to positive feelings about sexuality.

The Body at http://www.thebody.com provides information on AIDS.

Birthcontrol.com at http://www.birthcontrol.com provides information on a large selection of birth control products.

Café Herpé at http://www.cafeherpe.com has lots of herpes information.

The CDC's Guidelines for Treatment of STDs: http://www.cdc.gov/nchstp/dstd/STD98TG.HTM

Coalition for Positive Sexuality at http://www.positive.org is for sexually active teens.

Condomania at http://www.condomania.com provides information about and sells a huge variety of condoms.

The Go Ask Alice Web site at http://www.goaskalice.columbia.edu answers questions about health, dating, sexuality, drug use, and depression.

Sex, Etc. at http://www.sxetc.org is a very strong, well-done newsletter for and by teens about sexuality.

Safer Sex.org at http://www.safersex.org is devoted to discussing safer sex.

Society for Human Sexuality at http://www.sexuality.org gives info on safer sex without an anti-sex message.

The Stop AIDS Project's youth section, Q Action is at http://www.stopaids.org.

Teen Advice Online at http://www.teenadviceonline.org answers teenager's questions.

Teen Wire at http://www.teenwire.com is Planned Parenthood's candid site for teenagers.

Virtual Kid Health at http://www.virtualkid.com describes various STDS and how to protect yourself from them.

STD clinics locater at http://www.unspeakable.com

Books

AIDS: Readings on a Global Crisis by Elizabeth Rauh Bethel (Prentice Hall). Personal journals, essays, and scholarly investigations explore the topic and present multiple positions on AIDS.

Changing Bodies, Changing Lives by Ruth Bell (Times Books). Covers all aspects of teen sexuality, relationships, and coping with life.

Go Ask Alice by Columbia University's Health Education Program (Henry Holt). Answers questions about the whole range of health, sexuality, and emotional concerns.

The New Our Bodies, Ourselves by the Boston Women's Health Book Collective (Simon & Schuster). The bible on women's sexual health.

Smart Sex by Jessica Vitkus and Marjorie Ingall (Pocket Books). Smart, hip, straightforward info on sex.

201 Things You Should Know about AIDS and Other Sexually Transmitted Diseases by Jeffrey S. Nevid and Fern Gotfried (Allyn & Bacon). Full of valuable information.

For more resources and information, see http://www.dealwithit.com

Chapter 5

GETTING PREGNANT

If you're sexually active, there is a chance that you will get pregnant no matter which birth control method you use. The possibility is higher or lower depending on which method of birth control you use. But know that no birth control method, except abstinence, is 100 percent effective!

You can work toward 100 percent effectiveness by using one of the more effective hormonal methods or doubling up on two less effective barrier methods, like the condom and spermicide.

Pregnancies happen to girls who aren't careful and (less often) to girls who are. If it happens to you, you've got a very serious situation on your hands and a few different options to consider.

HOW YOU GET PREGNANT

Here is the only way you can get pregnant:

1. A sperm must make its way into your vagina, past your cervix, and up into the fallopian tubes.

2. There, it must meet and penetrate the outer wall of an egg that is making its monthly trip down the tubes to the uterus. That is fertilization.

Fertilization can obviously happen during intercourse, when a man's ejaculation sends literally millions of tadpole-shaped sperm into your vagina. It can happen even if a man pulls out early, since pre-ejaculate fluid (the stuff that comes out of the penis before he comes) can contain sperm.

It is also possible to get pregnant if a man spills some sperm near the opening of your vagina, after a hand job or withdrawal, for example, and just one of them makes its way into your vagina to the egg.

Immediately after one sperm penetrates the egg, the wall of the egg hardens and thickens so no more

For more on ovulation and the monthly cycle, see **pp. 20–21**.

sperm can get in. The fertilized egg makes its way down the fallopian tube to the uterus, which has been preparing for its arrival. The egg implants itself into the uterine lining and starts growing into an embryo.

2.

You cannot get pregnant from anal or oral sex (as long as the sperm is not near the opening of your vagina). You cannot get pregnant from any sexual act that does not involve a penis and sperm.

When you can get pregnant

1.

You can get pregnant any time there is the possibility that a sperm can meet one of your eggs in the fallopian tubes.

Eggs are only in the fallopian tubes during and right after ovulation. Sperm can live inside you for up to 5 to 7 days. So if you have intercourse up to 6 to 7 days before and a little after you ovulate, it is possible to get pregnant. In fact, most pregnancies result from acts of intercourse during the six days that end in ovulation.

Theoretically, if you knew exactly when you ovulated every month, you could make sure not to have sex during those times and avoid getting pregnant.

The problem is that it is almost impossible to predict exactly when you're going to ovulate. Hardly anyone has a completely regular cycle. And younger women usually have more irregular cycles.

How you know when you are pregnant

Early pregnancy symptoms (usually appear about 2 weeks after conception):

missed period breast tenderness
bloating **nausea** fatigue
increased or decreased appetite
frequent urination
light-headedness

Other factors besides pregnancy can delay a period, such as stress (including the stress of worrying that you're pregnant), sickness, recent weight gain or loss, and travel.

If your period does not come, or if there is just light spotting compared to the usual flow, and the other symptoms of pregnancy persist, you should take a pregnancy test ASAP—you may be pregnant.

You can take a home pregnancy test or go to your doctor for a test.

Home pregnancy tests are available over the counter at your local drugstore for around $9. They work by detecting the presence of the hormone HCG in a woman's urine. HCG is present in a woman's body only when she is pregnant. Home pregnancy tests are surprisingly accurate when used properly. So follow the directions carefully!

I was supposed to get my period yesterday and still haven't. There is the chance that I could be pregnant. What do I do? **- Gingersnp**

Ok, chickie, sometimes a girl will spend all this time STRESSing that she's pregnant. All that stress can alter your cycle by days, or more. Try to relax. **- wandawanda**

If you don't get your period in 2 weeks take a home pregnancy test or GO SEE A DOCTOR! That is the only way you will find out for sure. Speak to a counselor at your school, and ask them about clinics. Don't just think that you may have gotten lucky and "it won't happen to me." **- grouchi**

Although it is possible for a home pregnancy test to detect a pregnancy just a few days after conception, there is a chance of a false negative that early in a pregnancy. It's best to wait about 2 weeks after the intercourse. Or if you do one test early and it is negative, but your period still doesn't come, repeat the test a week or so later.

If the result is positive, or if you want to double-check a negative result, the next step is to head to the doctor for a definitive pregnancy test.

See Resources, p. 129.

Emergency contraception

If there is some kind of accident with your birth control (the condom breaks or slips off during sex, allowing ejaculation inside you) or you were forced to have unprotected sex against your will, and you are 100 percent sure that you do not want to be pregnant, you can get a form of emergency contraception.

"Morning-after pills" must be started within 72 hours of the unprotected sex— the sooner the better. You can get them only from a doctor or health clinic. You take two doses—12 hours apart—of hormones that cause changes in the uterine lining, making it inhospitable to a fertilized egg and in this way preventing pregnancy. This method reduces the chances of pregnancy by 75 percent.

sexuality

getting pregnant

Who would **help you** through an abortion?

What are your moral or religious convictions?

Why do you **want to keep** the baby?

If **you were** to have the baby, who would help you **raise it?**

How will you **pay for either option?**

What do you imagine your life would be like with a baby?

Why do you not want to keep the **baby?**

What are your motivations?

DECIDING WHAT TO DO

If you're sure that you're pregnant, you have to make a relatively quick decision about whether you will continue the pregnancy.

For some people, there is no decision to make. Their religious, moral, or personal beliefs make it unthinkable to intentionally terminate a pregnancy.

For others, abortion is an alternative that has been a safe and legal option in this country since 1973, when the U.S. Supreme Court ruled in **Roe v. Wade** that every woman has the right to decide to end a pregnancy in the first three months (and possibly later).

It's your body and your decision. No one can force you to have either an abortion or a baby. You need to make your own decision based on your own personal situation and circumstances.

There are tons of questions to ask yourself and to talk about with the baby's father and your family. If you can't talk to one or both of your parents, find some other trusted adult who can talk things over with you and help you make a decision with which you will be comfortable.

It is important to understand that nothing will alter your life as much as having a baby. Things that you might take for granted now—finishing high school, going to college, having a social life—all become difficult to impossible when you need to arrange and pay for child care.

Find some teenage moms and ask them what their lives are like!

For more on the abortion debate, see **pp. 270-71.**

124

Keeping the baby

If you decide to keep and raise your baby, get ready. Do as many things as you can early on to prepare yourself for this major, major change in your life. Assuming that you have a relationship with the father, it is essential that he be informed that you are pregnant. Will he be involved? (Legally, he has a financial obligation.) What will your support system be? How will you handle child care? Will you stay in school? How will you support yourself?

Start good prenatal care immediately with the help of an obstetrician/gynecologist and stop any potentially damaging habits like smoking, drinking, and taking any drugs, including nonessential prescription drugs, aspirin, and other over-the-counter medicines. Most likely, your doctor will pre-scribe special vitamins, and will give nutri-tional guidelines to follow throughout the 9 months (really 40 weeks) of pregnancy.

As the pregnancy proceeds, it's a good idea to begin preparing for the baby's birth. Take a parenting class. Go to the bookstore or library and read about basic child care.

See Resources for information on pregnancy and childbirth, **pp. 129–31.**

Teenage moms

Statistically, the odds are against teenage moms. According to SIECUS (Sexuality Information and Education Council of the United States) and the Alan Guttmacher Institute, which studies reproductive issues:

94% of teens believe they'll stay in school if they have a baby

70% of teen moms actually do stay in school

25% of girls who drop out of high school cite pregnancy as the reason

51% of teens believe if they had a baby, they'd marry the father

19% of teenage moms actually do marry the father

s
e
x
u
a
l
i
t
y

I'm only 15 and I made a total mistake. My boyfriend and I did it one time, and then I realized my period was late. We kept the baby, and it's been really hard. I'm still going to school, at a special one for girls with babies. But I'm warning you all, this can happen with one single sperm. Just one. So why are you taking the risk of a lifetime for an hour of pleasure?
— **staticqueen**

I'm an 18-year-old housewife and it sucks. I have graduated from school, and I haven't done much since then. My son is now 7 months old, and I'm so bored with staying home that I'm out looking for a job to keep me busy. I love my son, but being a housewife was never what I wanted for myself. Being a mother means that you have to give up spending time with your friends so you can care for your child. I don't even remember the last time that I went out with my friends. — **QuietStorm**

I got pregnant at 16. I gave up a life of hanging out with my friends when I wanted to or just chill-ing. I gave up being independent. I also ended up getting married that year. It's hard and almost every day I want to give up and run away. I'm not trying to tell you not to have a baby—it is your decision. I just want you to think about all the facts and stuff. — **fefifofum**

getting pregnant

In general, women who become teen mothers have more children, spend more time as single parents, and spend more time on public assistance than those who wait to have children until at least their twenties. Becoming a teenage mother means there's a good chance you'll be relegated to a lower socioeconomic status than you might otherwise have achieved or desired.

In addition, children born to teen mothers have a lot of strikes against them. They tend to do worse in school and have more learning disabilities, poorer health, higher rates of criminal activity, and higher rates of teenage pregnancy themselves.

This is not to say that the odds cannot be beaten. It is just to give you an idea of what you're up against. You are not a statistic. If you are pregnant and decide to have the baby, then you should be sure you have the support and the resources to beat the odds. Some teenage moms do eventually return to and complete school and pursue careers they may have postponed.

Having a baby is a huge and daunting responsibility for anyone, even for people who are married and economically stable. Understand the reality before making any decisions.

Adoption

If you don't want to have an abortion but are not prepared to raise a child at this time in your life, you can choose to have the baby and arrange to have it adopted.

Carrying a baby for 9 months and then letting it go can be a very difficult thing to do emotionally, even when you are certain that you're making the right decision for both you and the child. Being healthy and getting good prenatal care for the duration of the pregnancy are commitments you have to honor whether you're keeping the baby for yourself or giving it up.

The first step, if you don't already know someone who wants to adopt and raise your child, is to contact a state-approved adoption agency. The National Council for Adoption provides some guidelines. Adoption is a legal matter, so even if you know the people to whom you're giving your baby, you need a lawyer to draw up all of the necessary papers and a judge's approval. Be sure to keep good records and copies of all the forms. The baby's biological father also has to sign consent forms.

Adoptions range from the closed, traditional form of adoption, in which the birth mother retains anonymity, to the most open kind of adoption, in which the biological mom stays in touch with the adoptive parents and her child. In between the two extremes is a whole range of possibilities.

> I am 15 years old. About a month ago I had twins—a baby girl and boy. My parents were extremely mad when they found out, but after a lot of serious talks, they understood where I was coming from. And they were behind me every day. I gave my son and my daughter up for adoption. It's hard, but I'm glad I didn't abort them.
> — **slowpocoman**

For adoption resources, see p. 131.

Abortion

According to the Alan Guttmacher Institute and the National Abortion and Reproductive Rights Action League (NARAL):

50% of pregnancies are unintended

50% of unintended pregnancies end in abortion

55% of U.S. women getting abortions are under age 25

22% are teenagers

61% of all abortions are obtained by white women

Women who report no religious affiliation are **4** times more likely to get an abortion Roman Catholics are **29%** more likely than Protestants to get an abortion **1** in **4** pregnancies is terminated by abortion in this country, and **20** percent of all abortions are to women under the age of **19**. Approximately **300,000** American teenagers have abortions each year, although this rate, like the rate of teen pregnancy, is lower than it was in the 1980s.

Although you cannot help but be aware of the raging political debate about abortion, when you are the one who is undergoing an abortion, the struggle is more likely to be a personal one. Having an abortion can be an emotional and trying experience. Many women who have abortions feel relieved once it is over and say they have no regrets. Others do have regrets.

For abortion resources, see **p. 129.**

Ending the pregnancy
Abortion must be performed by a qualified, trained doctor in a clean, clinical setting. Do not, under any circumstances, try to perform an abortion on yourself or anyone else.

Your private doctor should be able to refer you to a clinic if he or she does not perform abortions. Any local chapter of Planned Parenthood can provide a list of safe abortion clinics.

Abortion clinics are also listed in the Yellow Pages, but it's better to get a referral. Occasionally, right-to-life or anti-abortion groups pose as abortion clinics or "abortion alternatives" in order to attract pregnant women and talk them out of getting an abortion.

It is a good idea to understand as much as you can about what will actually happen on the day of your abortion, so ask as many questions as you want beforehand. The more information you have, the more comfortable you will be with what you are going through.

Some things to ask:

1. What will happen during the procedure? How long will you be there? Can you bring someone with you? Is there anything you need to do to prepare?

2. Do you (or does your provider) have to tell your parents? See Abortion and Parental Consent, p. 128.

3. How much will it cost?

4. What are the risks involved? What happens if something does go wrong?

5. What happens after the procedure? Will you need to come in again? Do they provide counseling?

If something doesn't seem right to you, trust your gut instincts and call some other places.

Although you should not rush to a decision that you may regret later, there is a time factor involved in the decision to have an abortion. It is highly recommended that an abortion be performed in the first trimester of pregnancy (the first 3 months) or first 12 weeks after the start of the last menstrual period. These abortions are safer,

getting pregnant

easier, cheaper, and less controversial than those that occur later in the pregnancy.

A first-trimester abortion can be provided as soon as pregnancy is confirmed. In the first 6 weeks this can be done with manual vacuum aspiration (MVA) or medical abortion. During MVA, the cervix is dilated, a tube is inserted, and a manually operated pump is used to gently suck out the contents. For medical abortion, a doctor provides the woman with a dose of the drug methotrexate and a few days later with a dose of mispristol to terminate pregnancy. In 2000, the FDA is preparing to approve mifepristone, formerly called RU-486, which can also be used with mispristol for medical abortion.

A first-trimester surgical abortion, called dilation and curettage (D+C) can be done 6 weeks or more into the pregnancy. It takes 5 to 15 minutes, and can be performed with either local or general anesthesia. Usually, the cost at a clinic is $300 to $500. Some clinics have sliding scales (different costs for people who cannot afford them). If you are doing this on your own, don't be shy about asking for financial options.

In a D+C, the cervix is dilated (widened) and a vacuum tube is inserted to gently suck out the contents of the uterus. The walls of the uterus are then gently scraped with a surgical instrument called a curette. The clinic will usually keep you for an hour or two after the procedure, for rest and recovery. Bleeding and cramping usually follow, and there is a slight risk of infection, as with any surgery. Some doctors automatically prescribe antibiotics to prevent this. If you're not taking antibiotics, and you get a high fever immediately after, head to the doctor or nearest emergency room. For the next couple of days after your abortion, you need to take it easy.

It is harder to find doctors who perform second-trimester abortions (3 to 6 months into the pregnancy). The procedure, depending on how far into the second trimester you are, is also a lot more complicated. Usually, hospitalization and more instruments are required to extract the fetus. Sometimes medications are used to trigger the body to go into labor.

Getting a third-trimester abortion (6 to 9 months into the pregnancy), is increasingly difficult and very controversial. Many people who favor a woman's right to choose have qualms about third-trimester abortions, when the fetus is becoming more babylike, and could even survive outside the womb if born. Many doctors just won't do them. Seventeen states have banned these abortions, except when the mother's life is in danger.

Abortion and parental consent
States requiring parental consent before a minor can obtain an abortion: Alabama, Indiana, Kentucky, Louisiana, Maine, Massachusetts, Michigan, Mississippi, Missouri, North Carolina, North Dakota, Pennsylvania, Rhode Island, South Carolina, Tennessee, Wisconsin, Wyoming
States requiring parental notification before a minor may obtain an abortion: Arkansas, Delaware, Georgia, Idaho, Iowa, Kansas, Maryland, Minnesota, Nebraska, Ohio, South Dakota, Texas, Utah, Virginia, West Virginia
States in which parental consent laws are enjoined (on hold): Alaska, Arizona, California, New Mexico
States in which parental notification laws are enjoined: Colorado, Florida, Illinois, Montana, Nevada, New Jersey
States that require no parental involvement: Connecticut, Hawaii, New Hampshire, New York, Oklahoma, Oregon, Vermont, Washington

Medical abortions and RU-486
Medical abortion is administered in two installments. A woman takes the first pill in her doctor's office, then returns 2 days later to take another pill, which induces uterine contractions. Within a day or two, she starts bleeding in what seems like a heavy period but is a miscarriage. The bleeding can last 10 days. A third doctor's visit is required to make sure it worked and to check on the woman. Within the first 50 days of pregnancy, the success rate of medical abortion is 98.7 percent. Heavy bleeding is the only danger, which is why a doctor's involvement is so crucial.

Reproductive health, pregnancy, and decision making—National Organizations

Alan Guttmacher Institute offers information on reproductive health. Address: 120 Wall Street, New York, NY 10005. Phone: 212-248-1111 E-mail: info@agi-usa.org. Website: http://www.agi-usa.org.

American College of Obstetricians and Gynecologists (ACOG) provides free information and pamphlets on contraception, pregnancy, and prenatal care. Address: 409 12th Street, SW, Washington, D.C. 20024-2188. Phone: 202-638-5577. Website: http://www.acog.org.

Emergency Contraception Hotline will provide the name and number of a local emergency contraception hotline provider. Phone: 888-NOT-2-LATE or 1-800-584-9911.

National Abortion Federation will provide you with information about where you can get an abortion in your area and about abortion rights. Phone: 800-772-9100. Website: http://www.prochoice.org/.

Planned Parenthood Federation of America has chapters in every city and will direct you to a local chapter that offers prenatal care or assistance in terminating an unwanted pregnancy. National headquarters: 810 Seventh Avenue, New York, NY 10019. Phone: 212-541-7800 (national office) or 800-230-PLAN (for the Planned Parenthood health center nearest you). Website: http://www.plannedparenthood.org.

Sexuality Information and Education Council of the United States (SIECUS), 130 West 42nd Street, Suite 350, New York, NY 10036. Phone: 212-819-9770. E-mail: siecus@siecus.org. Website: http://www.siecus.org.

Reproductive health and decision making—Online

Feminist Women's Health Center Abortion Information at http://www.fwhc.org/ab.htm offers lots of information about abortions, the decision, the procedure, and personal stories from women who have gone through it.

Reproductive Rights Network at http://www.repro-activist.org/needab.htm provides links to useful sites if you need an abortion.

The RU-486 Files at http://www.ru486.org provides information about this non-surgical abortion option and its progress toward sales in the U.S.

Sex, Etc. at http://www.sxetc.org is a very strong, well-done newsletter for and by teens about sexuality.

What If I'm Pregnant? at http://www.plannedparenthood.org/womenshealth/whatifpregnant.htm on the Planned Parenthood site helps address options if you are pregnant.

Reproductive health and decision making—Books

Changing Bodies, Changing Lives: A Book for Teens on Sex and Relationships by Ruth Bell (Times Books). A superb book covering all aspects of teen sexuality, relationships, and coping with life.

sexuality

The Go Ask Alice Book of Answers: A Guide to Good Physical, Sexual, and Emotional Health by Columbia University's Health Education Program (Henry Holt). An excellent resource for all matters relating to health.

"I'm Pregnant, Now What Do I Do?" by Robert Buckingham (Prometheus Books). Comprehensive account of the options when you're pregnant.

The New Our Bodies, Ourselves by the Boston Women's Health Book Collective (Simon & Schuster). A comprehensive reference to women's health.

Pregnancy and parenting—Online

Baby Center at http://www. babycenter.com is for new and expectant parents and includes bulletin boards for teen parents and pregnant teenagers. A weekly teen parents support club meets online.

Childbirth.org at http://www. childbirth.org includes all types of information regarding pregnancy and how it will affect your life.

Teenwire at http://www.teenwire.com is Planned Parenthood's candid site for teenagers.

Dr. Koop at http://www.drkoop.com/ centers/Pregnancy provides information, message boards, and chats about pregnancy.

The Labor of Love at http://www. thelaboroflove.com includes articles, hints and tips, pregnancy journals, birth announcements.

Parenthood Web at http://www. parenthoodweb.com has young parents and single moms chats, among other resources.

Parents.com at http://www.parents. com provides parenting information and a helpful ob/gyn locator.

Parent Soup at http://www. parentsoup.com sponsors a teen parenting chat room and provides many parenting resources.

Sites by and for teen parents at http://www.designlinks.com/ teenlinks.htm provides links to lots of excellent websites by teenage parents.

Pregnancy and parenting—Books

The Hip Mama Survival Guide by Ariel Gore (Hyperion). A cool, eclectic reference.

Surviving Teen Pregnancy: Your Choices, Dreams, and Decisions by Penny Bergman (Morning Glory Press). Information and advice about this difficult decision.

What to Expect When You're Expecting by Arlene Eisenberg, Heidi E. Murkoff, and Sandee E. Hathaway (Workman). Considered the pregnancy bible.

What Now: Help for Pregnant Teens by Linda I. Shands (Intervarsity Press). For unmarried teens struggling with what to do.

The following titles deal with real-life experiences with teen pregnancy:

The Amazing "True" Story of a Teenage Single Mom by Katherine Arnoldi (Hyperion).

Annie's Baby: The Diary of Anonymous, a Pregnant Teenager, edited by Beatrice Sparks (Avon Flare).

An Actual Life by Abigail Thomas (Scribner).

Dear Diary, I'm Pregnant: Teenagers Talk about Their Pregnancy, compiled by Anrenée Englander (Firefly Books).

Listen Up! Teenage Mothers Speak Out by Margi Trapani (Rosen Publishing Group).

Adoption—National Organizations

National Council for Adoption, 1930 Seventeenth Street, NW, Washington, DC 20009-6207.

Open Adoption and Family Services can tell you about what your options regarding adoption are in the Northwest. Phone: 800-772-1115.

Spence-Chapin Agency will explain the adoption rules in the New York area and what options are available. Phone: 800-321-LOVE (800-321-5683).

Or contact **Catholic Charities**, the **Federation of Protestant Welfare Agencies**, or **United Federation of Jewish Philanthropies**.

Adoption—Online

Adopt: Assistance Information Support at http://www.adopting.org offers resources and information for those thinking about adoption.

Adoption.com at http://www.adoption.com is an excellent site on all aspects of adoption, including an area for birth-mothers.

Adopting.com at http://www.adopting.com/letters.html has letters to birth-mothers from prospective parents hoping to adopt.

Adoption Network at http://www.infi.net/adopt has a wealth of adoption information and chats on all subjects.

Friends in Adoption at http://www.friendsinadoption.com offers information for pregnant women about adoption and their options.

New Life Family Services at http://www.newlifefamilyservices.com is sponsored by an evangelical Christian organization and can arrange counseling and adoption services.

Adoption—Books

Pregnant? Adoption Is an Option: Making an Adoption Plan for a Child by Jeanne Warren Lindsay (Morning Glory Press). Everything you need to know when deciding whether to put your baby up for adoption.

For more resources and information, see http://www.dealwithit.com

Chapter 6

understanding
SEXUAL PReFeReNCe

Sexual preference is mostly understood to mean which gender you have sex with, prefer to have sex with, or fantasize about having sex with...though it's interesting to think about sexual preferences in a broader way too.

I prefer to make out with tall people.

I prefer to fool around with people who read the same books as I do.

I prefer to have sex with myself.

I prefer to have sex on the beach.

I prefer shy geeks.

SEXUAL PREFERENCE IS A CONTINUUM

Sexual preference is not simply a question of being gay or straight. Sexuality is a continuum and many people fall somewhere in between the two extremes. People move around on this continuum over time. Sexuality is constantly evolving—one of its many joys.

Curiosity and Questioning

As you develop sexual feelings and start to think about having sex, it's natural to think about what turns you on in a broad sense and to wonder who attracts you. A lot of girls begin to notice an interest in or an attraction to other girls or women (be it in real life, the media, celebrity crushes, dreams, or fantasies), and they wonder what this means about them and their sexuality.

I sometimes find that I like some of my girlfriends like that and think about kissing them, and then I'm stunned at myself and very confused because I like guys! — **blubuggy**

My best friend is HUGE in the chest and sometimes I think of having sex with her. Just thinking of her boobs against mine...it drives me nuts. But I also love guys. Am I bi-curious? or bi-sexual? I also like going to sites with naked women on them but I hate sites with naked guys.
— **Phoneixrose**

I don't blame you at all for liking girls and guys. I mean, come on, girls look better than a lot of guys!! You might become lesbian, stay bi, or even be straight. You never know how things are gonna work out. And it's ok, you aren't weird or anything for liking girls, and if anyone gives you crap about it, then they suck, ok? Remember that always! — **grrlzrule**

I think it is fine and normal to be confused about your sexuality. I am also and it is your right to either act on it or keep it a secret; but do NOT try to label yourself. Just be what you are—an indescribable human like everyone else. And don't feel you have to figure yourself out today, tomorrow, or this year! Give yourself time and accept your confusion until you do figure it all out! Good luck! I need it too!
— **fuschia**

since sixth grade i've dated girls exclusively (i'm now nearly 19). i've always said I would be open to dating a boy if he was really special...but i've still considered myself to be queer. now there's this guy who I'm kinda interested in but this would involve a complete reevaluation of my life/sexuality and I don't know if I'm up for that...*GRRRR* it's all so darn confusing sometimes.
— **rays**

I date **girls**, **but** boys are cute too.

Who knows?

Girls! Girls! Girls!

sexual preference

Why
would I rather
sleep with a woman?
Well, think of it this
way—who knows more about a
female than a female? We understand each other's emotions and
our bodies as well as theirs.
— **Nona**

WHY DO GIRLS LIKE GIRLS?

Of course, there is no one reason that girls like girls. For some people, the question is cause for debate. For others, who believe that we are attracted to individual people and not gender, the question is beside the point.

I'm not saying
anything against
being gay, but what
exactly attracts you to the
same sex? Why choose another girl
when you can have a man? Just
please clue me in, cause I
really don't understand
at all.
— **msbootsie**

It's just the way things are
& more than anything (more than
choosing, not choosing, being
horny...), it should be about LOVE.
Real love is about loving a person's
spirit, which I believe to be sex-
less. — **naTala**

Nature vs. nurture

Some people think homosexuality is a result of nature—you're either born gay or you're not. Some think it's nurture, a result of upbringing and environment—something in your life prompts you to make a conscious choice to be gay. Others think it's a combination of the two.

Since 1990, many studies have focused on what the potential biological causes of homosexuality might be. A 1991 study of 41 men has suggested physical differences in the hypothalamus (a specific area of the brain that governs sexuality among other things) of straight and gay men. In 1993, researchers found that female identical twins (who share the same genetic makeup) were 3 times as likely to both be gay as female nonidentical twins, suggesting a genetic component to lesbianism. Studies looking at male identical twins have had similar results. Other studies have looked at hormonal differences between straight and gay people.

None of these studies are conclusive and it is really impossible to judge them without knowing more about their objectives, the methods used, and the number of people involved.

Many people remain skeptical of this kind of research and are concerned that it could somehow be used against gay people. In the past, "scientific studies" that found biological differences between people were later acknowledged to be biased and inaccurate. For example. controversial studies as recently as 1997, by Philippe Rushton, have attempted to link skull size with intelligence in different races.

Some gay people support the nature argument because they feel that they really have no choice in the matter of the gender they're attracted to. If they did have a choice, they say, why would they choose to be part of a group that is often despised, discriminated against, and even attacked? In line with this reasoning, they like the term "sexual orientation" better than "sexual preference" since "sexual preference" implies a choice.

There are various psychological theories about homosexuality as well but they are all guesswork and not scientifically proven. In the late nineteenth century, when the terms "homosexuality" and "heterosexuality" were coined, homosexuality was considered to be a psychological illness. And for many years the American Psychiatric Association defined it as a disease, listing it in its Diagnostic and Statistical Manual of Mental Disorders (DSM) as a psychiatric ailment that could be "cured" with various treatments, from talk therapy to electroshock therapy. This characterization was finally determined to be prejudice, not science, and was removed from the book in 1973.

Animal sexuality

Homosexual behavior has been observed in the natural world among many species, including fish, reptiles, birds, and mammals.

One of the most famous instances of homosexuality in the animal kingdom is in the bonobo, a member of the great ape family. The bonobo is as close to the human race biologically as the better-known chimpanzee. Unlike chimpanzees, bonobos have sex often and in all different combinations: female-male, male-male, female-female. Female bonobos often mount each other and rub their clitorises together, a practice known as GG-rubbing (genito-genital rubbing). Primatologists have observed that bonobos use sex as a way to resolve tension and call them the "make love, not war" primates.

Researchers have observed sexual orgasm in sexual relations between pairs of female monkeys and between male dolphins. And in many species, it's not just about sex. Stable homosexual pairings between two males or two females occur in some species of birds, including gulls and certain waterfowl.

How do two girls have sex?

Two girls can engage in any sexual activities that don't involve a penis.

For more info on sex without intercourse, see **pp. 84-89.**

Safer sex between girls

When girls have sex with girls, they don't need to worry about birth control—but they most definitely need to worry about STDs! STDs and AIDS can be transmitted through vaginal fluid.

See What is Safer Sex? to understand how best to protect yourself, what risky behavior is, and what kind of barrier methods you can use, **pp. 108-10.**

I want to experience a friend of mine. She and I talked about it, and we're both just kinda experimenting. How do you go about it? Do you start off the same way a guy and girl start off? What should I do to get her really turned on. This isn't a joke...
— **itsybitsy**

experiment-
ing with a girl
is pretty much like
it is with a boy...you do
things you like when boys do
them to you and do things that
feel good to you...one of the cool
things about being with girls is
that you know what it feels like
when you touch them.
— **nikitachiquita**

I never really thought about being bi myself, but I have thought about other girls being lesbian. I've watched two girls dance really freaky at a party, and it kinda turned me on. What I want to know is, what do lesbians do when they're alone together? What do they get pleasure from? I mean, with guys, it's all about their dick. But what is it with girls?
— **Yvettey**

Clearly, a dick is NOT an essential part of sex! There are many things to do that don't require one! :) — **Simona**

My aunt (who I'm out to) was giving me a lecture about protecting myself from herpes and other STDs. I reassured her that I knew what I was doing and that she had nothing to worry about, and then I went home and said to myself, "Hey, self, you have no idea how to protect yourself from STDs!!!" Does the female condom work for lesbian oral sex, or is there some other way to do it?
— **Ethyl**

Here are some things you can use to have safer sex with women... If you're having oral sex, you can use dental dams, which are flat pieces of latex that you hold over the woman's genitals...if you can't find them, you can also use NON-MICROWAVABLE plastic wrap (the microwavable kind has pores in it large enough to let the HIV virus pass through). Also, if you ever use any kind of toys, you shouldn't share. If you DO share, you should put a condom on anything that is inserted, and change the condom in between people. Hope this helps.
— **missgarland**

138

DEFINING YOURSELF

Gay. Bi. Straight. Lesbian. Queer. Bi-curious. Bi-questioning. How we feel about our sexuality can and does change over time. Labels can seem like oppressive stereotypes or they can be a source of pride and comfort. There is a lot of pressure to define to yourself and to the world just exactly what your sexuality is at any time. People seem to have a hard time dealing with ambiguity.

Whether you're happy and proud to call yourself one thing or another, you're not ready to choose a label right now, or you're anti-label by nature, it's really up to you. In the end, your sexuality is your own work in progress, and you are the person who has to be comfortable with yourself.

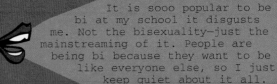

It is sooo popular to be bi at my school it disgusts me. Not the bisexuality—just the mainstreaming of it. People are being bi because they want to be like everyone else, so I just keep quiet about it all.
— **undertheRainbow**

i feel like i am at an AA meeting or something..."hi, i am trina, and i am bisexual." hehehe. i guess i have been forever, because when i had crushes they were on guys and on girls, and i have gone out with both guys and girls. i am open about it to people. some people just don't know bi people very well and are scared by us. being bisexual doesn't mean we are sex maniacs or anything, but that is what some people think. who cares? i like the way i am.
— **pandorasbox**

I don't think anyone is really "bisexual." Maybe I am wrong, but I think that is just something people say when they are confused about their sexuality. — **modernitie**

(1) do you like boys? (2) do you like girls? if you answered yes to both, chances are you are bisexual. that doesn't mean you have to label yrself as such. lots of people have pretty ambiguous sexualities. I like girls, physically, emotionally, spiritually, in every way. I prefer them. but that doesn't stop me from liking guys.
— **shaBoom**

Queer is the word that I identify with. Because it's a lot lighter than calling myself a lesbian, which makes me feel like a case study.
— **Padgett**

It's just the way I am. Deal with it. Gay, lesbian, dyke, homo, whatever you want to call it. Does that title tell you anything about me? Does that tell you that I'm an A student? That I'm a fanatical softball player? That I have a cat named Snowflake who I love more than anything in the world? That I'm a shy, scared girl who is just trying to be herself? No, I didn't think so. — **petulaC**

Gay high schools

Harvey Milk High School for gay, lesbian, bisexual, and transgender youth was founded in 1985 in New York City by the Hetrick-Martin Institute for Lesbian and Gay Youth. It started as a public school with 2 teachers and about 40 students. Some controversy attended its opening. Critics said public money was being used to subsidize homosexuality. (The school later became private.) Some also questioned separating gay kids from straight. But advocates said many of the students it served were in danger of getting no education at all. Many had been harassed at regular schools; others had dropped out or attempted suicide. Many had experienced humiliating sexual encounters on city streets. At the school they could find others who had had similar experiences without feeling like complete outsiders.

Two other cities, Los Angeles and Dallas, currently have high schools for gay youth. The Los Angeles Unified School District operates programs at four sites, called Eagle Centers. In Dallas a small private school, called the Walt Whitman Community School, opened in 1997.

HOMOPHOBIA

For girls who want to be with girls, it can be particularly hard and scary to think about all the various bad reactions people have to bi- and homosexuality. Homophobia takes different forms. It can range from mild disgust and fear of difference to the religious belief that homosexuality is a sin against God to physical violence. There is also self-hate, which some girls have to contend with, depending on the environment they've grown up in, as well as other factors.

Some girls have a harder time than others facing homophobia in themselves and in the world. It can be very helpful to talk to other girls (and boys) in your position for moral support. Girls who feel particularly alone or isolated can start to feel hopeless about their situations. They may get depressed or even start to think about suicide. Sadly, gay teenagers actually account for one-third of all teen suicides. Suicide is never a good option!

Also see Teenage Suicide, pp. 194–95 and Resources for dealing with suicidal thoughts, pp. 198–99.

I like girls and I don't know how to tell other people. I'm thinking about killing myself because no one understands me. What should I do? **— Cyla**

if you do kill yourself, then all those people who you think you can't tell & all the people who hate us b/c we like girls have won & bigotry wins out...i know it isn't easy. i know that people are assholes to us. i know what it is to be picked on, beat up, & on & on but we just have to keep on. if you need to, GET HELP!!! there are plenty of hotlines and books, etc. don't let them win & don't give up!! **— RaeDawn**

listen 2 me carefully! i don't know you and the only connection we ever have might be right now...but I know how u feel. i've tried committing suicide before and boy am i glad i failed! people always criticize what they don't understand, and what they don't understand is that we are all only human. maybe someday people can understand that maybe it's ok to love a person for who they are & not just for their gender. don't fret—there are people out here who DO understand!! **— Phaidra**

It can be very difficult to withstand the onslaught of homophobic negativity, but it is definitely possible!

I don't think we are against people who are attracted to the same sex. It's more that it scares us. I mean, what if everybody starts to become gay? How are we going to keep our world growing?
— **iluvrock**

In the Bible it says if a man sleeps with a man as he sleeps with a woman he shall be killed and the blood shall be on his own hands. Gayness is sick, gross, disgusting, and not normal. It should be stopped.— **Kasamira**

WOW! The ignorance is killing me. There is nothing wrong with being who you are. It's not sick or wrong or gross. You can't help who you are and shouldn't have to hide it. Find something better to do with your time than being rude to other people who aren't exactly like you.
— **susuki**

NEGA TIVITY

The Bible says a lot of things that don't make any sense. I'm not questioning the legitimacy of God's (or Goddess') existence or authority. I'm questioning the legitimacy of the Bible which was written by fallible mortal hand.
— **eartha**

You CANNOT and WILL NOT tell me or anyone else what is right and wrong!! Sin or no sin, we are following our hearts, just like straight people. Who created us?? GOD!!! If He didn't want us to be this way, then why did He create us this way??? answer that!
— **randomgrrl**

141

COMING OUT

As you start to understand your sexuality more fully, or become more comfortable with it, you may start to feel like you want and need to share this part of yourself with other people. It can be risky and scary to take this step because it's impossible to know how people will react. And you will most likely run into some homophobia along the way, be it from acquaintances, friends, or your own family. The people closest to you can be the hardest to tell because if they have bad reactions, it can feel totally devastating.

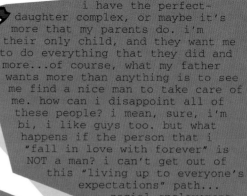

i have the perfect-daughter complex, or maybe it's more that my parents do. i'm their only child, and they want me to do everything that they did and more...of course, what my father wants more than anything is to see me find a nice man to take care of me. how can i disappoint all of these people? i mean, sure, i'm bi, i like guys too. but what happens if the person that i "fall in love with forever" is NOT a man? i can't get out of this "living up to everyone's expectations" path... social enslavement ...arrrgh!
— **seamless**

i've only come out to a few close friends, and i feel so fake around everyone else, like i'm constantly living a lie. it's so much stress to pretend all of the time. i never realized how much it affected how i act until i was around people who know. i can totally say anything I want around them and I feel so comfortable. but I'm scared to come out to anyone else because i lost my best friend last year by telling her.
— **HalieComeT**

You shouldn't give a rat's ass what anybody thinks. Your family's opinion might be important to you, but don't let anything stop you from being who you are! Your family should accept it because they love you and that means all of you. I went through a lot of shit and a lot of hiding my sexuality from people. Not anymore, though. I believe that I am my own person and I'll be whoever I want to be. Ever since I changed my attitude about the whole thing I don't know of anyone who isn't my friend or is ashamed in my family because I'm bi.
— **Wonderingrrl**

The very sorry fact is, not every-one is mature enough to handle their friends being gay. Like your best friend. It sounds to me like she wasn't really a good friend. Why don't you just concentrate on the friends you do have who know about everything. Maybe later you can come out to your other friends.
— **adasmith**

It took me a long time to even be able to say the word "lesbian" or write it down. Take your time and when you feel ready, you'll know.
— **lipservice**

I tried to tell my parents the roundabout way—going to AIDS marches, wearing red ribbons, bringing gay kids home to meet the family, joining PFLAG, and listening to feminist punk bands, but my parents were too dense to figure it out, and now I think they're curious but too scared to ask.
— **anichick**

i think i'm not going to tell my parents about my sexuality. it will just be easier that way. i have no problem with the closet, sorry.
— **amberrose**

Outing

In gay circles, there has been a lot of debate about whether gays and lesbians should remain closeted if they want to. Some people think that gay people, especially public figures, have a moral obligation to the gay community to come out and be counted. Others think that sexuality is a private issue and people should be able to deal with it as they see fit. There have been a number of cases in both gay and straight media in which public figures who had kept their sexuality private have been "outed" and confronted with evidence of their homosexuality.

Pride

all i have to say is grrrl luv = good luv! — **pattipie**

I think GURLS loving GURLS KICKS BUTT so rock on chics—you all rule :O)
— **SueG**

we can all relax!! grrrls like grrrls & its wonderful!!
— **jonigirl**

Ideally, girls who are bi or gay get through the struggle and reach a place of acceptance and pride about who they are. It's a huge relief to accept yourself and let go of shame. From there, you can move on to enjoy and explore your sexuality and yourself.

SHAME

Gay or bi friends

When friends (especially good friends) come out to you, it can bring up a bunch of different reactions and force you to really examine how you feel about bi- or homosexuality in general and your own sexuality in particular. It can be hard if you see your friend being hurt by other people's reactions, and it can be uncomfortable if you feel like your friend is sexually interested in you.

one of my really good friends is bi. i have no problem with that and we are still good friends. But another friend of ours said that being gay or bi is unnatural and she was against it. that got me mad. she doesn't really talk to our other friend anymore and she is always making rude comments. what should i do?
— **ahem**

I have friends who are totally disgusted with gays and lesbians too, but I just disregard their ignorance and try telling them that just because someone has a different choice of lifestyle doesn't change anything other than their relationships. If your friends can't deal, maybe you should hang around with people who can. — **Adenna**

my friend came out as bi to me. she was (still is!) my best friend in the whole world and i was like, eeewww, i hope she's not attracted to me, that would be soooo weird!!! Anyway, I guess I got used to it. I realized that I am friends with guys without worrying that they'll come on to me. There are different ways to have relationships with people.
— **spaceoddity**

sexual preference

Where to meet other girls

Being gay or bisexual can feel very isolating and lonely, especially if you don't know girls who feel the same way you do. Meeting other girls is important for moral support and also for fun!

Gay and bi community groups in your area (if they exist) are a great way to hook up with like-minded people. Also, the Internet has an excellent assortment of gay and bi sites to peruse and join. As always with cyber romances, if you do opt for a face-to-face meeting with someone you've met online, do so in a safe, very public place.

When it comes to girls you don't know from specifically gay settings, it can be difficult to gauge their interest, how they would react to your interest, and where they are with their sexuality.

i would really like to have experiences w/other girls. the problem is that i don't know where to meet anyone who has the same feelings as me. people always say to go to clubs but i'm underage. — **marsee**

You can meet other bi or gay girls at community support groups. Or if you're in college or high school, there's probably a support group for gay and bi students. Good luck! — **hotshotgirl**

I'm WAY curious about trying out a relationship with a girl. But I have no idea how to approach a girl. Wouldn't some girls get offended if I went up to them and asked them to be my lesbian lover? :) — **oPJo**

If you want to know if someone's gay, just mention something gay-oriented and see how she reacts. This seriously works. — **quake**

When it comes to picking up girls, I find that if I have the slightest inkling that they are curious, I go for it. I introduce myself, act casual and friendly. And eventually tell them I'm bi. If they're interested, they'll tell me. When girls know, its easier for them to approach you. — **AgathaC**

the wide world of homosexuality

Homosexuality certainly predates the ancient Greeks and written history; same-sex couplings even appear in some cave paintings. The Kamasutra, the sex manual of ancient India, contains descriptions of same-sex couplings.

Some cultures encourage same-sex experimentation among adolescents, as preparation for a grown-up heterosexual identity. Among certain highlander tribes in Papua New Guinea, boys practice oral sex on each other as a formal rite of passage. Many Latin and Muslim cultures wink at adolescent same-sex experimentation, although they remain intolerant of open, declared homosexuality. Definitions of homosexuality can vary. Among some Latin societies, men do not consider themselves gay unless they take the passive/receptive role during sex.

In countries like Pakistan and India, such experimentation may be okay, but it has to be kept quiet. The penalty for being a lesbian in Pakistan is 100 lashes in public.

National Organizations

Parents, Families and Friends of Lesbians and Gays (PFLAG) offers advice, general information, support groups for friends and family, and coming-out support. National headquarters: 1101 14th Street, NW, Suite 1030, Washington, DC 20005. Phone: 202-638-4200. Online: http://www.pflag.org.

Find a gay pen pal through **The Pen Pal Program, Youth Outreach, LA Gay and Lesbian Community Services Center**, 1625 North Hudson Avenue, Los Angeles, CA 90029, and/or International Pen Pal Program for Youth, P.O. Box 20716, Indianapolis, IN 46220.

The National Coming Out Project provides education about lesbianism, homosexuality, and bisexuality. Phone: 800-866-6263.

National Gay and Lesbian Hotline: 888-843-4564.

Online

Oasis at http://www.oasismag.com is a gay youth magazine.

¡Outproud! National Coalition for Gay, Lesbian, and Bisexual, and Transgender Youth at http://www.outproud.org.

Youth.org at http://www.youth.org is a gay youth organization.

Books

Bi Any Other Name: Bisexual People Speak Out by Loraine Hutchins and Lisa Kaahumanu (Alyson). Excellent introduction to bisexuality.

Free Your Mind: The Book for Gay, Lesbian, and Bisexual Youth—And Their Allies by Ellen Bass and Kate Kaufman (HarperPerennial). Facilitates acceptance of being gay.

Is It a Choice? Answers to 300 of the Most Frequently Asked Questions about Gays and Lesbians by Eric Marcus (Harper San Francisco). Answers to questions about homosexuality.

Two Teenagers in Twenty: Writings by Gay and Lesbian Youth, edited by Ann Heron (Alyson). Teens' stories about coming out and dealing with their sexuality.

Vice Versa: Bisexuality and the Eroticism of Everyday Life by Marjorie Gerber (Simon & Schuster). Cultural study of bisexuality, citing art, literature, pop culture, science, and psychology.

Some good fictional reads include:

The Nancy Clue Series by Mabel Maney (Cleis Press). A hilarious lesbian version of the Nancy Drew series.

Oranges Are Not the Only Fruit by Jeanette Winterson (Grove/Atlantic). Describes the adolescence of a ferociously bright and rebellious orphan adopted into a Pentecostal household as she comes to terms with her unorthodox sexuality.

Rubyfruit Jungle by Rita Mae Brown (Bantam Books). The classic coming-of-age gay novel.

For more resources and information, see http://www.dealwithit.com

sexuality

Chapter 7

SEX WHEN YOU DON'T WANT IT

Sexual encounters are only good when you are willing and prepared. Sex when you don't want it sucks. Sexual harassment, sexual abuse, sexual assault, and rape are about power and violence, not about sex. Being a victim of one of those acts is a horrible experience—and self-blame can often make it even more difficult, eating you up inside.

s
e
x
u
a
l
i
t
y

SEXUAL HARASSMENT

Sexual harassment takes many different forms—from unwelcome comments to unwanted physical contact to a hostile environment. Its legal definition is not crystal clear, and has been widely debated in the United States and the world.

Your rights to get an education and to work are regarded as civil rights, so sexual harassment at school or on the job is legally viewed as a kind of discrimination.

There are two basic kinds of sexual harassment, as defined by the Equal Employment Opportunity Commission (EEOC):

First, there is quid pro quo harassment, in which sex is traded for opportunities, grades, raises, or as a condition for keeping a job or not failing a course.

The second kind—"hostile environment" harassment—is harder to define, but includes unwelcome advances, requests for sexual favors, demeaning references to women, and the display of sexually explicit material.

What is important in the eyes of the law is the reaction of the woman, rather than the intent of the man. He may not mean to harass you, but if you feel harassed and say so, then it's legally harassment.

Sexual harassment is a civil, not a criminal, matter. In other words, you can sue someone for sexual harassment but not press charges in a criminal court. To convince a jury that you have been the victim of sexual harassment, you need to have witnesses, documents, and lots of evidence.

"Hostile environment" harassment

Different people have different levels of tolerance for graphic sexual talk and for teasing of a sexual nature. Some girls and women are more comfortable with it, while others find it more disturbing. There is no one right way to react, and each person needs to respond in her own way.

The goal is to find a way to resolve any sexual harassment problem to your satisfaction without causing yourself further problems. This can mean ignoring things because you don't want to waste your time, giving the offenders a piece of your mind, or reporting them to an appropriate adult. What you decide to do will vary depending on the circumstances. The better you understand your comfort level and the more that you communicate the things that piss you off, the better off you'll be. You have the right to move about your world freely and not be subjected to this type of crap.

Some young women have successfully sued their schools when their complaints about lewd graffiti and relentless sexual teasing in the hallways were ignored.

Power issues

Sexual harassment may involve an exchange of sexual favors for some benefit, for example when a person in a position of power, like a teacher or a boss, withholds good grades, a raise, or a new job from another person or threatens retribution unless that person agrees to sex. Even if the person who is not in power agrees to a relationship, this is still considered harassment.

Sexual relationships between teachers and underage students always present a legal issue, as well as a number of other problems, given the uneven power arrangement. Even if the two people involved are clear about and comfortable with the terms of their affair, it can be unfair to everyone around them. Regardless of whether or not the institution says it is acceptable, sex between an adult and someone under the age of 18 is always statutory rape.

Sexual assault

Unwanted contact with the breasts, genitals, or anus, short of penetration of the vagina or anus, is legally considered sexual

> The boys at my school are total scum-sucking incompetent idiotic jackasses! They will come up behind us at lunch, poke our backs with their fingers, and say, "That wasn't my finger—I'm a really tall man." CAN WE SAY SEXUAL HARASSMENT?! The worst part is, my friends just put up with it! GGGGRRRRRRRRRR! It really pisses me off!
> — **greenham**

> I agree with you: a lot of guys are major perverts and assholes. If you get sexually harassed, you should file a report so they don't think it's okay for them to do it again to you or one of your friends. You can't just sit there and watch your friends take it because it is majorly wrong. You have to convince them of this. One of my friends constantly got sexually harassed by this one guy...I overheard him saying he was going to invite her to his house and rape her. I was really scared for my friend. — **imanAlien**

I think I was
sexually harassed at
school. This guy who always
tells me I'm "sexy" or "the
cutest thing" put his arm out
for a hug. Normally I try to
avoid him because he's always
trying to touch me. Anyway, on Fri-
day I gave him a fake hug and
tried to get away but he held me
tighter. Then I could feel his
face getting close so I turned
my face really quick and he
ended up kissing me on my
cheek. What do you think—Sexual
Harassment, or in his words
was I getting "the wrong
impression"? I have told a
teacher and my friend's
father. Most of the guys
think it's funny but it's
really not.
— northernlight

It's
good that
you told peo-
ple. I know how
guys can be—the
only way you'll get
them to admit sexual
harassment is sexual
harassment is if you're
raped or something. If
this guy ever tries to
pull shit on you again,
just hurt him somehow,
or yell at him in
front of a bunch of
people and embarrass
the hell out of him.
Good luck!
— lovelylola

assault, a slightly lesser crime
than rape. But it is still a felony.

Victims of sexual assault can
feel extremely violated and vulnerable afterward and likely will benefit from counseling to deal with their
feelings. Sexual assaults, whether at
the hands of a stranger or an acquaintance, should be reported to authorities.
And, depending on the contact with the
attacker, a hospital visit may be in order.
Not reporting such incidents feeds into the
hands of sexual predators; it also keeps the
statistics on such crimes artificially low.

the wide world of rape

In about 14 Latin American
countries, including Argentina,
Brazil, Chile, and Costa Rica, a
rapist can escape penalty if he agrees
to marry the woman he raped. In these
countries, such a premium is placed on
virginity before marriage that a raped
woman is viewed as damaged goods and no
one else will marry her. Peru repealed this law
in 1997 after a public outcry.

In London, a rape victim is compensated 7,500
pounds (about $11,550) by the Criminal Injuries
Compensation Authority. When there are multiple
attackers, the price rises to 10,000 pounds
($15,400). The Criminal Injuries Compensation
Authority pays out about 200 million pounds per year.

In Turkey, a rapist automatically receives a
lighter sentence if the woman was not a virgin before
the attack or if the judge decides the woman acted
provocatively.

Under Kenyan law, if a man has intercourse with a
girl under the age of 14 against her will, he is not
accused of "rape." Instead, he is charged with the lesser
crime of "defilement." This has a maximum sentence of
5 years, as opposed to rape, which carries a maximum
penalty of life imprisonment.

In Pakistan, a married woman who says she has
been raped can have charges of adultery brought
against her and end up in jail herself. A female or
non-Muslim witness is not legally recognized, so a
man who rapes a woman in the presence of other
women cannot be convicted.

South Africa has the world's highest rape
rate, and in some poor black townships, rape is
seen as inevitable. There is one reported rape
every 14 minutes, and it is estimated that for
every reported rape, 20 to 35 other rapes
go unreported.

A high court in Italy ruled that if a
woman is wearing jeans, a man cannot be charged with raping her—
because she would have to help
undo the jeans and there-
fore consent to the act.

sex when you don't want it

RAPE

Although rape involves a sexual act, it's not really about sex—it's a brutal show of power.

It is common for women who are raped to blame themselves, and in many ways society encourages that reaction. Law enforcement officers, even family and friends, sometimes question why a woman was not being careful enough. Some people may question why she did not fight off her attacker. Some people still believe that what the woman was wearing is somehow relevant to the crime. Rape is the only crime where the victim is blamed to this extent.

Perhaps this is why rape also continues to be the least reported violent crime: 30.5 percent of all rapes and sexual attacks are reported, compared with 59.1 percent of aggravated assaults and 55.8 percent of robberies.

Rape kit procedure

The rape kit procedure may seem like it's prolonging your ordeal, but it is a vital step in reporting and stopping rape, both of which can be powerful tools in your recovery. Even if you are not totally certain that you are going to bring criminal charges, you should take this step. Without it, if you should change your mind later, the rape will be a lot harder to prove and the rapist a lot harder to identify. Because rape is such an intimate crime, the rapist leaves evidence of himself on your body. With all the advances in DNA testing and identification, these microscopic traces of your attacker are your best chance for nailing him.

Rape kit procedure includes photographing any cuts and bruises; taking a saliva sample; combing your pubic hair for any evidence (like his pubic hair); conducting a pelvic exam; checking your underwear for semen stains, which can be used for valuable DNA tests; and cleaning under your fingernails. You will also be asked to relate what happened, and someone, usually a doctor will write it all down. If the hospital has a rape crisis volunteer or staff member on call, they can be in the room with you during this procedure.

What to do if you are raped

If you are raped, there are certain things you have to do immediately to increase the chances that your attacker will be apprehended and hopefully put away.

1. Do not immediately bathe, wash, or dispose of the clothes you wore during the attack—your body and clothes can provide important evidence for catching and prosecuting the rapist.

2. Tell someone—the police, a doctor, a friend, or a counselor at a rape crisis center. There are rape crisis centers in every city, at most hospitals, and on most college campuses. The national rape crisis phone number is 800-656-HOPE and they will refer you to the closest center in your area. It might feel strange to contact some center for help where you don't really know the people who will be helping you. However, the beauty of a rape crisis center is that the staff and volunteers are trained to deal with these situations. They don't need personal information from you. They are there to help you.

3. As soon as possible, get yourself to a hospital or clinic. There you will receive the standard rape kit procedure, collecting evidence of rape. You will be given the chance to talk to a counselor and told

Rape: The aftermath

In addition to self-blame, rape victims commonly experience extreme feelings of help-lessness, overwhelming fearfulness, crippling anger, guilt, and/or depression. A rapist can rob a woman of the sense that she has any control over what happens to her and that she can move about the world free of fear.

Some victims of rape fear and distrust men for a long time afterward, and they may find it very hard to have sex again without reliving their attack. Every victim has her own timetable for recovery and needs plenty of love, patience, and support. Most victims of rape do manage to recover, survive, and move on, doing all the things they want and need to do with their lives.

I was raped when I was 15, by a man I didn't know. Afterward, I did a lot of stupid crap, and my grades dropped all over the place. It's very difficult to see yourself as "clean" or "pure" after it's happened. I completely shut down toward men for a while, and then when that didn't work (like ignoring the problem ever does), I slept around—a lot. I thought that every person after him would erase the memory of his face, but it doesn't. Pulling your stuff together and rebuilding your life so that you're stronger and wiser than you were is possible.
— Altheasays

Reporting and pressing charges

There is no question that pursuing a rape case can be a harrowing ordeal, involving confronting one's attacker in a courtroom, identifying him, and to some degree reliving the attack. It can also be a pivotal and therapeutic part of getting over a rape, a way of taking back control and refusing to be shamed into silence. After all, he's the one who committed the crime and should be ashamed, not you.

Many police departments have gotten more sensitive to sex crime victims. Some have set up specialized divisions in which cops—often female ones—with special training deal with such complaints. Sex crimes prosecutors have been hired specifically to go after rapists (and other sex offenders), and having a cooperative victim is vital to the success of any rape case. However, part of the process may still feel extremely alienating and upsetting.

In the eyes of the criminal justice system, your importance is not just as a victim, but as a witness, and your credibility will be an issue. It is no longer legal to question a woman about her sexual past in a rape trial. But the rapist's lawyers may do everything in their power to tarnish your reputation anyway. Despite some pitfalls, women who pursue rape cases are seldom sorry they did. Taking action can help to complete the process of getting over a rape.

 where you can get some follow-up counseling, which is highly recommended. Also, you will be offered emergency contraception and antibiotics to fight potential STDs.

4. In the weeks and months following a rape, get tested for STDs, pregnancy, and, about 6 months after the attack, HIV infection.

5. Consider continuing counseling. After going through counseling, eventually it may be useful to join a rape support group. It is common to feel some sense of alienation from people who have never been through the sort of nightmare that you have endured after a rape, so meeting with a group of other rape survivors could be useful.

Date rape

Around 80 percent of all rapes, defined as unwanted sexual penetration, occur between people who are at least acquainted with each other. This has been defined as date rape.

There are many date rape scenarios. It can happen on a first date with someone or much further along in a dating relationship, possibly even after there's already been sex. Or it can happen between friends. Date rape can be so shocking and upsetting because you knew and trusted the person and can't believe that you misjudged him or didn't see the signs.

Alcohol is a factor in about two-thirds of all instances of date rape and sexual assault. Alcohol and other mood-altering drugs can cloud judgment. They can also affect a woman so much that she becomes too drunk or high, possibly even to the point of unconsciousness, to consent to sex.

Statistics suggest that the highest incidence of date rape is in the senior year of high school and freshman year of college, both times when there may be more drugs and alcohol around and people take chances they would not otherwise take. The first month or so of freshman year is the most dangerous time for date rape. In many instances of date rape, the woman was willing to be sexual up to a point and found that when she decided it should stop, the man would not cooperate and instead forced or intimidated her into having sex with him. Saying a no-nonsense "no," and repeating it if necessary, ought to be enough to stop a sexual encounter, no matter how far it has gone. But it is important, both legally and in terms of being clear in your communication, to say "no" out loud.

It is important to understand how often these incidences occur: just being aware can help prevent this from happening in your own life. Think carefully about who you feel safe with and why. Pay attention to how people treat you. If a guy you are getting involved with constantly insists on going somewhere that the two of you can be alone or displays aggressive sexual behavior during which his personality seems to change, take note! And keep away.

Supporting other people who have been through this horrible experience is important. It is a lonely, difficult thing to go through, and there has been too much silence and shame for too long.

Date rape: The debate

Under the law, there is no distinction between stranger and acquaintance rape: rape is rape. But in the eyes of a jury and some people, the two kinds of rape can look different. Since date rape involves two people who know each other, and usually there are no bruises or witnesses, it

> my bf almost raped me today. i didn't want to have sex with him, but he kept protesting and whining and made me feel guilty about not having sex with him. i did it for a few reasons: (1) to make him happy, and (2) because I was scared he was going to rape me if i didn't. i don't know what to do. i love him to death. he has never done anything like this before. can anyone help me?
> — **terriscary**

> You should really tell someone—a teacher, parent, or other adult you trust. I understand that you love him, but if he pushes you to do things that you aren't really ready for, you should rethink this relationship because to me, an outsider looking in, this seems to be a really unhealthy relationship.
> — **mopey**

i got sort of
raped last night, and i
don't know if i should
say anything or not,
because i was pretty
drunk.
— **GirlfromIowa**

Tell someone, girl. Even
if you were drunk, that guy took
advantage of you, and you don't
want him to do it to anybody
else. What if you're pregnant?
I've been sexually abused by one
of my best guy friends. I told
even though I was afraid that I'd
lose his friendship.
— **lilithfiend**

can become a case of "he said/she said" very quickly. If it is reported and charges are brought, the guy and his lawyers will often argue that sex did indeed happen, even potentially "rough sex," but that it was consensual and that the woman wanted it just as much as the man. A disturbingly large number of men who are accused of date rape, about 80 percent, do not even recognize that they raped the woman.

People have successfully argued that the woman in question falsely accused the man of date rape as revenge for being jilted after having sex. Often the woman who brings date rape charges is made to feel that she is the one on trial. It is true there have been instances of false accusations—but this doesn't change the fact that date rape happens and that it can be every bit as violent and upsetting as rape by a stranger.

No one has the right to have sex with a woman against her will, not even her husband. Chances are that a guy who date-rapes one woman will do it to other women because he thinks he can get away with it. It may be both therapeutic to the victim and helpful to other women to report such incidents.

The date rape drug

The "date rape drug" is a powerful sedative, 10 times more powerful than Valium, called Rohypnol, or "roofie," for short. It is illegal in this country but legal in Europe and Latin America, so people can still get hold of it. Rapists have been known to slip these into unsuspecting women's drinks. The women feel paralyzed, experience blurred vision, get the spins, and may black out or enter a dreamlike state where their memory is seriously impaired. Many women who are victims of date rape while on this drug don't even have a clear memory of being assaulted. Be careful about taking drinks from men you don't necessarily feel safe with.

Just the facts about
...Rape

According to the National Victim Center and Crime Victims Research and Treatment Center, 12.1 million American women report having been forcibly raped at least once in their lives—in the vast majority of cases, by men that they knew. Of these women, 39 percent said they have been raped more than once.

According to the Justice Department:

A woman is raped every **2** minutes somewhere in America.

In the course of **4** years at college, **14** to **20** percent of young women will have some experience of date rape or sexual assault on a date.

One out of three American women will be the victim of rape. The U.S. rape rate is **13** times that in England and **20** times that in Japan.

About **38** percent of rapes occur in the victim's home; **38** percent in the homes of friends and relatives.

Self-defense: Preventing rape

It's unhealthy to let the fear of being raped take over your life, but it's important to find a balance between leading a full and adventurous life and taking sensible precautions. There are behaviors you can adopt to lower your chances of being victimized:
1. Whenever possible, walk with other people. There's safety in numbers.
2. Know where you're going and act like it. If you suspect that your evening's plans may include some walking, wear shoes that you can easily walk—or run—in. Walk purposefully with your head up and a strong stride.
3. Cultivate an alertness to dangerous situations and avoid them, if possible.
4. Know the places and people in your life that are safe and unsafe.
5. Follow your instincts. If a situation, a street, or even a party gives you a bad feeling, leave. Run if necessary, or make a scene.

Self-defense classes are widely available. They usually include instruction in being assertive on the street and getting away from an attacker, as well as some physical self-defense techniques. Some of these classes include rape enactments, during which a well-padded teacher plays the role of rapist. Students learn how to injure vulnerable parts of the attacker's body, with the least risk to themselves.

Physical confrontation is riskier and should be a last resort. In the event of an attack, two things are important: doing what comes naturally to you and doing whatever you do with absolute conviction. It's a good idea to have a plan in mind in the event of the attack. As for weapons like pepper spray, mace, and even guns, women are buying these in increasing numbers, but they pose a big risk. They can give a false sense of confidence and are all too often turned on the victim. Getting away and surviving are your first priorities, not inflicting damage on your attacker.

If you are driving alone, a good habit to get into is keeping all doors and windows locked at night. If you suspect that someone is following you, or if another car bumps yours, don't pull over. Drive to a well-lit or populated area—a police station ideally. And honk your horn until someone comes out or the suspicious car goes away. Don't give rides to strangers. And don't hitchhike.

154

INCEST

Incest is sex between family members. Parents, grandparents, uncles, cousins, stepparents and siblings can all be perpetrators of incest.

Being the victim of ongoing childhood sexual abuse at the hands of a close and trusted relative can have damaging, long-term psychological effects. Survivors suffer from higher rates of depression, eating disorders, alcohol and drug addiction, suicide, low self-esteem, and difficulty in maintaining healthy adult relationships.

Anyone who has ever been victimized in this way needs to tell someone, get help, and talk to a therapist who specializes in such matters. There are huge issues to sort out, including guilt, complicity, and trust. There is no such thing as an inappropriate feeling stemming from incest, from anger to enjoyment. This is not something that a person can ever handle alone. Incest survivors who join support groups to talk about it discover that they do not feel as alone anymore.

If your parent abuses you or any other family member in any way, you have to find someone outside—a trusted older friend, teacher, guidance counselor, or therapist—who can give you a safe emotional space, and help you find some solutions.

Among incest victims under 12 years old, 90 percent know the man who attacked them, and half of the attackers are close relatives. One in five victims under 12 is raped by her father.

Between 200,000 and 360,000 cases of child sexual abuse occur each year in the United States, and 80 percent of these involve incest.

For more on sexual abuse in the family, see p. 229.

At night my dad goes into my little sister's bedroom and touches her in places that she doesn't want him to. I don't know if I should tell anyone about what he has been doing because he might hurt me. Please help!!! — SadYgirL

i hope you do tell someone really soon cause if not, your sister will have tons of trouble when she grows up. it happened to me by my dad and it's not easy telling someone but you need to. i have been living the pain of not telling anyone until i was 12 and i have had some really hard times growing up. — dottee

When I was young my grandfather molested me. It just stopped about 3-4 years ago. This year I told my parents about it. They told me that I could press charges. I don't know if I should. If I do, my grandmother will be torn! I still love him because he is my grandfather but I have no respect for him and hate being around him. This also happened to my cousin, her dad talked to him about it and he denied it! I'm afraid that if I do press charges he will deny it! — VelmaV

I was also molested when I was younger. I know the feeling of helplessness that it brings. You need to turn him in so that he won't do this to anyone else. As you've seen with your cousin, he won't stop if he doesn't have to. — mascaramama

155

MOLESTATION

Molestation is contact of a sexual nature with a child, including indecent exposure, genital contact, fondling, and penetration. It happens not just to children but to teenagers. If you are the victim of incest or molestation, tell someone. If you can't tell your parents, tell a trusted adult. Children who are the victims of any kind of inappropriate sexual contact suffer reverberations throughout their lives. So if you've been abused in any way, at any time, it's essential to get professional help.

Child molesters depend on their victims' silence. They often bribe, threaten, and cajole their victims into keeping quiet. They tell them that no one will believe them or that the victims will be blamed. Child molesters and incest perpetrators sometimes justify their actions by convincing themselves and their victims that the children want and enjoy the sex as much as they do. They are sick people and need to be stopped.

RESOURCES

Rape—National Organizations

The Rape, Abuse & Incest National Network (RAINN) is a nonprofit organization that operates America's only national hotline for survivors of sexual assault. The hotline offers free, confidential counseling and support 24 hours a day, from anywhere in the country, as a service for survivors who cannot reach a rape crisis center through a local call, as well as those who might not know that a local center exists. Address: 635-B Pennsylvania Avenue, SE, Washington, DC 20003. Phone: 800-656-HOPE. Website: http://www.rainn.org. E-mail: RAINNmail@aol.com.

National Coalition Against Sexual Assault is an organization working to end rape and improve services for victims and survivors. Also provides guidelines for choosing a self-defense course. Phone: 717-728-9764. E-mail: ncasa@redrose.net.

Rape—Online

Sexual Assault Information Page at http://www.cs.utk.edu/~bartley/saInfoPage.html is one of the top sites on the Internet for finding answers to many questions about sexual assault, harassment, incest, and date rape. Lists resources like rape crisis centers and self-defense classes.

Rape—Books

After Silence: Rape and My Journey Back by Nancy Venable Raine (Crown). A personal memoir of recovery.

Against Our Will: Men, Women and Rape by Susan Brownmiller (Fawcett Books). A classic sociological look at rape in society.

Backlash: The Undeclared War Against American Women by Susan Faludi (Anchor). Intelligent, aggressive examination of attacks on women's rights, including discussion of media, myths, sexual harassment, and assault.

Before He Takes You Out: The Safe Dating Guide for the 90's by Scott Lindquist (American Vigilance). How to protect yourself from date rape.

Street Smarts: A Personal Safety Guide for Women by Louise Rafkin (Harper Prism). Practical advice for keeping safe.

Surviving the Silence: Black Women's Stories of Rape by Charlotte Pierce-Baker (Norton). Stories of rape survivors.

Telling: A Memoir of Rape and Recovery by Patricia Weaver Francisco (Cliff Street Books). Author says talking—to her rapist as he raped her and about her rape afterward—saved her life. Beautifully written, poetic account.

Self-Defense—National Organizations

Martial Hearts. Self-defense for women and children. Address: 10930 Crabapple Road, Roswell, GA 30075. Phone: 770-640-6986. Website: http://www.cs.utk.edu/~bartley/index/prevention/martialHearts/. E-mail: kkollman@ix.netcom.com.

Also, to find **self-defense courses geared for women,** consult your local YWCA and your Yellow Pages for Model Mugging courses.

Incest—National Organizations

Society's League Against Molestation provides counseling and nationwide referrals over the phone. Phone: 609-858-7800.

Incest—Online

VOICES in Action: Victims Of Incest Can Emerge Survivors at http://www.Voices-action.org. provides many useful links to other related groups.

Incest—Books

Bastard Out of Carolina by Dorothy Allison (Plume). Harrowing, beautifully written account of childhood pain, rape, and betrayal.

Betrayal of Innocence: Incest and Its Devastation by Susan Forward and Craig Buck (Penguin USA). Study of the trauma caused by incest.

Breaking the Silence: A Personal Story of Incest and Recovery by Melody Platt (Rainbow Books). Memoir of sexual abuse at the hands of a father from infancy on. The book resulted from a journal kept while the author was in therapy.

The Courage to Heal: A Guide for Women Survivors of Child Sexual Abuse by Ellen Bass and Laura Davis (HarperPerennial). Most widely read self-help text for incest survivors.

The Kiss by Kathryn Harrison (Bard). A memoir of one woman's love affair with her father.

Push: A Novel by Sapphire (Vintage Books). A young woman's raw account of sexual abuse.

Secret Survivors: Uncovering Incest and Its Aftereffects in Women by E. Sue Blume (Ballantine Books). Resource especially for unconscious survivors of childhood sexual abuse. Shows how survivors frequently suffer from depression, addiction, and eating and panic disorders.

For more resources and information, see http://www.dealwithit.com

Boys

(what the guy is
dealing with)

ANATOMY AND PHYSIOLOGY (BOYS' BODIES)

The **bladder** stores urine until it is excreted.

The **urethra**, inside the penis shaft, is the tube that carries urine and semen out of the penis through the meatus. (A valve inside the bladder ensures that urine and semen do not travel through the urethra at the same time.)

penis

shaft
(the length of the penis)

the coronal ridge
(the ridge of tissue between the head and the shaft)

head
(the glans)

the frenulum
(a notch in the head, on the underside of the penis; this is where the skin of the shaft extends)

The ridge, head, and frenulum are full of nerve endings and are the most sensitive areas of the penis.
The skin covering it all is relatively loose and expandable, to accommodate the growth of the penis when erect.

The **meatus** is the opening for both urine and semen to come

The **scrotum** (aka balls) refers to the two sacks that hang underneath the penis. The scrotum is covered with loose, coarse skin, a bit of hair, and a

Spermatic cords attach the testes to the body.

The **testes** are the two testicles which reside in the scrotum and are extremely sensitive.

The **prostate gland** surrounds the urethra, and produces semen, the thick fluid that carries sperm from the testicles.

The **seminal vesicles** carry sperm into the urethra from the vas deferens.

The **vas deferens** (located inside each spermatic cord) is where seminal fluid, or semen (the stuff sperm travel in), is made.

A few words about
the penis...

penis schlong dick cock tool weener weenie peepee willie

The penis is an extremely loaded symbol—what it represents goes far beyond what it really is.

In our society, many objects that are longer than they are wide (skyscrapers, swords, and guns, to name a few) are seen as phallic symbols and are thought to represent power and strength. Phallic comes from phallus, the Greek word for the penis.

Your first encounter with a penis in real life (not counting baby penises) may feel strange. It might be weird to come across a body part that you don't have yourself but have heard so much about. If you want to know what feels good for a boy and his penis, it's always helpful to ask. Boys' desires and preferences are as individual as girls'.

Some parts of puberty, like skin problems, hair growth, and general physical maturation affect boys and girls with relatively equal impact, though the way they manifest themselves varies greatly. Boys start puberty slightly later than girls (on average) and, as with girls, mature at different rates. Boys' sexual development is usually broken down into five stages:

1. From birth to puberty, boys' genitals grow slightly. Then, during puberty, boys go through the next four stages.

2. The onset of puberty occurs anywhere between ages 9 and 16. At a signal from the hypothalamus (a region of the brain) and the pituitary gland, boys' bodies start producing hormones, like testosterone, in their gonads (reproductive glands). Testicles grow and start hanging lower down. Pubic hair appears. Testosterone also begins changing the shape of the body by adding muscles in the chest and shoulders. The areas around the nipples (areolae) get bigger and darker.

3. Beginning between ages 11 and 16, the penis gets longer and a little wider, and the penis and scrotum get darker. More pubic hair appears. Shoulders broaden, hips narrow. Facial and underarm hair may develop. The voice may begin to deepen.

4. Between ages 11 and 17, there's another growth spurt for the penis, which gets considerably longer and wider. Lots more body hair appears. Sperm production has begun, followed by the first ejaculation. Increased facial oils may produce acne.

5. Adult proportions are reached. This phase is usually completed by age 18, and may continue into the early twenties. The penis assumes its full length and width; the scrotum is fully developed. Pubic hair has spread to thighs and up toward belly. Chest hairs appear. Shaving is more frequent.

WHAT HAPPENS TO BOYS DURING SEX?

Erection

erect penis

An erection (boner, hard-on, woody, stiffy) occurs when blood rushes into and fills the spongy cylinders of the penis, enlarging it and stiffening it (a condition that is technically called vasocongestion). Tightened muscles at the base of the penis hold the blood in, which keeps the penis erect. The testicles are also drawn closer to the body, instead of hanging loosely.

Erections often occur in response to some sexual stimulation or thought—but not always. They can also be spurred by unrelated things, like fabric brushing against the penis, having to pee really badly, or nothing much at all. It's more or less a reflex. Boys have lots of erections in their sleep and often wake up with erections. Erections are not within a boy's control, and they can occur at extremely inopportune moments, when they aren't wanted. Imagine if every time you had a sexual thought or a split-second feeling of being turned on, your body responded in a way that was noticeable to the rest of the world. Pretty embarrassing... If you notice that a guy you know has an erection at an inappropriate time, be merciful and ignore it. That way, he can ignore it, and it will go away.

Erections, though they can come on suddenly, can also build up in stages, from limpness to sort of semi-erect to very

flaccid penis

hard. As more and more blood flows into the penis, it darkens in color and gets stiffer and stiffer. The head also fills with blood and can get larger. In this highly aroused state, a small amount of clear fluid, called pre-ejaculate, often squeezes out of the tip of the penis. It can contain some sperm and can theoretically fertilize an egg. This is one reason early withdrawal is not an effective method of birth control.

For more information on birth control, see pp. 104–107 and 114–18.

Erections resolve themselves in one of two ways:

1. They go away by themselves. When the erection "realizes" no one is paying attention to it (or is discouraged for some other reason), the muscles at the base of the penis relax and let the blood out, leaving the penis in its unaroused state (smaller and softer).

2. They go away after ejaculation. The male orgasm culminates with the penis emitting semen in a series of muscular contractions, after which the muscles at the base of the penis relax and the penis returns to its unaroused state.

Does a guy get an erection when you are making out?
— **samiam**

I think that you would notice if he had a hard-on, like it would be sticking out for a little bit. — **warningwarning**

What is a boner exactly? And is it the same as a schlong? — **gotfreckles**

A boner is slang for an erection, when blood flows to the penis and makes it hard. A schlong, a rather vulgar word, is the penis itself. — **mssaigon**

Circumcision

It is common in this country, and nearly universal among Jewish and Muslim families, for boys to be circumcised. Usually done on newborn babies, circumcision is a procedure during which the foreskin, which covers but is not attached to the glans (the head of the penis), is cut away. On an uncircumcised penis, the glans is still covered by the loose, sleevelike foreskin, which can be retracted or slid back. Circumcision alters the appearance of the penis but not the way it works.

There is some debate about the value of circumcision. The penis is easier to keep clean without the foreskin, so until 1998 the American Academy of Pediatrics endorsed circumcision for health reasons. More recent evidence suggests that provided the penis is kept clean, an uncircumcised man is at no greater risk for infection than someone who's circumcised. And there is a bit of debate about whether circumcision may cause some reduction in sexual sensation.

Erection problems

Premature ejaculation is when a boy ejaculates before or immediately after penetration in intercourse. It happens a lot more in boys who haven't been having sex for very long or who haven't done it in a while. It can also happen when the excitement level is extremely high for some other reason. Many guys have problems with this at some point in their teen years. Using condoms can sometimes help.

Problems getting or maintaining an erection: Penises do not always cooperate with the situation at hand, and when a boy can't get an erection (or keep one), it can be difficult not to take it personally. You might assume that he doesn't want to have sex with you, is not turned on, "can't get it up for you." But, in fact, lack of interest or desire is rarely the cause of these erectile problems (which are sometimes called impotence, but usually only in older men when the situation is chronic).

Most frequently, the problems are caused either by performance anxiety or by other emotional factors. If this happens to someone you are fooling around with, it can be awkward. It helps to remember that it most likely has nothing to do with you. If you feel comfortable talking with your partner about his feelings, you might ask him if he's feeling upset about anything else. (Sometimes other issues in relationships or in a guy's life can influence sexual functioning.) Or you might just want to ignore it and move on to other things. This stuff happens, and it's more uncomfortable for him than for you.

Wet dreams

Also known as nocturnal emissions, wet dreams are what happens when a boy ejaculates in his sleep. Most boys have their first wet dream sometime between the ages of 11 and 16, when they first begin producing sperm. Wet dreams alleviate the buildup of sperm and may or may not be the result of an explicitly sexual dream. They're most frequent during puberty (when some boys have them), and almost all men have a wet dream sometime in their lives. Masturbation during the day or an active sex life may help curb the frequency of wet dreams.

Ejaculation

blowing your wad
shooting your load
cuming climax

Although people tend to think of ejaculation as part of the male orgasm, it is actually a separate biological function—it's even possible for the two to occur independently of each other. Inside the testicles are specialized cells (Sertoli cells) that continuously produce sperm. Ejaculation happens when the sexual tension builds to the point where it absolutely has to be released, causing sperm and semen to spurt out of the tip of the penis.

When a guy ejaculates, first muscles in his prostate gland push semen into the urethra, and then contracting muscles in the penis and urethra force it out the opening. About a teaspoon of this fluid comes out, containing as many as 600 million sperm. Semen (aka cum, seed, jizz, wad), a combination of seminal fluid and sperm, is usually white, yellow, or gray and generally sort of thick and mucusy or "creamy." Seminal fluid, which is made in the seminal vesicles, both nourishes the sperm and helps it to swim faster.

Ejaculation usually happens at the same time as a series of rhythmic contractions in the pelvic muscles (this is the orgasm part). Male orgasms, like female ones, vary in intensity.

After ejaculation, there is a resolution period before another erection can occur. The length of this period varies from person to person and occasion to occasion.

MALE MASTURBATION

jack off pull your pud
spank the monkey jerk off
beat your meat beat off

Most boys and men, well above 90 percent, masturbate from time to time, or frequently. There are several popular techniques for male masturbation. Probably the most common is holding the penis shaft with one hand and rhythmically pulling up and down, while occasionally stroking the head, building momentum until climax and ejaculation. Some guys also rub against something, the bed or another inanimate object.

EMOTIONAL RESPONSES AND ISSUES (BOYS' HEADS)

It sometimes seems that boys let their sex drive make decisions for them. But that's a pretty gross generalization. What is true is that during puberty boys are inundated with hormones that have a huge impact on the desire for sex. Testosterone, the hormone responsible for the sex drive in both men and women, is the dominant male sex hormone. The exact impact of testosterone on male behavior is a subject of some debate.

Performance anxiety: It is natural for boys to get nervous about sex and their role in it. Boys worry about many of the same things that girls do: what their partners will think about their bodies, their odor, the appearance of their sex organs, and their level of experience. In boy-girl intercourse, a guy may feel anxious about not "satisfying" his lover because of lack of endurance, fear that his penis isn't the right size or shape, or not knowing how a girl's body works sexually. The more comfortable a boy can be with his sex partner, the less nervous he will be. Communication is what makes sex good.

Penis size anxiety: Boys are just as anxious as girls are about their bodies. In a way, a boy's anxiety about the size and shape of his penis is like a girl's concern about her breasts, because it is similarly affected by societal ideals and images.

Does size matter? Like most questions of this nature, this one is pretty subjective. The "normal" range of an erect penis is between 4 and 10 inches, with most falling in the 5- to 7-inch range. Size definitely does not affect sexual function. And, except for extreme situations, penis size has very little effect on sexual pleasure. (A super-large penis can be painful for a girl during intercourse, and a super-small penis might not deliver enough stimulation.) Most often, for most people, size makes no difference.

PART 3

brain

Your brain (and the hormones it releases) is responsible for all of the changes going on in your body. And the changes in your body are responsible for many of the changes in your life. As you grow into an independent person, you and your brain must try to figure out what's going on and how to respond.

Inevitably, everyone faces challenging emotions, decisions, and situations. Your reactions can range from happiness to fear to anger to grief. Asking for help, from the people around you or from other resources, is always helpful when things seem hard.

No two people share the same thoughts and feelings—the way you think about and react to things is part of what makes you unique. Being aware of what you feel and trying to understand why is a way of learning who you are.

Chapter 1

PSYCHOLOGY

People are moody. And teenagers are especially moody. Some of it has to do with hormonal changes, some of it has to do with life changes and the stresses and pressures that go along with them, and most of it is a combination of the two. All of these factors cause a variety of emotional responses, ranging from familiar feelings to ones you haven't yet experienced. Often, emotions come jumbled together, so that it's hard to distinguish one from the other. Or they come in cycles, one after the other, after the other.

Pleasurable emotions, like happiness, love, and satisfaction, are great and fun to feel. It's the painful emotions that are harder to deal with. Everyone experiences and reacts to these emotions in her own way.

Emotions are feelings, not actions. And while you can't control the way you feel, you can control what you do. If any of your emotions get to the point where you think you can't handle them, or if you find yourself acting out your emotions on yourself or others in ways that are destructive, it's important to ask for help and try to figure out what's going on.

See therapy, p. 175
and Self-Destructive Behavior, pp. 183–99.

b
r
a
i
n

ANGER

Anger is an inevitable part of everybody's life, and learning how to deal with it effectively can be difficult. Suppressing your anger can lead to physical and emotional problems (headaches, stomachaches, tantrums, depression). Figuring out safe, nondestructive ways to express your anger is important to your health!

> when i get mad i don't like to be around anyone, then my friends take it the wrong way and get all pissed off at me. plus when i'm mad i can't think straight or anything and i'm hyper-sensitive. lately i've just started crying over little things, math (which is my best subject), guys, basketball, even when teachers lecture me.
> — **platform_shoes**

> Crying is like a release for me. For anyone really. Some people take their anger out by exercising and calm themselves by reading a book. I, on the other hand, cry.
> — **resemblence**

> i have had anger issues too in the past month or so. i find myself getting angry at myself a lot, and also at my family. i don't know if this has anything to do with my home life or not but it's kinda scaring me because i'm not usually an angry person.
> — **xylish**

> If you feel like yelling, count to 10 and wait for the feeling to go away. If it won't, just excuse yourself, go to the bathroom or somewhere and just scream. It helps. — **fire123**

> A lot of people have that same problem. I think there's something under the surface that makes people short-tempered. Your first step would be to figure out what that is...it could be something like loneliness, being upset about something, being unhappy with yourself, etc. Usually if people have something else on their mind, they take it out on any little thing they come across.
> — **bracelet**

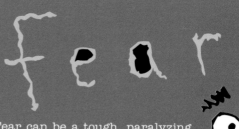

fear

Fear can be a tough, paralyzing emotion. Some fears are well-founded and can be useful in certain situations (if you're extra careful in a potentially dangerous environment, for example). Other fears can hold you back from doing what you want to do. Luckily, many fears can be overcome. At the very least, you can learn to recognize the ways in which they control your behavior.

ANXIETY

i have all these fears, and most of them are really stupid but i'm still scared. like, i'm afraid to be around people i don't know (and most of the people that i know). some of my other fears are: big dogs, cats, loud people, rabid animals, rape, pain, shots, breaking a bone, and sex. — **aTeaM**

Sometimes I feel like I'm losing my mind, especially lately. Day after day I have terrible nightmares, and when I wake up I feel sick. Then I get ready for school or wherever I am going and all day long my heart beats fast, sort of like I'm nervous. I've suddenly developed an unreasonable fear of spiders and I want to cry all the time. I'm going to be graduating soon and I have a feeling that this has something to do with it. — **campy**

I'm totally freaking out about starting school. I was crying all yesterday and today. I'm going to be a junior this year and my boyfriend is going to be a senior. All I keep thinking about is that all my friends (and my boyfriend) will be gone in just a year. I feel old and I'm scared of the future. This has been the best summer of my entire life and I feel like once school starts everything will just go bad. — **T.G.I.F.**

Anxiety is a state of uneasiness and distress about what the near or distant future may bring. It can be an intense, specific fear or a general feeling of dread that lacks a specific cause.

Finding ways to relax and calm yourself is helpful. But if your anxiety about things feels uncontrollable, or is getting in the way of your ability to function, it may be helpful to talk to a professional counselor. Anxiety disorders are quite common and treatable.

Sometimes I get so nervous that I can see and hear myself shaking. Like if I talk, my voice is really shaky and I can see my hands and my whole body shaking. Is there something wrong with me? — **fastrhythm**

Just lie down and think of nothing to get through it but if you can't do that then i suggest trying to calm your nerves with breathing in deeply. It works for me. Ever heard of panic attacks??? I mean I can't really tell you that that's what's wrong, but I used to have them, only I was afraid of different stuff. — **giga8pet**

For the past year I've had this obsession with dying. I've had quite a few friends die (murder, car accidents etc.). And I'm scared of dying now. Every time I go in the car I sit there and think about how I could shield myself if we crashed and if I see a truck or something I get scared it will veer into my lane. I'm also scared someone will break into my house and murder me. I'm also scared about not knowing what happens when I die. And I'm scared that I will die painfully.
— **kIwI_LuVer**

i am such a nervous person. last year i was so paranoid, i had to inspect all of my food before i ate it. i thought that i was going to be poisoned. whenever i heard a plane, i was afraid of bombing. this year i am not so bad. however, i often get afraid that i have cancer or some other life-threatening disease. aye! i don't go places a lot because i am nervous.
— **think-pink**

boredom

Boredom can spur you to do something new, or if you just can't get excited about anything, it can be a sign that other things are wrong. Or it can simply be boredom.

does anyone think it's weird to feel angst and restlessness all the time? i just tend to get bored very easily. i have a restless soul, i know this. but i'm unimpressed with routines, bored with the familiarity of everything around me...ya know?
— **pixi_stick**

It can't be *weird* to feel that way because whatever you feel is what you feel, weird or not. I feel that way sometimes, like I don't care about anything, not even people I love or anything I enjoy, not even sleeping.
— **no-curfew**

LONELINESS

Teenagers can be particularly vulnerable to feeling lonely because their relationships to the world and people around them are in a state of flux. But loneliness is really part of the human condition. :-(

I'm feeling really lonely right now. I don't think I've felt wanted since August when I moved 700 miles away from comfort. — **RaveOn57**

last night i broke down crying. I felt so damn empty and lonely. I kept saying that i wanted to die. I cried allllll night...i don't know how much more pain and stress and anger i can take! — **millenium_gurl**

I've been feeling like i'm alone in the world. it's like a feeling that no one understands me and everyone seems to be ignoring me.
— **GoldBeads**

JEALOUSY

Everybody gets jealous. Thinking about what you want in a positive way and learning to be generous about other people's happiness can be more constructive than spending a lot of negative energy on wanting what other people have.

I get jealous of everything! And everybody! I am so jealous of everybody I see, like if they are prettier, skinnier, more popular, flirt too much, wear cooler clothes, etc. it just bugs me. I make faces and walk away!
— **septgirl**

lately i've been jealous about everything, and i know it's not very attractive. i'm sure it's because i'm going through a low point right now, so i'm not feeling very confident. i'm even jealous towards my friends—i should be happy for them! my close friend got an A on her test, i got a B-. we studied together. i felt bitter.
— **rriot**

GRIEF

When someone you know dies, it can have a huge impact on you. How close you were to the person, the circumstances of his or her death, and your previous experiences with death can all play a part in your reaction, which may include feelings of deep sadness, loss, anger, guilt, or anxiety about your own health. If someone has committed suicide, these feelings can be even more complicated.

Grieving takes time, energy, and caring. And everyone grieves differently and at their own pace. Many people find talking to other people (friends, family, counselors) very helpful.

Eventually, the intensity of the grief will subside, but there will always be memories of the loss and the person you are mourning.

Grief is not specific to death. The loss of anyone or anything very meaningful to you—the end of a relationship, moving to a new home, graduating from school—can produce feelings of grief.

I can't seem to deal with death at all. About 1/2 yr. ago, my sax teacher died, who was like a father figure to me after my father moved out. I still cry about it, but i should really be over it by now. what to do?
— **CyCy**

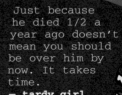

Just because he died 1/2 a year ago doesn't mean you should be over him by now. It takes time.
— **tardy_girl**

My best best guyfriend just died and I still miss my dad who also died. All I need is someone to tell me that it will be okay, like my guyfriend always used to, and I'll feel a lot better.
— **TraciS**

One of my closer guy friends died last summer in a car crash. It was such a shock to me and I cried for days on end. I tried to use my grief constructively and wrote a poem for him and it did wonders for me. I still get sad when I think about him and his amazing smile as he used to throw Swedish fish at me after lunch, but life does go on for us and although I didn't think so at first— everything is alright now.
— **ani_S**

Just because a person dies and leaves your life doesn't mean that they aren't with you anymore—they are still there. My aunt died 6 yrs. ago and then my grandmother died 3 yrs. later. Whenever I go to my Dad's house (where my grandmother used to live) I always know they are there watching me. I can feel them and I know whenever I am in a bad mood they are there to hold me, even though I can't feel them.
— **iluvsoccer**

my grandpa just recently passed away. I know you are really hurting, but don't try to hold it in. Let everything out and let other people know how you feel. Trust me it will help. It will take a long time. I still cry all night thinking about how I could've been a better person in getting to know my grandpa, but I also know that he is feeling better than he has in years. — **caracara**

it sucks when friends die. i know one thing that has gotten me through 2 suicides of my friends in the past year was God. my family and other friends helped too. maybe try going to a counselor or reading books about death and how to cope. it'll be one of the hardest things that you'll go through but just stay strong and you'll be alright. — **youngh**

DEPRESSION

Most people are familiar with depression, either their own or someone else's. It may be caused by particular events, like breakups or family problems. Or there may not be any specific reason for feeling low.

Facing it, knowing you will live through it, coming up with ways of coping with it, and talking to people are all ways of getting through the hard times.

If you notice changes in both your eating and sleeping patterns, if you find yourself turning to self-destructive behavior, and/or if you have seriously contemplated suicide, get help!! You may be suffering from clinical depression, a mood disorder that's said to afflict over 10 million Americans.

See Depression, p. 176.

172

I have depression. I have been fighting it pretty good, but lately I don't feel like fighting it anymore. I just want to give in and let the depression overtake me and whatever happens, let it happen. I've tried to kill myself before, but always stopped, crying that "I don't want to die, but I don't want to live either." — **moot-point**

Just so you know, we all feel this way sometimes. I have felt this way many times, and its perfectly normal for a teenage girl to THINK about things like this. BUT, if this is how you feel constantly then you have a problem and you need to get help. — **iLLuminator**

I just got over depression. The second bout in my life. It runs in my family, so chances are it'll return. But I know how you're feeling. I went through 6 hellish months of it. But I got through it, just like you will. You'll get through it with help. Talking to other people (especially a therapist) and journaling helps. — **Ladybuggie**

i feel what i think is described as depression on a regular basis. the odd thing is that i am not experiencing any specific event that would normally cause depression. things are normal, except i find myself feeling inferior as a result of little things. like when i don't understand the math homework, i'll just start crying. can any of you gurls relate? — **ToFuLover**

Music helps me when i'm depressed. When i'm angry i listen to metal to release my anger. I listen to something with a nice beat when i'm sad. — **discoforeva**

I can't find anything to give me any joy. I can't sleep, I don't feel like eating, I don't care about school. I feel like crying all the time. I've felt like this for almost a year. What shall I do? — **undercat**

I used to be really sad, and I found screaming into a pillow was okay, and once I started writing in a diary more I just became more at peace with myself. Another thing I did was get into weight lifting and running. It gives you a great sense of power, positive self-esteem and you have something to be PROUD of. Believe me, it's the best thing I EVER did for myself! — **Meshes**

this happens to me—nothing particularly upsetting, but i get so hung up about little things. talk to somebody you feel close to—it just might help. also, crying is healthy for you. — **mary2K**

Also see Teenage Suicide, pp. 194—95, and Resources on pp. 196—99.

b
r
a
i
n

psychology

one minute i'll be really happy about something, and then someone gives me a dirty look and i'm down and depressed. When i'm mad i feel like i could rip someone's head off, and when i'm sad i just wanna lay down and die. — **cocoqueen**

My friend was the same way. Her parents took her to a shrink and now she is no longer going in and out of mood swings impulsively. I think you should check it out. She is a lot happier now. — **pYramid**

MOOD SWINGS

Moodiness and mood swings are common teenage occurrences. Emotions can change suddenly and then change back again. Sometimes it may be hormonal changes, sometimes it may be PMS, sometimes it may be the circumstances of your life....

If you feel like your emotions are truly out of control, and you are powerless to stop them, talking to someone about it is always a good idea. People who suffer from serious highs and lows continually may want to talk to a therapist.

See PMS, pp. 24–25.

See Manic-depressive illness, p. 176.

I have been having the most unbelievable range of emotions! I'm a really happy person. But, I get SO depressed and I don't know what to do. I will suddenly start crying for no reason. Sometimes, I feel like there's just NOTHING to live for. My emotions go uP and DOwn. — **PsandQs**

I'm sorta on an emotional rollercoaster but to keep my sanity and to keep from killing myself I write and draw. It helps me. Get a journal and write and express all your feelings to it.
— **harvestmoon**

Self-esteem

Many girls start to suddenly get down on themselves around the ages of 11 or 12, believing that they don't measure up physically, socially, academically, or in some other way. And these perceived shortcomings make them feel bad about themselves. This loss of self-esteem in girls is very common. Several recent studies (most famously by Carol Gilligan at Harvard University) have documented that adolescent girls, in particular, suffer from low self-esteem.

Why? Researchers point to teachers who call on boys more in class, to parents who push brothers more to succeed, and to societal emphasis on what a girl looks like rather than on who she is and what she can do. Simple awareness of this trend can go a long way toward resisting it.

Low self-esteem can lead to low self-confidence, low self-worth, and depression at any age. If you are having a hard time believing in yourself or if your confidence level seems low, ask yourself why. Understand the obstacles in your path and try not to be too distracted by negativity while you remain focused on following your own interests.

People cope with bad feelings in a variety of ways:

Asking for help

If things seem too difficult, ask for help. Who you ask—a friend, boyfriend, sibling, parent, parent's friend, doctor, teacher, school psychologist, social worker, or counselor—is up to you. The really important thing is that it is someone you trust. Also remember that the relationship you have with the person you ask affects the way that person will respond to your needs. A parent, for example, will feel differently about your problem than a friend.

Writing about it

Writing your feelings out may help you make sense of them. Just the act of putting it all into words distances you from the chaos and can allow you to regain some perspective and control. Keeping a journal also gives you a record of how you feel over the course of time. Going back to read it later can help you figure out what makes you feel a certain way and why.

Taking action

Do something fun. Change your environment. Volunteer. Get a new perspective.

Therapy

Talking to a professional is often helpful when you are feeling like things aren't going right or when you don't feel comfortable sharing what's going on with the people in your life. This is what therapists (counselors) are for. Their role is to provide an ear, and sometimes advice, and help people work through the hard stuff that goes on in their lives.

A common misconception about therapy is that only people who are "beyond help" need it. Going to see someone who is professionally trained is not a sign of being crazy. It's a sign that you are taking control of your life and figuring out how to make it better, with assistance from someone with that very purpose. The role that a therapist plays is very different from that of a friend or anyone else. No matter how much your friends care about you, or how smart and intuitive they are, the fact that they are part of your life prevents them from being objective.

People usually find therapists through other people's referrals—friends' therapists, school counselors, doctors, referral services. Even if your parents select the therapist, you have the right to ask questions and speak up if you don't feel comfortable with the situation. Therapy is most effective with a therapist you trust and respect.

Also, see family therapy, p. 227.

I was incredibly depressed last year. Once I sat down and finally told my parents everything that had been going on, they took me to a psychiatrist, which really helped me sort things out in my mind. — **tatooed**

I have been diagnosed as clinically depressed. I've gone through a lot of crap, but I keep on ticking. My advice to EVERYONE is this: 1) Find an outlet—whether it be music, art or a sport, get your feelings out in the open or down on paper!! 2) Talk to a counselor or psychologist. They can help! A doctor may be able to prescribe something for you. (I am currently taking prozac, and it helps.) 3) If you are depressed, don't feel ashamed of it, it's no fault of your own. 4) Don't give up on life!!!!! This is the most important!!! — **crinkletoes**

brain

Common psychiatric illnesses

Manic-Depressive Illness (Bipolar Disorder)

What it is: Mood swings from extremely elevated (happy) to severely depressed. Each phase may last up to three months individually, or a person might feel both extremes at once. Medically known as bipolar mood disorder, it usually starts in adult life before the age of 35. It may start in adolescence or earlier. People whose parents have it are more likely to develop it themselves.

Symptoms (of the manic stage):

- severe mood changes; excessively good, happy, or irritable
- unrealistically high self-esteem, often with grandiose delusions of a close connection to God or celebrities
- hyperactivity; talking quickly, jumping from one topic to another without appropriate connections, refusal to allow interruptions, making plans to do too many things at once; spending large amounts of money
- inability to concentrate
- decreased need for sleep
- sudden irritability
- high risk-taking behavior, such as sexual promiscuity or reckless driving

Symptoms (of the depressive stage):

- depression, indifference, feelings of sadness and worthlessness, unexplained crying spells
- loss of pleasure from previously enjoyed activities
- frequent complaints of physical ailments, aches, and pains
- low energy
- loss of memory or concentration
- thoughts of suicide or death
- major changes in diet or sleep patterns

Treatment: With education, medicine, and therapy, this is one of the most treatable of psychiatric illnesses. The patient and family are educated about the disease, and sometimes family therapy is warranted. Medicine such as lithium and other mood-stabilizing drugs can reduce the number and severity of the manic episodes and help prevent depression. Use of lithium must be carefully monitored to prevent serious adverse side effects. Psychotherapy may help the patient adapt to stress and understand herself better, decreasing the likelihood of attacks.

Obsessive-Compulsive Disorder (OCD)

What it is: This anxiety disorder often begins in adolescence or young adulthood. It is characterized by recurrent obsessions (persistent, unwanted impulses or images) or compulsions (repetitive behaviors or rituals to help alleviate anxiety) that cause major distress and anxiety and significantly interfere with one's daily routine or relationships. For example, an obsessive fear of germs might coincide with compulsively washing one's hands. The ritualized behavior does not necessarily have

Depression

What it is: Feelings of depression that persist for at least two weeks and interfere with the ability to function—not just feeling "blue." One of the most common mental illnesses, depression tends to run in families and can strike at any age. Depressive disorder is any form of depression serious enough to require treatment. There are several forms of depression, including bipolar, seasonal affective disorder (SAD), unipolar, and dysthymic disorder (neurotic depression), and they can overlap with one another.

Symptoms:

- frequent sadness or crying
- feelings of hopelessness
- lack of energy, feelings of fatigue and "burnout"
- feelings of worthlessness and of inappropriate guilt
- lessened pleasure in previously enjoyed activities
- persistent boredom
- social isolation and poor communication
- recurring suicidal thoughts, wishing to die, or attempting suicide
- increased irritability, anger, or hostility
- physical symptoms like frequent complaints of headaches and stomachaches
- inability to concentrate or indecisiveness
- change in appetite and unexplained significant weight loss or gain
- change in sleeping patterns

Treatment: One of the most treatable mental illnesses; between 80 and 90% of all depressed people respond to treatment, which consists of psychotherapy or antidepressants (tricyclics, serotonin reuptake inhibitors, monoaminine oxidase inhibitors, and lithium), or both. The usual treatment for SAD is light therapy.

anything to do with the fear of infection; more commonly, the person suffering from this disorder believes that by repeating the behavior, she may be able to ward off fears.

Symptoms:

- unrealistic or excessive worry
- repeating ritualized behaviors
- cleaning to the point of excess
- checking and rechecking (an alarm clock, the oven)
- completing a series of things in a specific order, and if interrupted, beginning again until completion is achieved
- being meticulous
- avoiding specific things (sidewalk cracks)
- hoarding
- slowness
- difficulty sleeping
- shakiness
- upset stomach
- high pulse and/or breathing rate

Treatment: OCD is a brain disorder that can be treated with behavior therapy such as exposure-and-response prevention, which is successful in 50–90% of sufferers. Some medications, like serotonin reuptake inhibitors, are very helpful. Family support, education, and therapy are also essential for successful treatment.

Panic Disorder

What it is: Repeated periods of fear or discomfort that develop without warning, along with a racing heartbeat. Panic attacks can cause sufferers to feel anxious all the time, or to avoid places or activities where attacks often set in, disrupting daily life and often causing depression. This depression may lead the sufferer to turn to drugs or alcohol, which actually worsen anxiety and increase the panic attacks. The disorder is more common in women and usually begins when victims are in their twenties, often after a traumatic event.

Symptoms:

- intense apprehension, fearfulness, or terror
- racing or pounding heartbeat
- dizziness or lightheadedness
- chest pain or heart palpitations
- shortness of breath or feeling of smothering
- sweating
- trembling or shaking
- nausea or abdominal distress
- hot or cold flashes
- sense of unreality
- fear of dying, losing control, or going crazy

Attention Deficit/Hyperactivity Disorder (ADD or ADHD)

What it is: A teenager with ADHD has problems paying attention and concentrating, and/or with hyperactive and impulsive behavior. Sufferers often act before thinking, commonly causing problems with their peers, parents, and teachers. It is most common in boys, and is usually diagnosed first during the elementary school years. Its symptoms frequently become less severe in late teen and young adult years. There are four types of ADHD— inattentive, hyperactive, combined, and not otherwise specified (including some characteristics, but not enough for a full diagnosis).

Symptoms (inattentive type):

- failure to pay attention to details
- distraction or difficulty sustaining attention
- appearing not to listen
- struggling to follow instructions
- difficulty keeping organized
- avoidance of sustained mental effort
- frequent loss of necessary items
- forgetfulness in daily activities

Symptoms (hyperactive/impulsive type):

- fidgeting or squirming
- difficulty staying seated
- excessive running or climbing, or feelings of restlessness in adults
- difficulty engaging in activities quietly
- acting as though driven by a motor
- excessive talking
- not waiting for a question to be finished before blurting out an answer
- difficulty waiting turns
- frequent interruption of others

Treatment: A combination of parent training, behavior management strategies, individual and family counseling, and sometimes medicine is required to treat ADHD effectively. Psychostimulants or stimulants are the most frequently used medicines, and are effective in approximately 70–80% of those treated.

Treatment: Combination of medication and psychotherapy can help prevent panic attacks, and cognitive and behavioral therapy can help alleviate anxiety when panic attacks do occur. Drugs commonly used to treat depression help 75–90% of panic attack victims.

Psychiatric drugs

Antidepressant medications are often used by doctors and psychiatrists (only MDs can prescribe them) to treat depression, panic disorder, and OCD. Most of them work by altering the action of the neurotransmitter serotonin. It is believed that moods, feelings, levels of vitality, and sleep depend—at least to some degree—on your serotonin levels. Serotonin is associated with a calming, and somewhat sedative, effect on people.

Selective serotonin reuptake inhibitors (SSRIs), such as Prozac (fluoxetine), Zoloft (sertraline), and Paxil (paroxetine), interfere with your body's reabsorption of serotonin, which makes it more available to brain cells and probably reduces anxiety and depression. They may take several weeks to begin working, and must be taken long enough to stop the symptoms, usually 3 to 6 months or longer. SSRIs have side effects, which your doctor can tell you about.

RESOURCES

To find a therapist, ask friends, family members, or someone at school for a recommendation or look under Mental Health, Social Services, or Family Services in the Yellow Pages. Your doctor can also refer you to a therapist.

General—National Organizations

American Psychological Association, 750 First Street, NE, Washington, DC 20002. Phone: 800-374-2721. Website: http://www.apa.org/psychnet.

American Academy of Child and Adolescent Psychiatry, 3615 Wisconsin Avenue, NW, Washington, DC 20016. Phone: 800-333-7636. Website: http://www.aacap.org.

American Psychiatric Association, 1400 K Street, NW, Washington, DC 20015-2403. Phone: 888-35-PSYCH. Website: http://www.psych.org.

Depression: Awareness, Recognition and Treatment (DART), 2235 Cedar Lane, Vienna, VA 22182. Helpline: 800-421-4211.

National Alliance for the Mentally Ill offers information and resources for the mentally ill and their families. Address: 200 North Glebe Road, Suite 1015, Arlington, VA 22203-3754. Phone: 800-950-NAMI.

National Association of Social Workers, 750 First Street, NE, Suite 700, Washington, DC 20002. Phone: 202-408-8600. Website: http://www.naswdc.org.

For the largest **mental health referral organization** in the country, ring 800-THERAPIST. This free service will refer you to a local certified therapist who specializes in your area of need.

National Foundation for Depressive Illness gives referrals to doctors and depression support groups, publishes a quarterly newsletter, and runs an outreach program for teens. There is also a recorded message with information on the signs of depression. Address: P.O. Box 2257, New York, NY 10116. Phone: 800-239-1265. Website: http://www.depression.org.

General—Online

Suicide @ Rochford at http://www.rochford.org/suicide contains a variety of information about suicide and prevention.

Adolescence Directory On-Line (ADOL) is a guide to adolescent issues at http://education.indiana.edu/cas/adol/adol.html.

Mental Health Net at http://www.cmhc.com is a large online mental health community and resource guide.

National Alliance for the Mentally Ill at http://www.nami.org offers information, resources, and links for the mentally ill and their families.

General—Books

Almost Lost: The True Story of an Anony-mous Teenager's Life on the Streets, edited by Beatrice Sparks (Avon). Deals with a suicidally depressed teenage boy, his struggle to survive on the streets, and his battle with self-hatred.

The Bell Jar by Sylvia Plath (Bantam Books). The classic autobiographical novel about a young woman's mental break-down.

The Complete Poems by Anne Sexton (Houghton Mifflin). The stuff of Sexton's life, painfully honest and emotionally moving.

Darkness Visible by William Styron (Vintage Books). A profound memoir of depression.

Feeling Good Handbook by David D. Burns, M.D. (Plume). Drug-free self-help for depression.

Girl, Interrupted by Susanna Kaysen (Vintage Books). A riveting tale of how the author was hospitalized while grow-ing up because she refused to conform.

Listening to Prozac by Peter D. Kramer (Penguin USA). A comprehensive and scientific look at antidepressants.

Meeting at the Crossroads: Women's Psychology and Girls' Development by Lyn Mikel Brown and Carol Gilligan (Ballantine). Groundbreaking look at the challenging passage from girlhood to adolescence.

Prozac Nation by Elizabeth Wurtzel (Riverhead Books). A twentysomething woman's memoir of depression, drugs, and the wonders of Prozac.

Reviving Ophelia by Mary Pipher (Ballantine). Investigation into why girls lose rather than gain self-esteem as they become women.

Welcome to My Country by Lauren Slater (Anchor). Takes you into the therapist's POV as she works to understand and interact with her patients suffering from mental and emotional distress, schizo-phrenia, and depression.

ADHD—National Organizations

Children and Adults with Attention Deficit/Hyperactivity Disorder (CHADD), 8181 Professional Place, Suite 201, Lan-dover, MD 20785. Phone: 800-233-4050. Website: http://www.chadd.org.

National Institute of Mental Health pro-vides extensive information about OCD, among other mental health issues. Address: Information Resources and Inquiries Branch, 5600 Fishers Lane, Room 7C-02, Rockville, MD 20857. Phone: 301-443-4513. Website: http://www.nimh. nih.gov/publicat.

ADHD—Online

Psychweb.com at http://www.psychweb. com provides information and other online ADHD resources with chat rooms and other services.

ADHD—Books

ADHD Handbook for Families: A Guide for Communicating with Professionals by Paul L. Weingartner (Child Welfare League of America). Written by a doctor and sufferer of ADHD, this book gives practical advice for dealing with health care professionals regarding ADHD.

Adolescent ADD: Gaining the Advantage by Patricia O. Quinn (Magination). Straightforward book addressing the con-cerns of adolescents suffering from ADD.

Making the Grade: An Adolescent's Struggle with ADD by Harvey C. Parker and Roberta Parker (Specialty Press). The story of a seventh-grader's struggle with ADD. Also includes techniques to help and cope with ADD.

Depression Awareness Recognition & Treatment (D/ART), 5600 Fishers Lane, Room 14C-03, Parklawn Building, Rockville, MD 20857. Phone: 301-443-4140.

National Depressive and Manic-Depressive Association (NDMDA) provides education for sufferers and their families. Address: 730 North Franklin, #501, Chicago, IL 60610. Phone: 800-826-3632. Website: http://www.ndmda.org.

Sympatico's HealthyWay at http://www.ns.sympatico.ca/healthyway/DIRECTORY/B4.html offers hyperlinks to various mental health sites, including depression sites (with reviews of each site).

Moodswing.org at http://www.moodswing.org. Online resources for people with bipolar disorder and their friends and family members.

For more information on Prozac and other antidepressant drugs, go to the **Food and Drug Administration (FDA) Center for Drug Evaluation and Research Online:** http://www.fda.gov/cder.

Bipolar Disorders Portal at http://www.pendulum.org is a rich site providing information, links to other websites, books, articles, and more for victims of bipolar disorder.

Society for Manic Depression at http://www.theport.com helps bipolar people educate themselves and move to remission. Includes a chat room.

The Beast: A Journey Through Depression by Tracy Thompson (Plume). An eloquent, unflinchingly honest autobiography that recounts this journalist's struggle with depression, which culminated in a terrifying bout with suicide, and her search for an understanding of and a cure for it.

How to Cope with Depression: A Complete Guide for You and Your Family by J. Raymond DePaulo and Keith Ablo (Ballantine). A guide to the available treatments and guidelines for phases of therapy.

Overcoming Depression by Demitri Papolos and Janice Papolos (HarperCollins). The book often recommended by doctors to their patients, now updated and revised, including suggestions for dealing with managed care.

Anxiety Disorders Association of America educates victims and their families about anxiety disorders. Also includes a chat room. Address: 6000 Executive Boulevard, Suite 513, Rockville, MD 20852-3801. Phone: 301-231-9350. Website: http://www.adaa.org.

National Institute of Mental Health provides extensive information about OCD, as well as other mental health issues. Address: Information Resources and Inquiries Branch, 5600 Fishers Lane, Room 7C-02, Rockville, MD 20857. Phone: 301-443-4513. Website: http://www.nimh.nih.gov/anxiety/library/brochure/ocdbro.htm.

Obsessive-Compulsive Information Center. Address: Dean Foundation for Health Research and Education, 2711 Allen Boulevard, Middleton, WI 53562. Phone: 608-827-2390.

Anxieties.com at http://www.anxieties.com provides step-by-step help for fear of flying, panic attacks, OCD, and more.

The Boy Who Couldn't Stop Washing: The Experience and Treatment of Obsessive-Compulsive Disorder by Judith L. Rapoport (New American Library). The groundbreaking book that brought OCD to national attention.

Getting Control: Overcoming Your Obsessions and Compulsions by Lee Baer (Plume). Self-help for sufferers of OCD.

The Sky is Falling: Understanding and Coping with Phobias, Panic & Obsessive-Compulsive Disorders by Raeann Dumont (Norton). Well-written guide for the victim of anxiety disorders.

Panic Disorder—National Organizations

Anxiety Disorders Association of America educates victims and their families about anxiety disorders. Also includes a chat room. Address: 6000 Executive Boulevard, Suite 513, Rockville, MD 20852-3801. Phone: 301-231-9350. Website: http://www.adaa.org.

Freedom from Fear offers a free newsletter and a referral list of specialists. Address: 308 Seaview Avenue, Staten Island, NY 10305. Phone: 718-351-1717.

National Alliance for the Mentally Ill offers information about anxiety diseases and links for other resources. Address: 200 North Glebe Road, Suite 1015, Arlington, VA 22203-3754. Phone: 800-950-NAMI. Website: http://www.nami.org.

National Institute of Mental Health Panic Campaign provides extensive information about panic disorder and other mental health issues. Address: 5600 Fishers Lane, Room 7C-05, Rockville, MD 20857. Phone: 800-64-PANIC. Website: http://www.nimh.nih.gov.

Panic Disorder—Online

Anxieties.com at http://www.anxieties.com provides step-by-step help for fear of flying, panic attacks, OCD, and more.

tAPir (the ANXIETY-PANIC Internet Resource) at http://www.algy.com/anxiety is a comprehensive resource.

Panic Disorder—Books

Don't Panic: Taking Control of Anxiety Attacks by R. Reid (HarperCollins). Self-help program for dealing with and eliminating panic attacks.

Life with the Panic Monster: A Guide for the Terrified by Evelyn B. Stewart (Rutledge). A woman's story of her disabling panic attacks and eventual relief from them.

The Sky Is Falling: Understanding and Coping with Phobias, Panic & Obsessive-Compulsive Disorders by Raeann Dumont (Norton). Well-written guide for the victim of anxiety disorders.

For more resources and information, see http://www.dealwithit.com

b
r
a
i
n

Chapter 2

SELF-DESTRUCTIVE BEHAVIOR

Self-destructive behavior is the act of putting yourself in emotional or physical danger. It is usually a response to painful events and emotions in a person's life.

Self-destructive behavior can take different forms, from underachieving to deliberately injuring yourself. It can also happen for different reasons. Some people sabotage themselves as a way of avoiding future pain and risk. Others hurt themselves to gain control over some part of their lives, even though that control is put to a destructive use. The urge to create a physical manifestation of a disturbing emotional or psychological state is another possible motivating factor.

Some self-destructive behaviors have more severe consequences than others. But all should be taken seriously. If you realize that you are hurting yourself in some way, it is very important to understand why you are doing this as a first step to stopping your behavior. Talking to a professional about what you are going through is often an essential part of this process.

See Therapy, p. 175.

brain

self-destructive behavior

UNDERACHIEVING

Sometimes simply not living up to your potential is a way of acting destructive toward yourself. The way some people deal with all the external and internal stress and pressure in their lives is to just shut down and stop trying. You may intentionally or unintentionally not do the things that you could be doing because you feel bad about your life and yourself. This can happen in small ways or on a large scale.

Though it is hard to see too far down the road, what you decide to fail at today could limit opportunities in the future.

Healthy eating
Everyone is unique in her body and in her eating habits.

Normal eating is being able to eat what you like when you are hungry and continue eating until you are satisfied. It means choosing healthy food but not being so restrictive that you never indulge yourself.

See Body Image, **pp. 51–57** and Taking Care of Yourself, **pp. 58–65.**

Normal eating can be three meals a day, or several small meals and snacks throughout the day. It is leaving some cookies on the plate because you know you can have some tomorrow, or it is eating more now because they taste great.

Normal eating is giving yourself permission to eat sometimes because you are happy, sad, or just because it feels good.

In short, normal eating is flexible. It varies in response to your emotions, your schedule, your hunger, and your proximity to food. It is part of your life, but shouldn't run your life.

EATING DISORDERS

About 2 million Americans, mostly women and girls, suffer from eating disorders. A further unknown number have dangerous eating and dieting habits—taking diet pills, laxatives, or diuretics and following extreme fad diets—which may not be as dangerous as an eating disorder, but can still have significantly bad effects.

Since the 1980s, eating disorders have gained exposure in the media. Some people have blamed the media for glorifying super-thin young models and for pressuring young women to achieve these "ideal" body types.

For more on drug use and abuse, see **pp. 200–213.**

Eating or not eating in an obsessed manner has little to do with true hunger. It can be a way to feel in control, to get attention, to punish parents, or even to reward yourself. Or you may have the mistaken impression that weight will influence your popularity. Whatever the reason for them, eating disorders are very dangerous behavior patterns that in the end only bring pain.

In the most extreme cases, people starve or overeat themselves to death. Sufferers of eating disorders can be any weight (but their weight fluctuates radically). They may even appear "average"—it does not mean they suffer less or are in any less danger.

Here are four common types of
eating disorders.

Anorexia nervosa

What it is: This potentially fatal condition
involves an intense fear of gaining weight
or becoming fat. A distorted perception of
body weight, size, or shape leads an
anorexic person to restrict food intake to
the point of deliberate starvation. Anorexics can be as much as 15 percent under
their normal body weight and still perceive
themselves as overweight. One percent of
teenage girls in the United States develop
anorexia nervosa and up to 10 percent of
those may die as a result.

Anorexics usually strive for perfection.
They set very high standards for themselves and feel they always have to prove
their competence. If they can't control what
is happening around them, they feel they
can at least control their weight.

**Some common physical effects and
health risks (may be one, a few, or all):**

- loss of hair on head
- growth of soft, downy hair ("lanugo")
  on face, back, and arms (the body needs
  this hairy layer for body warmth)
- loss of menstruation or irregular periods
  (without food, hormone levels drop, alert-
  ing the body it cannot support a fetus)
- dry skin and brittle hair and fingernails
- cool grayish or yellowish skin
- lowered body temperature and blood
  pressure
- slowed reflexes (from slowed heart rate
  and thyroid function)
- premature loss of bone density
- constipation
- swollen joints
- muscle atrophy
- kidney and heart failure in the most
  extreme cases

Anorexia can eventually lead to death by
starvation and organ failure.

How to identify anorexia: Anorexia may
not be noticed in the early stages because it
often starts as an innocent diet. As it pro-
gresses, the disease still may not be noticed
by family members or friends because the
anorexic usually wears layered and baggy
clothes. Even emaciated, anorexics continue
to feel "fat" and want to hide their "ugly,
fat body."

An anorexic may avoid any eating situations. If she can't avoid these situations,
she will often play with, hoard, or conceal
food instead of eating it.

**Common behavior patterns
(may be one, a few, or all):**

- obsession with the body and food
- need for perfection and control
- rapid mood swings
- anxiety
- suicidal tendencies
- lethargy
- insomnia
- depression
- daily use of laxatives or diuretics in an
  attempt to control weight
- rigid schedule of obsessive exercise,
  even if in physical pain
- ritualized eating
  habits (eating at
  precise times of
  day, chewing
  each bite a spe-
  cific number of
  times, etc.)

Treatments: Treatment is often difficult because many anorexics are in denial and don't accept the need for help. If an anorexic is in danger of near-starvation, immediate hospitalization is often recommended to meet basic nutritional needs. Patients are placed on a balanced diet, with the goal of gradually restoring their weight to a normal range.

Treatment is often based on rewards—eat and don't purge in order to receive something that she wants (like a CD). Once they reach their target weight, they graduate into an outpatient program, where fluid intake and weight continue to be tracked.

Therapy is usually recommended. Because distorted self- and body images are common among anorexics, this is often an initial focus of therapy. The patient is reeducated on how to recognize normal weight and body fat and relate that information to her own body. Family therapy is sometimes recommended, since a person's feelings about her body may stem from messages she got from her parents. Group therapy is also used, as it provides instant support and gives the patient perspective about her relationship with her body.

Relapses are common with anorexics, so recovery can be slow and frustrating. An individual's prognosis for recovery from an eating disorder is increased if the person does not binge or purge and has had the disorder for less than 6 months.

Some medications can be extremely helpful in treating anorexia nervosa. Because the disorder is often associated with depression, drugs like antidepressants may speed up the recovery process.

Bulimia

What it is: Bulimia typically involves frequent and persistent binge eating. This binge eating is usually followed by purging through self-induced vomiting and/or laxative and diuretic abuse. A binge is different for every individual. For one person a binge may range from 1,000 to 15,000 calories; for another, one cookie may be considered a binge. These binge-purge episodes are usually done in secret. Bulimics are rarely overweight, although they perceive themselves to be fat.

Bulimics are insecure, unsure of their own self-worth, and tend to do things to please others rather than themselves. They think that food is the one comfort they have, and they give it to themselves in excess.

Like anorexics, bulimics cannot recognize their true body size and often feel too fat and ashamed over their lack of control when eating. So purging gives them back a sense of being in control, a way of fixing their "disgusting" behavior.

Some common physical effects and health risks (may be one, a few, or all):

- noticeable weight fluctuations in short periods of time
- period disappears for more than three cycles
- constipation
- damaged and discolored teeth (stomach acids erode tooth enamel)
- heartburn and/or bloating

- lung irritation and damage (choking while vomiting causes food particles to lodge in lungs, causing inflammation)
- weakness
- irregular heartbeat
- kidney damage caused by chronic loss of body fluids
- salivary gland enlargement (looks like a bad case of the mumps)
- puffy eyelids and face
- bloodshot or watery eyes from vomiting
- sores or calluses on back of hand used for purging (where teeth scrape skin)
- dehydration and depletion of important minerals
- hormonal imbalance
- chronic sore throat

Like anorexia, bulimia can kill.

How to identify bulimia: Because bulimics "binge and purge" in secret and maintain normal or above-normal body weight, they can often successfully hide their problem from others for years. Bulimics use the bathroom frequently after meals to vomit—often immediately after eating. They may take a lot of laxatives or diuretics. Bulimics may have puffy faces, red eyes, sudden bad breath, or tooth problems (due to the effect of stomach acid on tooth enamel). Bulimics feel out of control while eating and may have mood swings since their bingeing and purging are often followed by feelings of shame and/or depression. Some bulimics may act these feelings out and shoplift, be promiscuous, and abuse alcohol, drugs, and/or credit cards.

Common behavior patterns (may be one, a few, or all):

- binge-purge episodes
- daily use of laxatives and/or diuretics in an attempt to control weight
- obsession with the body and food

Treatments: The use of laxatives or vomiting as a method of controlling overeating can lead to serious medical complications such as dehydration or kidney failure. Bulimics may require hospitalization or close medical monitoring.

Therapy (individual, family, or group) is also necessary. Many of the same issues of distorted self-esteem and self-perception that are relevant to anorexia treatment appear in bulimia treatment. Sessions often involve examining how one's attitudes about food, dieting, weight, and body shape may affect behavior. Therapy is used to focus on interpersonal relationships and how they affect eating habits and attitudes.

Antidepressants such as Prozac, Paxil, and Zoloft are sometimes used to help treat signs of severe depression, which often accompanies bulimia. Antidepressants can sometimes help a person binge/purge less frequently.

Treatment also includes dental check-ups, since frequent vomiting can lead to tooth decay as a result of enamel erosion from stomach acids.

Often bulimics have been purging and bingeing for a long time before they are detected. But their hope for recovery is increased if they have had the disorder for less than 6 months. A good support system is also essential to quick recovery, which is why support groups are often recommended.

- tendency toward perfectionism
- rigid schedule of obsessive exercise, even when in physical pain
- rapid mood swings
- anxiety
- suicidal tendencies
- lethargy
- insomnia
- depression

Binge eating disorder

Although probably the most common eating disorder, this problem has only recently been recognized by the medical profession.

Most people with binge eating disorder are obese (more than 20 percent over the healthy body weight), but normal-weight people can be affected also. Binge eating disorder probably affects about 1 million to 2 million Americans. Up to 40 percent of people who are obese may be binge eaters.

What it is: Binge eaters suffer from a combination of symptoms similar to those of compulsive overeaters and bulimics. They periodically (on average, at least 2 days a week for 6 months) go on large binges, uncontrollably consuming an unusually large quantity of food in a short period of time (less than 2 hours), eating until they are uncomfortably full. Unlike bulimics, bingers do not follow their binges with some type of purging behavior (like self-induced vomiting or laxatives).

The causes of binge eating disorder are still unknown. Up to half of all people with binge eating disorder have a history of depression. Whether depression is a cause or an effect of binge eating disorder, though, is unclear. It may even be unrelated.

Bingers may be people who will never fit the impossible cultural ideal, so they diet, get hungry, and binge. Or, like compulsive overeaters, they may eat for emotional reasons, to comfort themselves, avoid threatening situations, and numb emotional pain. Anger, sadness, boredom, anxiety, or other negative emotions can trigger binge episodes.

Bingeing can be a way to keep people away. Some bingers may feel they don't deserve love and may be subconsciously trying to fulfill the notion that "if I'm fat, no one will like me."

Currently, researchers are looking into how brain chemicals and metabolism (the way the body burns calories) affect bingers.

Some common physical effects and health risks (may be one, a few, or all):

- severe weight gain
- radical weight fluctuations
- body odor
- swollen limbs
- bad skin
- high blood pressure and/or high cholesterol
- all the diseases that accompany obesity, including diabetes, gallbladder disease, heart disease, and certain types of cancer

How to identify binge eating disorder: Most of us overeat from time to time, or eat when we aren't hungry or because we're bored or upset, and many people feel they frequently eat more than they should. This does not mean that a person has binge eating disorder. Bingers feel unable to stop eating voluntarily, even though they know that their eating patterns are abnormal. But this does not stop them from doing exactly the same thing the next time. They may eat healthy foods, but they are just as likely to eat huge amounts of junk foods. Some people miss work, school, or social activities to binge.

Most bingers have tried many diets without success. The more weight they gain, the harder they try to diet—and dieting is usually what leads to the next binge, which can be followed by feelings of powerlessness, guilt, shame, and failure. So they may end up in a cycle of losing and regaining weight (yo-yo dieting).

Obese people with binge eating disorder often feel bad about themselves, are preoccupied with their appearance, and may avoid social gatherings. Most feel ashamed and try to hide their problem. Often they are so successful at this that close family members and friends don't know they binge.

**Common behavior patterns
(may be one, a few, or all):**

- bingeing
- frequently eating alone (out of embarrassment over quantity)
- depression
- preoccupation with weight
- feeling disgusted, depressed, or guilty after overeating

Treatments: Dieting worsens rather than helps binge eaters. People with binge eating disorder may find it harder than other people to stay in weight loss programs, and may be more likely to regain weight quickly.

For these reasons, people with this disorder may require treatment that focuses on their binge eating before they try to lose weight. Many of the treatment methods for bulimics appear to help binge eaters. Hospitalization is rarely necessary, but it may be required for depression or self-destructive behavior.

Several therapy methods are used to treat binge eating disorder. One of these is cognitive-behavioral therapy, learning to be aware of how you act and using some sort of trigger to retrain that action. Bingers are taught techniques to monitor and change their eating habits as well as the way they respond to difficult situations.

Family or group therapy can also be helpful, encouraging people to examine their relationships with friends and family and to make changes in problem areas.

Treatment with medications such as antidepressants may aid some individuals, since it helps the depression often associated with bingeing and also seems to suppress the need to binge. Self-help groups also may be a source of support. Often, a combination of all of the above methods is the most effective in controlling binge eating disorder.

Compulsive overeating

What it is: Compulsive eating or overeating may be a distraction—a way to relieve anxiety or avoid doing something you think you'll fail at. Or it may be a form of revenge ("You're making me fat!") or a substitution for something that's missing in the person's life.

Compulsive overeating involves constant eating (and sometimes bingeing) without the purging typical in bulimia. Although compulsive overeaters are often overweight, not all people who are obese are compulsive overeaters.

Compulsive overeaters have what is characterized as an "addiction" to food—they eat for emotional rather than nutritional reasons, often consuming large quantities of "junk" food to fill a void and avoid feelings. They often turn to food for comfort when stressed, hurt, angry, or upset. The food can block out feelings and emotions.

Compulsive overeating usually starts in early childhood, when eating patterns are formed. Most people who become compulsive eaters have never learned the proper way to deal with stressful situations and use food instead as a way of coping. Fat can have a protective function for them, especially those who have been victims of sexual abuse. They sometimes feel that by being overweight, and thus supposedly less attractive, they'll keep others at a distance.

Like anorexics and bulimics, some compulsive overeaters abuse laxatives and/or diuretics in an attempt to control their weight. However, unlike with anorexia and bulimia, a high proportion of compulsive overeaters are male.

Some common physical effects and health risks (may be one, a few, or all):

- severe weight gain
- moderately to excessively overweight
- constipation
- swollen joints
- muscle atrophy
- bad skin
- unhealthy hair
- puffy look from poor circulation (caused by constricted veins and arteries)
- high blood pressure and/or high cholesterol
- breathlessness
    - stomach cramps
    - gas
    - bone deterioration
    - diseases that accompany obesity, such as heart attacks, strokes, and kidney damage or failure

How to identify compulsive overeating: People suffering with this eating disorder often eat nonstop throughout the day and panic if they think they will be in a situation where they won't be able to eat. They also have a tendency to be warm or hot regardless of the weather—either because their constant eating has led to them being overweight or simply because of their increased digestive activities.

**Common behavior patterns
(may be one, a few, or all):**

- lethargy
- increased feelings of worthlessness and hopelessness
- lack of self-pride
- negative attitude
- tendency to blame others
- feeling disgusted, depressed, or guilty after overeating
- procrastination
- awareness that eating patterns are abnormal

Treatments: Dieting and bingeing can go on forever if the emotional reasons for the bingeing are not dealt with. Unfortunately, compulsive overeating is not taken seriously enough yet. Sufferers are directed to diet centers and health spas instead. But like anorexia and bulimia, compulsive overeating is a serious problem and can result in death. With the proper treatment, which should include therapy and nutritional counseling, it can be overcome.

Hospitalization is rare. More often, the compulsive overeater is given a diet plan to follow, a support group to join, and therapy to readjust her food-self values. Sometimes medication is prescribed as well. It is increasingly recognized that obesity is not a failure of will or behavior, nor is it a disorder of body weight regulation. It is a chronic medical condition, like diabetes. In the obese person, body weight is just as carefully regulated as it is in non-obese persons, but a chemical imbalance in her levels of serotonin may mean that she is unable to control her intake in much the same way as an alcoholic relates to a drink. Therefore, medications known as serotonin-reuptake inhibitors—which may suppress craving and promote weight loss—are recommended in some to rectify the chemical imbalance and help control compulsive overeating.

Diet Drug Abuse

Over-the-counter diet aids are abused by many people. Bulimics and anorexics, for instance, sometimes use laxatives and/or diuretics to purge their body of extra weight from waste and fluids. But you don't have to have an eating disorder to abuse these drugs—anyone who exceeds the recommended dosage in an attempt to control her weight is at risk.

Popular diet pills such as Acutrim and Dexatrim contain a combination of phenylpropanolamine and caffeine, both of which can have dangerous side effects at high doses. Ephedrine, a so-called "natural" herb found in many diet pills and food supplements, also can cause adverse reactions. Many people find that after prolonged use of laxatives they cannot move their bowels without them. Laxative abuse can also cause bloody diarrhea, uncontrollable gas, dark and blotchy skin, abdominal cramping and pain, nausea and vomiting, muscle pain, and permanent damage to the bowels.

But most seriously, overuse of either diuretics or laxatives can result in electrolyte imbalance and dehydration, which can cause kidney damage and organ malfunctions. Once the electrolytes go out of balance, the person is at a very high risk for heart failure and sudden death.

Diet pills and laxatives are not even an effective way to lose weight. By the time laxatives work, the calories have already been absorbed. The person usually feels like she has lost weight because of the amount of fluid that is lost, but this is only temporary because the body will start to retain water within 48 to 72 hours. This usually leaves one feeling bloated. In fact, the retention can sometimes cause a dramatic weight "gain" of as much as 10 pounds as well as severe constipation, which leads to repeated use of these products. The same fluid loss/water retention cycle occurs with the use of diuretics.

b
r
a
i
n

self-destructive behavior

RISKY BEHAVIOR

Risky behavior is not all self-destructive. Sometimes, doing things you might normally be afraid to do can be a way to stretch your limits and explore your possibilities.

However, doing things that may have serious and dangerous consequences—drug and alcohol use, reckless or drunk driving, unprotected sex, shoplifting, skipping school—can be destructive to you now and in the future.

Peer pressure, feelings of invincibility, and an adrenaline rush, among other things, may make it difficult to think clearly about the consequences while in the moment. Unfortunately, one risky act can really change your life. If you notice yourself engaging in self-destructive behavior, try to understand why you are doing it and think hard about the potential consequences.

> I am 16, an honor student, and I lead a satisfying life. However, I party a lot, and in the past few months I have gotten more drunk and stoned than usual. What's worse is that every time I get wasted, I fool around with people who either I don't know or are older. I don't want to do these things, but they always seem to happen. What should I do? It's scaring me.
> — **HotPicante**

> I have a friend who I'm really close with and care about a lot but lately she's started to steal small things...like candy, rings, etc. She's not poor at all so I don't get why she's stealing! She claims she's addicted to it, she can't control herself...but I find that to be one of the lamest excuses. — **QofHearts**

For more on drug abuse, see **pp. 200–213.**

SELF-MUTILATION

Anything that involves the deliberate, repetitive, impulsive, non-lethal harming of yourself can be characterized as self-mutilation.

Some common behaviors are

obsessive face picking

obsessively pulling out head and body hairs—a condition known as trichotillomania

carving words or pictures into your body using razors, knives, paper clips, bobby pins, pens, scissors, combs, pieces of glass, or fingernails

compulsive cutting

The key to understanding self-mutilation is to understand its cause. What is behind the anxiety, anger, depression? What makes it so bad that self-inflicted pain seems like a way to cope with or manage all this pain? Some self-abuse is linked to alcohol or drug abuse, physical or sexual abuse, or an eating disorder. Many people who self-mutilate suffer from what's called dissociation—an altered state of consciousness, a feeling of being outside of your body, of being unreal. It can be a way of "leaving" an unbearable situation, at least psychologically. This is a numbing defense common to victims of trauma, including sexual abuse. But what works as a coping strategy during a traumatic event can become a habitual response to stress. So some people end up cutting themselves in order to feel something, to know that they're still alive.

Other cutters may be using self-mutilation for different purposes—injuring themselves to vent angry feelings, or wanting to make a physical manifestation of their pain for others to see. There is evidence that when faced with intense emotions or traumatic situations, self-injurers are overwhelmed and unable to cope. Instead of acting out, they act in. They choose to harm themselves because it brings them a rapid release from tension and anxiety and quickly calms the body. The self-injurer may feel guilty or angry afterward.

Sometimes self-mutilation is a way of punishing oneself for being "bad." Or it seems to help maintain a sense of security or feelings of uniqueness. Or it helps the person express or cope with feelings of alienation. It may also be an attempt to escape from emptiness or depression or an effort to regain control of one's life—although in reality the self-injurer loses control to the self-abuse, which becomes an ugly habit that she or he cannot stop.

> i dunno how to say this but i have this huge problem with cutting myself...it kind of scares me but it's like my only escape...
> — haZel88

> first of all, i just have to say that i have been there. not only do you have to stop cutting yourself, but you need to find the root to the problem. without narrowing down what it is that is causing you to cut yourself, you may just never stop. i myself used to cut myself because i was angry—i hated my family, school, church, God, etc. i felt like nothing was going right in my life.....cutting myself was my own twisted way of expressing my anger towards others.
> — MissV

brain

> Well, I have been cutting myself for a year! I have contemplated suicide! and I have come close so many times! I have told my best friends and they just get mad at me! What should I do?? HELP!
> — Alex_V

See Self-Mutilation Resources, p. 197.

> hey you got a BIG @$$ problem. you have what is called self-mutilation. you need to get help and right away. listen, call a hotline for suicide or self mutilation. they can tell you what to do. please seek help, you need it. if you don't get help now it might get worse. please don't let it get any worse.   — dreamdream

self-destructive behavior

TEENAGE SUICIDE

Suicide is an ugly, horrible act. There's no way around that. Teens who kill themselves don't just hurt themselves. Everybody around them is left feeling angry, guilty, helpless, and depressed.

Sometimes things seem hopeless, but a permanent step like suicide is not the solution. If you have any serious thoughts of suicide you MUST talk to someone. Talking to a friend, trusted adult, therapist, or a suicide prevention hotline can be very helpful.

Most teenagers have been exposed to some discussion of suicide, which is the third leading cause of death among people aged 15 to 19 and the second leading cause of death among those 19 to 24. If you have a friend who has talked about suicide, take it seriously. You can ask your friend straight out if he or she is considering suicide and then urge him or her to call one of the resource numbers at the end of this chapter. If your friend flat-out refuses to get help, alert an adult to the situation or call a suicide hotline on your friend's behalf and get advice from a professional.

Signs that someone is considering suicide seriously include a preoccupation with death, giving away valued possessions, a plan for how to kill themselves, possession of pills or a weapon, a previous history of hurting themselves, and an inexplicable sense of calm after a long depression.

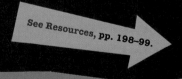

See Resources, pp. 198–99.

If someone you know commits suicide

If a friend commits suicide, it's important to remember that it isn't your fault. As in the case of any death of a loved one, the survivors grieve. In the case of suicide, the grief process often also includes feelings of shame, guilt, failure, rejection, and anger—

> Help me!! Yesterday one of my really good friends admitted to me that she was seriously considering suicide. Her parents don't treat her well and her life isn't the greatest, but I would really miss her if she takes her life. I've tried talking to her, but she always changes the subject. What do I do now? How am I supposed to get through to her? :o(
> — **sing-a-long**

> I also confided in my friend when I was suicidal. A lot of what she needs is just support, and someone to talk to. She should talk to doc too. If you've been talking to her about it and she still insists on ending her life, you should really tell someone (like a trusted adult) that can also help you. Your friend may get mad at you for doing this (I was mad at my friend for a few days) but would you rather lose a friend temporarily, or lose a friend FOREVER??!?!?!
> — **Volunteer**

toward the person who committed suicide, yourself, God, or others. Sometimes you may be able to understand the pressures that caused someone to commit suicide; other times the cause is a complete mystery.

Survivors need to know that it is OK to grieve, cry, laugh, and heal. Moving on does not mean that you loved the person any less or that you've forgotten about her or him. It may be helpful for survivors to grieve and talk about the suicide with each other. The mourning process for death by suicide may be considerably longer than for other types of death.

many times i have felt so
insecure about myself i have thought about
committing suicide. i don't know what to do!
— **scRawl**

Please do not kill yourself. I know
that no matter what anyone tells you right
now, it seems as though it couldn't get ANY worse
and that suicide is the only way out. I've been there.
I've been way over into that side and I'VE COME BACK. It will
get better, you will get better, you can be happy. But you
must realize this yourself, because you are the only one who
can help yourself right now. All I ask is that you wait—a
day—a week...things will not seem as bad afterwards. You
must believe in yourself. — **silvershark**

i'm sure you've heard this countless
times, i have heard it too, but, i've been there. it seems there are
about as many depressed girls as there are coins in a wishing well. i am
depressed all the time, and i still think about suicide. it's hard to live
for me, but i'm trying. i know sometimes it seems like life is too hard, but
aren't there things you want to do and be and see in your lifetime?
suggestion—write a list of about ten things you want to have, do, see, etc.
before you die. you cannot kill yourself before you achieve those things.
chances are that once you achieve them, you will be happier and you will
not want to die so badly. trust me. it is selfish to commit suicide,
living people will mentally die with you. there are infinite ways to
seek help, but you have to seek help, you can work on it yourself,
you can talk to people online, you can read about things to do
for yourself, you must try to help yourself reach a
better place alive. — **patientchik**

b
r
a
i
n

I live in a
very small town, so
when a boy in my grade committed
suicide 2 years ago it was a big deal. It also
made one of his friends decide to kill himself too b/c he
thought it was his fault for not helping out. My town has never
really gotten over it. Believe me, people care. Life IS worth living. — **powerFLY**

self-destructive behavior

Eating Disorders—National Organizations

The American Anorexia/Bulimia Association, 165 West 46th Street, #1108, New York, NY 10036. Phone: 212-575-6200. Provides referrals to therapists, support groups, and other resources in your area. This service is confidential and free.

Bulimia/Anorexia Self-Help Hotline: 800-227-4785.

National Association of Anorexia Nervosa and Associated Disorders (ANAD), P.O. Box 7, Highland Park, IL 60035. Phone: 847-831-3438. More than 300 affiliated groups providing information on self-help groups, therapy, and referrals to professionals.

National Eating Disorders Organization (NEDO), 6655 South Yale Avenue, Tulsa, OK 74136-3329. Phone: 918-481-4044. Website: http://www.laureate.com. An educational organization for people suffering from anorexia, bulimia, and eating disorders, as well as for their families and friends. Offers support groups, information (newsletter, audiotapes, etc.), and referrals.

Overeaters Anonymous, 6075 Zenith Court NE, Rio Rancho, NM 87124. Phone: 505-891-2664. Website: http://www.overeatersanonymous.org. A self-supporting group (there are no dues or fees for members) made up of individuals who, through shared experience, strength, and hope, are recovering from compulsive overeating.

Eating Disorders—Online

About.com's Eating Disorder Site at http://eatingdisorders.about.com includes essays on how victims of eating disorders relate to their bodies, crisis help, pen pal matchmaking, chat rooms, links, and FAQs on specific eating disorders and dieting.

Anorexia Nervosa and Related Eating Disorders at http://www.anred.com provides information about anorexia, bulimia, binge eating, compulsive exercising, and other lesser-known food and weight disorders.

Anorexia.org at http://www.anorexia.org/services is an eating disorder support group providing information, discussions, chat, and anonymous e-mail.

Eating Disorder Recovery Online at http://www.edrecovery.com is maintained by an eating disorder and trauma recovery center. They provide services and information to assist people with eating disorders. Phone: 888-520-1700.

Eating Disorders Association Resource Center at http://www.uq.net.au/~zzedainc hosts a website with resources for anorexics and bulimics.

Eating Disorders Website at http://www.angelfire.com/ca/AnorBulim includes information about eating disorders and links to related sites.

Feminist.com at http://www.feminist.com for information and resources on eating disorders.

The Food and Drug Administration (FDA) has information on over-the-counter dietary supplements at http://www.fda.gov/cder/drug.htm.

Hugs International at http://www.hugs.com is the center for information and resources about non-dieting.

Something-Fishy Website on Eating Disorders at http://www.something-fishy.org offers first-person accounts from people who suffer from eating disorders, information, and chat and resource links.

Eating Disorders—Books

Fat Is a Feminist Issue by Susie Orbach (Berkeley). The classic book examining the role food plays in women's lives.

Hunger Point by Jillian Medoff (Harper Mass Market). A novel that attempts to unravel the familial and social pressures that drive two sisters into a life of serious food abuse (one survives, the other doesn't).

Life-Size by Jenefer Shute (Avon). A harrowing novel about a girl suffering from anorexia and almost starving herself to death.

My Sister's Bones by Cathi Hanauer (Dell). A novel about a few months in the life of a girl who is coming of age just as her beautiful older sister begins to succumb to anorexia.

Wasted: A Memoir of Anorexia and Bulimia by Marya Hornbacher (HarperCollins). A passionate and eloquent account of a young woman's near-death self-starvation.

Self-mutilation—National Organizations

SAFE (Self-Abuse Finally Ends) gives referrals to local programs dealing with self-abuse and self-mutilation and information on treatment options. Phone: 800-DON'T-CUT (800-366-8288).

Trichotillomania Learning Center acts as a clearinghouse for information on compulsive hair-pulling and can refer people to support groups. Address: 1215 Mission Street, Suite 2, Santa Cruz, CA 95060. Phone: 408-457-1004.

Self-mutilation—Online

Pioneer Clinic at http://www.pressenter.com/~cnovakmd. This trichotillomania treatment and education center is a great starting point to learn more about trichotillomania.

Self-Injury Home Page at http://crystal.palace.net/~llama/psych/injury.html gives good information and links to other resources.

SelfHarm.Com at http://www.selfharm.com provides information about self-harming behavior, self-injury, self-mutilation, self-abuse, and cutting, plus coping skills, alternatives to self-injury, support groups, personal cutting stories, and ways to stay safe.

Self-Injury Discussion Board at http://www.psychtests.com/wwwboard_self_injury deals with the various emotional issues and questions related to self-injury.

To read poetry by people who suffer from self-mutilation, log onto http://www.geocities.com/~anansie/lck/lyrics/self.html.

Trichotillomania Learning Center at http://www.trich.org acts as a clearinghouse for information on compulsive hair-pulling and can refer people to support groups.

Self-mutilation—Books

Bodies Under Siege: Self-Mutilation and Body Modification in Culture and Psychiatry by Armando R. Favazza (Johns Hopkins University Press). The first survey of self-mutilation with information on classification and treatment of self-injurious behavior.

brain

A Bright Red Scream: Self-Mutilation and the Language of Pain by Marilee Strong (Viking Press). A compassionate study of self-mutilation ("a bright red scream" is how one of the subjects describes the sensation of intentionally inflicting pain upon oneself).

Cutting: Understanding and Overcoming Self-Mutilation by Steven Levenkron (W.W. Norton & Co.). A comprehensive book on the causes and effective treatments of this disorder.

The Luckiest Girl in the World by Steven Levenkron (Penguin). A good nonfiction read on self-mutilation.

Women Who Hurt Themselves by Dusty Miller (Basic Books). The look at the suffering experienced by women who suffer from addictive and self-hurting behavior.

You Are Not Alone: Compulsive Hair Pulling, the Enemy Within by Cheryn Salazar (Cheryn International). Offers a handle on hair tugging.

Suicide

Use local and national suicide hotlines. Check the Yellow Pages under Crisis, Counseling, Social and Human Services, Mental Health, or Suicide, or look in the front pages under these headings.

Call your family doctor. Or contact an adult you respect and can trust.

Dial the police emergency number—usually 911.

Important: Do not give up if you get a busy signal, especially on a hotline. Keep trying.

Go to a hospital. Emergency rooms are open 7 days a week, 24 hours a day.

Suicide—National Organizations

Call a national suicide hotline (the calls are confidential and usually free). Usually staffed by trained volunteers and professional counselors who help callers identify their problems, explore options, and develop a plan of action, these hotlines also offer referrals to community-based services, support groups, and even shelters if necessary.

Boys Town National Hotline: 800-448-3000 (24 hours). Provides a bilingual suicide prevention hotline, for boys and girls.

Covenant House Nine Line: 800-999-9999 (24 hours). A youth crisis hotline for talking about any problem.

KID SAVE: 800-543-7283 (24 hours). Gives information and referrals to shelters, mental health services, sexual abuse treatment, substance abuse, family counseling, residential care, adoption/foster care, and the like for teens in crisis.

TEEN LINE operates every night from 6 p.m. to 10 p.m., Pacific Standard Time. In California, call 800-TLC-TEEN (800-852-8336). In other states, call 310-855-4673. Somebody will immediately call you back so there won't be a big charge.

The Samaritans Hotline: 212-673-3000 (24 hours). The Samaritans Hotline is a non-religious, completely confidential hotline.

If someone you know has taken their own life (or died any other way), contact one of the following groups for information on coping and referrals to a local support group:

American Association of Suicidology, 4201 Connecticut Avenue, NW, Suite 408, Washington, DC 20008. Phone: 202-237-2280. Website: http://www.suicidology.org.

SA\VE (Suicide Awareness\Voices of Education), P.O. Box 24507, Minneapolis, MN 55424. Phone: 612-946-7998. Website: http://www.save.org.

Suicide—Online

For more information on suicide, to chat with someone who is going through similar experiences, or to read about another teen's own suicidal feelings, log onto these sites:

Suicide Help Page at http://mailhost. infi.net/~susanf/suihelp.htm includes suicide prevention information, steps for helping someone who is suicidal, and help for those left behind after a suicide.

Suicide @ Rochford at http://www. rochford.org/suicide an essential resource for anyone contemplating suicide.

For valuable advice on how to help someone who is threatening suicide, log onto http://www.ohd.hr.state.or.us/ cdpe/chs/suicide/help.htm.

The Samaritans Online at http://www. mhnet.org./samaritans. This Samaritans website provides crisis support through e-mail.

TEEN LINE at http://www. teenlineonline.org. a website for teens in crisis staffed by trained teen volunteers.

Suicide—Books

You Mean I Don't Have to Feel This Way? by Colette Dowling (Bantam Books). Helps readers to deal with suicidal depression.

Some reads on why some people commit suicide and how it affects those left behind:

Another Country by James Baldwin (Vintage Books). A classic novel in which a black jazz musician commits suicide, compelling his friends to search for the meaning of his death and, consequently, for a deeper understanding of their own identities.

Face at the Edge of the World by Eve Bunting (Clarion Books). A novel in which the main character, haunted by the suicide of his best friend, attempts to re-create his friend's last weeks and discover why he took his own life.

What Are They Saying about Me? by Maureen Wartski (Juniper). A moving story of how gossip makes a teenage girl not want to live.

For more resources and information, see http://www.dealwithit.com

brain

self-destructive behavior

Special Section
Altered States

Part of growing older is dealing with the inevitable issue of drugs, whether it's alcohol, cigarettes, pot, or any other mind-altering, mood-altering substance you may encounter. In order to make decisions for yourself in a responsible way, it's important to understand your own motivations and to be aware of the dangers of drug and alcohol use.

WHAT IS A DRUG?

A drug is a substance—other than food—that, when taken, has some effect on your body and/or your mood. Drugs affect everyone differently and the effects of many drugs can be unpredictable and catch people completely off guard. Many drugs, such as speed and heroin, can have very dangerous effects, even on the first try. It is far too easy to take too much of a drug, which can have majorly bad effects. Overconsumption is always a bad idea. Be aware of the effects and risks of every drug and keep in mind that many drugs are illegal.

For effects, risks, and legality of various drugs see chart starting on p. 202.

WHY PEOPLE TAKE DRUGS

Experimentation: People take drugs to see how the drugs will make them feel.
To feel a certain way: People take drugs because they like the way the drug affects their mood or senses.
Peer pressure: People take drugs because their friends are taking drugs and they

> I've been hanging out with the same group of friends, all through high school. But now my "friends" are drinking a lot, and doing stupid things to get in with the "popular" people. They all say that I'm ruining the friendship because I won't drink with them, or try to hang out with the in crowd.
> **— FourStars**

> Don't let your so-called friends pressure you into something you don't want to do. Tell them that you really don't want to do it, and if they can't get that through their heads, then give them the boot! Who needs them? Find some people that you have more in common with and that respect your decisions. **— olives**

don't want to be left out or ridiculed.
Escapism: People take drugs to get away from bad feelings in their lives.

If you are thinking about drinking or taking drugs, or if you already do, it's important to understand your motivations. If you might be using drugs as an escape from something wrong with your life, then by all means get help! Women who are pregnant or think they might be should never use drugs!

See Resources in Self-Destructive Behavior, p. 196.

ADDICTION

People also take drugs because they are addicted to them. Addiction is the repetitive, compulsive, psychologically dependent use of a substance that occurs despite negative consequences to the user. Addiction has the power to destroy lives and families. People can get addicted to any drug (and arguably to behaviors such as eating, having sex, taking risks, or gambling). About 6 million

Americans are addicted to some substance.

Psychological addiction is the state of needing to get high to function "normally." This can easily translate into physical addiction, where your body becomes so accustomed to having a particular drug in your system that you would actually suffer physical symptoms (ranging from chills and headaches to hallucinations) if you stopped taking it. You can be psychologically dependent without being physically dependent, but not vice versa.

Here are some not so clear-cut signs of addiction:

- you get high more than two times a week
- you do it without thinking about whether you want to do it
- you don't have any friends who don't get high
- you're using more and more drugs to get the same high
- you get high on your own
- you get high to get high—not to socialize

If a cluster of these symptoms applies to you or a friend, see Resources p. 213.

Risks of addiction

It's important to understand where you and any drug you may consider using stand in terms of addiction risk.

Certain drugs, such as heroin and cocaine (especially crack cocaine), carry a very high risk of addiction. People who have become addicted to these drugs have reported a compulsion to use them again even after one or two experiences with them. See the drug chart for information on addiction potential of each drug.

Additionally, although anyone who uses drugs can get addicted to them, certain people are more at risk for addiction than others. People at greatest risk have typi-cally grown up in a family with a drug-abusing parent, have a past history of physical or emotional abuse, and are depressed. If there is addiction in your family tree, you may have a genetic tendency toward chemical dependency—which means experimentation can be a more dangerous activity for you than for someone else.

Breaking an addiction

If you find that you can't stop taking drugs even though they are having a bad effect on your life, admitting that you have a problem is a necessary and very difficult first step. Recovering from a drug addiction is a long and trying process, but there are many excellent support groups and resources available to help people recover from addictions. Also know that if you do decide to quit using any addictive sub-stance, cravings for that drug become even stronger during withdrawal, and you can feel quite ill for some time, depending on how long and how seriously you've been using the drug. Even withdrawing from something as seemingly benign as caffeine can cause serious headaches for some people.

For more information on breaking addictions, see Resources, p. 213.

If you recognize addictive behavior in a friend or relative, it can be very frustrating. Addiction is not an easy thing to admit to oneself. And your friend or relative may not be ready to take this step. Getting someone to admit he or she has a problem is the first and hardest step in overcoming any addiction.

Although you can try talking to or confronting this person about her or his drug abuse, ultimately you are not responsible for that person's behavior. Finding resources such as Al-Anon—a national network of support groups formed specifically for loved ones of alcoholics—to help you deal with a friend's or relative's addiction is definitely a good idea.

COMMON DRUGS

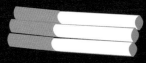

Nicotine

Found in: cigarettes, cigars, chewing tobacco, nicotine gum, and patches.

In 1995:
19% of eighth-graders smoked cigarettes
27% of tenth-graders smoked cigarettes
34% of twelfth-graders smoked cigarettes

Source: Tobacco plant.

Legal code: Legal if you're over 18.

History: Tobacco was used in the 1500s to treat headaches, colds, and other medical problems and was even thought to be holy because of its healing reputation. This view gradually gained opposition and by 1890 nicotine was discontinued as a medicine in the United States, although tobacco remained very popular, particularly chewing tobacco. Cigar and cigarette smoking caught on in America in the 1900s and rose to a peak in the mid-1960s, when 40 percent of all adults were smokers. This number has declined to 25 percent in the 1990s for a few possible reasons: the ban on cigarette advertising on TV; authoritative studies linking smoking to very serious health problems, especially deadly cancer; and an effective educational campaign using this knowledge.

Effects: Nicotine stimulates the heart and circulation. It can increase concentration and attention. Smokers report that it helps to relieve anxiety and stress.

Risks: Cigarette smoking is the major cause of preventable deaths in America. Tobacco users or those living with smokers have nearly all the cases of lung cancer, a two times greater risk of fatal heart disease, a two to three times greater chance of peptic ulcers, and a several times greater risk of throat, mouth, esophageal, pancreatic, kidney, bladder, and cervical cancer. On average, people who smoke die 5 to 8 years earlier than people who do not smoke. Smokers get more colds, tend to have a year-round cough, and eventually develop emphysema. Sooner or later they also experience a deadened sense of smell and taste, premature and more face

wrinkles, yellow teeth (and fingertips from tobacco stains), and increased heart rate and blood pressure.

Nonsmokers also experience some of these risks if they are constantly exposed to second-hand smoke. Part of the rationale behind nonsmoking bars and restaurants is consideration of the health of people who work in these environments.

Risks for teens: People who start smoking as teenagers put themselves at much higher risk for nicotine addiction. Recent studies show that early smoking permanently scars the DNA structure of the lungs, leaving them vulnerable to future lung disease even if teen smokers quit later in life.

Adolescent smokers are twice as likely to suffer a major episode of depression. Teens with long-term depression are more likely to be smokers.

Dangerous nicotine overdose may be very rare, but it's possible.

Nicotine poisoning can cause nausea, weakness, and dizziness.

Nicotine can cause serious and permanent damage to an unborn fetus. If you think you may be pregnant, do not smoke!

Do not combine with: Cocaine or other drugs that increase heart rate or blood pressure—it can increase risk of heart attack.

I smoke on the weekends and at parties but I never crave cigarettes. Am I just considered a social smoker? — **beepbeep**

If you just smoke socially, it is really not very smart of you. That's how about 99% of teens get addicted. You start smoking socially b/c you think it's cool, and then, without you noticing, you find yourself smoking when you're alone, when you're upset, whenever...and TA-DA you're addicted. I have been an addicted smoker for 2 years. I quit a month ago. Don't start. It's the hardest thing in the world to quit. — **calliopejane**

Addiction rating: High.

Quitting: Serious cravings for nicotine decrease quickly within days of quitting, and nicotine gum or the patch can help during this time. Much harder to deal with are the habits and psychological associations people have developed around smoking over time (certain friends, places, and routines can trigger the urge). And many people worry about weight gain after quitting. Smoking both accelerates the body's metabolism and gives you something non-caloric to stick in your mouth. Although weight gain is usually only temporary and can be kept to a minimum, the best solution is to substitute exercise for smoking.

There are many programs available to help you quit if you find that you can't do it alone.

For help on quitting, see Resources p. 213.

I smoke and really want to stop because i'm afraid i'm very addicted to cigarettes. I don't want to have to ask my parents to buy something for me to help me quit (because i don't want them to know i smoke). Is there anything else I could do to stop smoking?
— **bravissimo**

I quit a month ago, after 3 years, b/c I was spitting up blood in the mornings and getting sick all of the time. Smoking does that to you. I would suggest this: **1)** Make the decision to quit. **2)** When you decide to quit, finish the pack you have and promise not to smoke anymore. **3)** Tell your friends you're quitting so they won't offer you cigarettes. (When everyone else is smoking and they offer you one, it's all too easy to take it.) You will realize after the first 3 days how dependent you were on the nicotine. You will be a bItCh, but your friends will understand. **4)** Give yourself rewards as you go along. **5)** Just notice how much healthier you feel. You'll be surprised.
— **Lugenia**

Alcohol

Found in: Beer, wine, liquor.

About 90% of high school seniors have tried alcohol. Nearly a third report drinking heavily (more than 5 drinks in a night) in the past 2 weeks.

Alcohol content in various beverages
Beer: 5% or less alcohol
Ale, porter, wine: 9% to **12%** alcohol
Liquor (hooch, whiskey, spirits):
40% or more alcohol
Bottle labels usually indicate the percentage of alcohol the liquid inside contains.

Source: A variety of organic substances including grapes, berries, potatoes, sugars, corn, and grains—all left to ferment.

Legal code: Legal if you are over 21.

History: Alcohol has been around for thousands of years, used both recreationally and as part of religious ceremonies. Some of the earliest known writings include references to drinking. In the Middle Ages, alcohol was thought to be able to cure almost every health problem.

Effects: Many people feel a sense of well-being, self-confidence, and stimulation while drinking. This feeling is often replaced by drowsiness and sedation as the alcohol leaves the body. Alcohol dulls awareness, reflexes, and judgment. Alcohol is absorbed very quickly into the blood from the stomach, in as short a time as 5 to 10 minutes. The effects can last for several hours depending on the amount, how quickly it was drunk, and the body size of the drinker.

A few studies have reported that drinking in moderation (a glass of wine a day) can actually be healthy.

Risks: Dangerous overdoses are possible when people drink a lot of alcohol very quickly. This type of overdose is most common in younger (especially college-age) drinkers. Drinking on an empty stomach is particularly dangerous. If someone passes out and can't be woken up or seems to have trouble breathing, call for help immediately. An unconscious person may literally choke on his or her own vomit.

Moderate drinking can cause hangovers, including headaches, and nausea.

Excessive drinking can compromise memory, abstract thinking, problem solving, attention, and concentration. It can also cause loss

brain

altered states

of appetite, vitamin deficiencies, stomach ailments, skin problems, sexual impotence, liver damage, and damage to the heart and central nervous system.

More than six thousand 15- to 20-year-olds were killed in alcohol-related deaths in 1998. **Risks for women:** Women get drunk faster than men: after drinking the same amount of alcohol, a woman's blood alcohol level may be 25 to 30 percent higher. This is in part because women are smaller. More significantly, women produce less of the enzyme that metabolizes alcohol, alcohol dehydrogenase, so a greater percentage of the alcohol consumed goes directly into a woman's bloodstream.

This means that women are more vulnerable to the negative effects of alcohol, in both the short and the long term. Women are more prone to liver damage from excessive alcohol. After drinking the same amount as a man, a woman's ability to determine the safety of a situation (Can I drive? Should I have sex with him? Do I have to use a rubber?) is also more compromised. The more alcohol a woman drinks, the higher her chances are of being sexually assaulted. Birth control pills slow down the rate at which alcohol leaves the body.

Alcohol can cause serious and permanent damage to an unborn fetus. If you think you may be pregnant, do not drink! Some studies suggest that women who have three to nine drinks per week are more likely to develop breast cancer than women who don't drink at all. This research is very preliminary, but women who do decide to drink should pay attention to it and any forthcoming breast cancer studies.

Risks for teens: Since your brain does not finish developing until you are 20, it may be more vulnerable to alcohol's damaging effects than mature brains.

Genetic risks: Children and siblings of alcoholics are estimated to have a seven times greater chance of becoming alcoholics than children and siblings of nonalcoholics. (The males in a family are more prone to these genetic risks.) If you have a close relative who is an alcoholic, it is extra-important to make smart decisions about drinking.

Do not combine with: Any other downers. Each downer increases the other's effects. Two or more downers taken together can be extremely dangerous and even deadly.

Addiction rating: Medium (high if you have a genetic predisposition toward alcoholism).

Drinking and driving: If you decide to drink, be responsible and don't ever drive drunk! Legally, if you're caught driving with a .08–.10% blood alcohol concentration (the exact percentage differs by state), you may be arrested and charged with

---

I started drinking over the summer, but before I go out and get totally wasted, I want to know the dangers and effects of drinking. I only drink every once in a while—stuff like margaritas, beer, gin and tonic, and wine. — **GraceM**

I really don't think drinking's that big of a deal if you do it only occasionally, but some of the long-term effects of excessive drinking are really bad. Some of the effects can happen from short-term drinking too—permanent brain damage affecting vision, memory, and learning ability (this summer, I drank every day, and my memory is horrible now); bladder damage (experienced this one, too); and depression (been here, too). — **vintageme**

What is excessive drinking?

There is no easy answer to this question. There are a few screening tests that are widely used by clinicians as first attempts to understand if someone has a drinking problem.

CAGE is the most widely used test:

C Have you ever felt the need to Cut down on your drinking?

A Have you ever felt Annoyed by someone criticizing your drinking?

G Have you ever felt Guilty about your drinking?

E Have you ever felt the need for an Eye opener (a drink at the beginning of the day?)

If someone says yes to two or more of these questions, she may have a problem. This test is by no means definitive. Only a health care professional trained in addiction can make the determination that someone is addicted to alcohol or any other substance.

If you think you have a problem, see Resources, p. 213.

DWI (driving while intoxicated). You also jeopardize your own life, and the lives of anyone else on the road.

Marijuana

pot weed
hash doobie
reefer
herb grass
mary jane
bud ganja

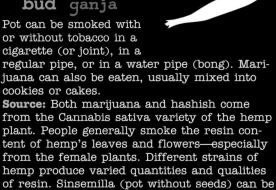

Pot can be smoked with or without tobacco in a cigarette (or joint), in a regular pipe, or in a water pipe (bong). Marijuana can also be eaten, usually mixed into cookies or cakes.

Source: Both marijuana and hashish come from the Cannabis sativa variety of the hemp plant. People generally smoke the resin content of hemp's leaves and flowers—especially from the female plants. Different strains of hemp produce varied quantities and qualities of resin. Sinsemilla (pot without seeds) can be as potent as hash.

THC (tetrahydrocannabinol) is the active ingredient of marijuana.

THC content
Low-grade marijuana: 1% or less THC
High-grade marijuana or sinsemilla: 4% to 8% THC
Hashish: 7% to 14% THC
Hash oil: up to 50% THC

Legal code: Generally illegal, although marijuana has been legalized in some states only for use as a treatment for AIDS, anorexia, multiple sclerosis, epilepsy, and the effects of chemotherapy. Physicians risk federal prosecution even in these states if they prescribe it.
History: The cannabis plant has been cultivated for thousands and thousands of years for its fiber and for its healing and intoxicating effects. In the 1800s European artists embraced the drug for its supposed creative powers. Although the cannabis plant has been in America for hundreds of years, it was mainly harvested for fiber to make clothes and rope. It was not until the 1900s that Americans really began to use the cannabis plant as a drug. Marijuana was made illegal in the Harrison Narcotics Act of 1914, though it didn't really hit the public consciousness until the 1920s, during the Jazz Age. The federal government then tried to portray it as an evil weed that would lead to all kinds of deprivation, including other drug use, orgies, and murder.
Effects: Effects vary from person to person, depending on the situation and the amount of THC in the pot. Many people report feeling happy, stimulated, or relaxed at first, followed by a feeling of drowsiness or calmness. Others get tired or headachy immediately.
Many people get hungry (the "munchies"). Emotions can swing wildly during a high, depending on what's going on. Hash or high-grade marijuana can have hallucinogenic effects. When pot is eaten, its effects are delayed and can be stronger. Some people report feeling intellectually stimulated and having greater sense perception and feeling more open to emotions. About half of the THC passes out of the body within a day. The rest can stay in your system for up to a month or longer.
Risks: Overdose is not possible. People can get paranoid and anxious. The best treatment for this is generally a reassuring talk from a friend.
It is impossible to really understand all the effects of pot, especially the long-term ones, because smoking it releases hundreds of chemicals besides THC, which haven't been fully identified or investigated. Moderate pot smoking can cause short-term memory loss, decreases in attention and concentration, and slowed reflexes. As with tobacco, chronic pot smoking can damage your lungs, mouth, and throat. It may also compromise memory, cause personality changes, and reduce fertility.
Risks for women: Long-term pot smokers may experience irregular periods, which can make it harder to get pregnant. Marijuana may cause serious and permanent damage to an unborn fetus. If you think you may be pregnant, do not take pot in any form!
Risks for teens: Pot affects the brain, though how is not conclusively known. And it may have more damaging effects on brains that are not fully developed.
Do not combine with: Cocaine or heart or blood pressure medications.
Addiction rating: Low.

UP

Uppers, or stimulants, make the body work faster by increasing the heart rate and pumping adrenaline into the system.

Caffeine

Found in: Coffee, tea, soft drinks, pain relievers, over-the-counter stimulants, chocolate.

Caffeine content of common substances: Chocolate bar—30 mg; stay-awake pill—100 mg; cold-relief tablet–30 mg; coffee (8 oz.) brewed or dripped–115 mg; coffee (8 oz.) percolated–80 mg; instant coffee (8 oz.)–60–80 mg; caffeinated soft drinks (12 oz.)–30–45 mg; tea (8 oz.) brewed–40–60 mg.

Source: Found in the leaves, seeds, or fruits of more than sixty plants, including coffee and cocoa beans, kola nuts, and tea leaves.
Legal code: Legal (it's consumed by an estimated 90% of the world's population).
History: People have been taking caffeine in the form of tea, coffee, and chocolate for thousands and thousands of years. Tea drinking was popular in China in the fourth century for its healing properties. Coffee was grown in the sixth century in Yemen and was known for its ability to stimulate and combat fatigue. Europeans embraced coffee in the 1600s, and coffeehouses became known as places to enjoy coffee along with stimulating, often political, discussion. Americans have an interesting historical relationship to coffee, since they turned to it as a form of protest against the British tax on tea, beginning in the late 1760s. Coffee drinking reached a peak in the United States in 1940 and has declined since then, though soft drinks have picked up a lot of the caffeine slack.
Effects: Caffeine is a mild form of speed, stimulating the heart and respiratory system. It can increase concentration and attention, and can also slightly enhance endurance.

Caffeine takes only about 15 minutes to be absorbed into the bloodstream.
Risks: Higher doses may cause nervousness, anxiety, irritability, headache, disturbed sleep, and stomach upset or peptic ulcers. Overdoses are extremely rare. Caffeine can aggravate stress and contribute to panic attacks. It has also been associated with (but not definitely connected to) cardiovascular disease, fibrocystic breast disease, birth defects, and cancer. Taken in conjunction with exercise, caffeine can increase the risk of dehydration and can be a stress on the heart rate.
Risks for women: Excessive caffeine consumption may aggravate PMS or reduce chances of getting pregnant. It may also result in benign breast cysts.
Do not combine with: Other drugs that increase blood pressure or stronger stimulants.
Addiction rating: Medium.

Cocaine

coke blow crack rock snow C

Cocaine is either snorted, injected, or smoked (in the form of crack).
Source: Cocaine is a white powder that comes from the leaves of coca plants, often from South America. Crack is a super-addictive smokable form of cocaine that's been chemically altered.
Legal code: Illegal.
History: Native cultures in South America have chewed coca leaves for their stimulating effects for thousands of years. When the Spanish discovered South America, they brought cocaine back to Europe, where its use spread very rapidly. It was even used as an anesthetic in surgery, and in America the Coca-Cola Company's original secret formula included cocaine. Cocaine was classified as illegal in 1914 by the Harrison Narcotic Act.
Effects: People report a sense of well-being, increased endurance and energy, reduced appetite, heightened alertness, and elimination of fatigue, which can quickly turn into anxiety or panic. The physical effects of coke include an increase in blood pressure, heart rate, breathing rate, and body temperature. The effects of snorted cocaine peak in about 15 to 30 minutes and then fade, which often encourages users to repeat the dose in order to maintain the effect. Most of a crack high (which happens faster and is more intense) is usually finished after 15 minutes. In either

case, the high is followed by a crash.
Risks: There's a serious risk of overdose, leading to seizures, heart attack, strokes, and death. Repeated use of high doses can lead to a psychotic paranoid state. Cocaine use can cause irregular heartbeats and insomnia. Stress on the heart leads to a higher chance of heart attacks, strokes, and respiratory failure. Heavy users are susceptible to hallucinations and "coke bugs"—the sensation of imaginary insects crawling over the skin. Cocaine and crack use have also been a contributing factor in a number of drownings, car crashes, falls, burns, and suicides.
Injectors risk: Hepatitis or AIDS.
Risks for women: Cocaine and crack can cause serious and permanent damage to an unborn fetus. If you think you may be pregnant, do not use cocaine!
Do not combine with: Decongestants, high doses of caffeine, MAO inhibitor antidepressants (such as Nardil or Parnate), or anything that affects heart rate or makes people more prone to seizures.
Addiction rating: High.

Amphetamine and methamphetamine

speed **meth** crank **crystal** ice dexies **black** beauties hearts **whiz**

Users snort, smoke, swallow, or inject speed.
Found in: Diet pills and certain prescription medications as well as in undiluted forms.
Source: The lab.
Legal code: Only legal by prescription—to help control weight or treat attention deficit hyperactivity disorder or the sleeping disorder called narcolepsy.
History: These drugs were developed in the 1920s in an attempt to make a synthetic form of ephedrine to treat asthma. Amphetamine in the form of nasal inhalers (Benzedrine) became very popular very fast for its euphoric effects.
Effects: Users describe a sense of well-being, increased endurance and energy, short-lived euphoria, heightened alertness, and elimination of fatigue. These feelings of happiness and confidence usually lead to a high risk of dependence. Speed increases heart and respiratory rates and can decrease appetite. Effects last for 4 to 6 hours.
Risks: There's a serious risk of overdose, with

convulsions, high fevers, coma, and possibly death from heart failure, ruptured blood vessels in the brain, or hypothermia. Speed can produce an irregular heartbeat, increased sweat, higher body temperature, and insomnia. When used in conjunction with exercise, speed can become fatal because of the increase in body temperature. Repeated high doses can lead to a psychotic paranoid state. Long-term use can lead to hallucinations, delusions, and violent and self-destructive behavior. Injecting speed puts the user into AIDS and hepatitis risk territory because of contaminated needles.
Do not combine with: Decongestants or MAO inhibitor antidepressants.
Addiction rating: High.

Ecstasy (MDMA)

X XTC E

Source: Pills made in illegal labs by altering the molecular structure of both legal and illegal drugs.
Legal code: Illegal.
History: Developed in 1914 in Germany as an appetite suppressant; nobody paid much attention to Ecstasy until the 1980s, when it was seen as a potentially therapeutic drug because of its empathic effects.
Effects: Users report a sense of energy and alertness similar to that from amphetamines, as well as a feeling of happiness, openness, and caring for everyone. Ecstasy causes a rise in body temperature, usually resulting in acute dehydration. Effects begin in 20 minutes to an hour and last for 4 to 6 hours, with the peak experienced in about an hour.
Risks: There's a serious risk of overdose, leading to heart attacks, dangerously increased body temperature (which can lead to lethal dehydration), seizures, and death, especially when used in conjunction with a lot of physical activity. High doses can lead to teeth clenching, shakiness, dry mouth, nausea, and cramping.

Not much is known about the long-term effects of taking Ecstasy, although there is some concern that it can cause liver problems and damage to the brain.
Do not combine with: MAO inhibitor antidepressants.
Addiction rating: Unknown.

b
r
a
i
n

altered states

OUT

Hallucinogenic drugs distort the perception of objective reality. Under the influence of hallucinogens, the senses of direction, distance, and time become disoriented.

There are three categories of hallucinogens: **serotonin hallucinogens** (LSD, psilocybin, mescaline, and DMT); **belladonna alkaloids** (prescription medications and jimsonweed. Jimsonweed is the active ingredient in some prescription medications for asthma and certain stomach conditions. Jimsonweed tea or seeds can cause hallucinations at dangerously high levels); **horse tranquilizers** (PCP and ketamine).

LSD (lysergic acid diethylamide)

acid trip blotter

LSD is either (1) absorbed in its liquid form onto a piece of paper (known as a blotter) or a sugar cube and chewed or (2) taken as a tablet or capsule.

Source: The lab.

Legal code: Illegal.

History: Created as a drug in the lab in 1938, it was tested as "truth serum" by the government in some experiments (these tests are described in Tom Wolfe's novel **The Electric Kool-Aid Acid Test**). Fairly quickly, the experimenters realized how damaging the drug could be. LSD went on to be used illegally and recreationally to induce hallucinations.

Effects: LSD overloads the brain's sensory switchboard, causing sensory distortions or hallucinations. Everyone who tries acid experiences this differently—it all depends on the person, the dose, and the particular situation. Significant mood swings are common. Many

people report a sense of detachment from their bodies, an intensification of colors, distortion of vision and/or hearing. Emotional effects include a heightened self-awareness and ecstatic experiences. Effects, which begin in 1/2 to 1 hour and peak in 2 to 6 hours, can last for up to 12 hours or more. LSD may produce sweating and palpitations or trigger nausea.

Risks: LSD users run the risk of having a "bad trip," most commonly experienced as acute physical and psychological anxiety—this can be a very serious and frightening experience. More seriously, while under the influence, people have experienced convulsions, coma, heart and/or lung failure, and have even died. Also, because judgment is impaired—with slowed reaction times plus visual distortions and hallucinations making even the most basic tasks difficult to impossible to perform—many people have accidentally injured or killed themselves while on LSD.

Flashbacks—visual and often frightening memories that are replayed after the trip at unpredictable times—are common among heavy users. Psychotic reactions are possible but rare.

It is fairly common for LSD to be laced with other dangerous substances, like strychnine (rat poison), PCP, or amphetamine, in which case it could be deadly or cause permanent brain damage.

Do not combine with: Anything, and never use if you're alone.

Addiction rating: Controversial: LSD is a highly potent drug that doesn't cause physical dependency but can cause psychological dependency.

Psilocybin mushrooms

'shrooms "magic" mushrooms

Mushrooms are dried and eaten whole or pulverized and mixed into drinks or food such as brownies.

Source: The mushroom family.

Legal code: Illegal.

History: Mushrooms have been around for ages and ages. Archaeologists have found sculptures of mushrooms in Central and South America from as far back as 500 B.C. Used by some Native Americans in religious rites, their use outside of that community is entirely recreational.

Effects: Immediate effects can include mild feelings of nausea and increased blood pressure, heart rate, and breathing. Overall, the effects are similar to those of LSD but usually last for 4 to 6 hours.

Risks: Though mushrooms are thought to be a "natural" alternative to LSD and other lab-produced hallucinogens, they have many of the same negative side effects, such as dangerously impaired judgment and bad trips.

A real risk is that you'll eat the wrong kind of mushroom—many species that look similar to psilocybin mushrooms are extremely dangerous and can be fatal.

Addiction rating: Low.

PCP (phencyclidine)

angel dust **ketamine** Special K

Taken as pills, snorted, smoked, or injected.

Source: The lab.

Legal code: Illegal, except by prescription for use as an anesthetic for large animals.

History: PCP was originally developed as a general anesthetic. But when a number of patients reported hallucinations and delirium, doctors stopped using it. Ketamine is now used only as a veterinary anesthetic.

Effects: Mostly taken for its euphoric effects, it also causes drunken and hallucinogenic effects as well as a numbing, dissociative high. Effects last for 4 to 6 hours, but significant amounts of the drug stay in the body for the next 2 days.

Risks: There's a serious risk of overdose, leading to seizures and comas, even death. PCP increases blood pressure and body temperature. Coordination, thought, and judgment are all compromised, if not shut down. Users become completely out of touch with their surroundings. Regular use can eventually lead to violent reactions, agitation, confusion, and communication difficulties.

Do not combine with: Alcohol or other downers—this can kill you! Eating or drinking before taking it may also induce vomiting, which can be very dangerous in a dissociative state.

Addiction rating: Unknown.

Peyote or mescaline

Dried cactus buttons eaten whole or pulverized and mixed into drink or food.

Source: A cactus that grows in northwestern Mexico.

Legal code: Illegal, except in the Native American Church.

History: Archaeologists in Central and South America have found evidence showing the use of peyote in drug rituals thousands of years ago. The use of peyote as part of the religious rituals of the Native American Church has been protected by the First Amendment.

Effects: Peyote increases blood pressure and heart rate. It can produce visual distortions and hallucinations or nausea and vomiting. Everyone's experience of this is different, depending on the person, the dose, and the particular situation. Significant mood swings are common. Many people report a sense of detachment from their bodies. Some report deeply spiritual experiences. Effects can last up to 12 hours or more.

Risks: Though peyote is thought to be a "natural" alternative to LSD and other lab-produced hallucinogens, it has many of the same negative side effects, including dangerously impaired judgment and bad trips.

Do not combine with: Stimulants.

Addiction rating: Low.

DMT (dimethyltriptamine)

yopa **cohoba**

Usually taken as tea or with marijuana.

Source: Originally from a vine, now it's created in the lab.

Legal code: Illegal.

History: DMT was used by South American natives in snuff form (either inhaled through the nose or placed between the cheek and gum).

Effects: DMT causes hallucinogenic reactions similar to those from LSD, but the effects end in less than an hour.

Risks: In addition to the same dangers as LSD, this drug carries an increased risk of anxiety attacks.

Do not combine with: Stimulants.

Addiction rating: Controversial: DMT is a highly potent drug that doesn't cause physical dependency but can cause psychological dependency.

down

Downers, or depressants, have two major effects: their sedative effects decrease anxiety and their hypnotic effects encourage sleep. Many drugs have a sedative effect at low doses and a hypnotic effect at high doses. There are two main kinds of downers. **Opiates** include opium, heroin, morphine, codeine, painkillers like Demerol and fentanyl, and methadone. Morphine, the major active ingredient in opium, is used in prescription painkillers. Codeine is a slightly milder form of morphine. Methadone, a less destructive and dangerous drug than heroin, is sometimes used to wean heroin addicts off heroin. **Sedatives** include barbiturates, quaaludes, and Valium and other benzodiazepines.

Opium

O gong Chinese molasses

Can be smoked or taken as tincture of opium.

Source: Poppy seeds.

Legal code: Illegal.

History: Since prehistoric times opium has been used in a tea made from opium poppies. It was used medicinally in the Middle East up to 4,000 years ago. Archaeologists have discovered opium pipes dating back to 1000 B.C. Between A.D. 600 and 900 opium was introduced by the Arabs to China, where it was used medicinally at first and then for pleasure, resulting in a huge number of opium addicts. China banned opium in the 1800s, causing a war with England, which had a huge opium business in China. President William Howard Taft, after he witnessed firsthand how opium destroyed China's advanced civilization, pressed Congress to pass legislation restricting narcotics—efforts that culminated, after his term in office, in the Harrison Narcotic Act of 1914. Opium has been around in the United States for hundreds of years and was available in many household medicines until it was outlawed in 1914.

Effects: Opium users describe a pleasurable rush and then a dreamy state with very low sensitivity to pain.

Risks: There's a high risk of death by overdose, even on the first try. Overdoses are more common with injection but are possible from snorting and smoking. Breathing slows, to the point where it may stop altogether. Other side effects include dry and itchy skin, pinpointed pupils, delayed periods, loss of sex drive, nausea, vomiting, and chronic constipation. Opium carries a very high risk of addiction, and withdrawal is miserable.

Do not combine with: Anything that also slows breathing, including alcohol, barbiturates, quaaludes, or Valium.

Addiction rating: High.

Heroin

smack mojo horse junk kag

Purer forms of this white powder mean that many users can now get high by snorting or smoking the drug's cooked byproducts, but the most intense high comes from injecting heroin directly into the veins (usually in the arms and legs, although necks, groins, and penises are also injected, especially if addicts overuse more accessible veins).

Source: The lab where it's created from the dried "milk" of the opium poppy plant.

Legal code: Illegal in the United States and most other countries, heroin is still used in some European countries, such as the United Kingdom, to help relieve pain in cancer patients.

History: Heroin was first developed in a lab around 100 years ago by Bayer Company scientists who were trying to make morphine more effective. Before the danger of addiction became clear, it was touted as a miracle cure—a boon in treating the effects of tuberculosis and pneumonia because of its respiratory relief and pain-killing properties.

Effects: Users report a pleasurable rush of drowsy, warm euphoria and then a dreamy state with very low sensitivity to pain. It depresses the nervous system, including functions such as coughing, breathing, and heart rate. These effects are immediate if the drug is injected or smoked and take about 15 minutes if it is snorted.

Risks: There's a high risk of death by overdose, even on the first try. Overdoses are more common with injection but are possible from snorting and smoking. Heroin is highly addictive, and withdrawal is miserable.

First-time users usually don't get an immediate high—they get sick. Their noses run uncontrollably, and they get severe stomach cramps (constipation is one side effect of heroin, which is why users often become dependent on laxatives as well).

If you inject, HIV/AIDS and infectious hepatitis are big concerns. Other side effects include dry and itchy skin, pinpointed pupils, delayed periods, loss of sex drive, and chronic constipation.

It is not uncommon for heroin to be laced with quinine and other dangerous substances.

Do not combine with: Anything that also slows breathing, including alcohol, barbiturates, quaaludes, or Valium, all of which increase the chances for overdose.

Addiction rating: High.

Sedatives, barbiturates, and quaaludes

Source: The lab.

Legal code: Legal by prescription.

History: In the mid-1800s, scientists synthesized chloral hydrate, the first chemical sedative. The first barbiturate was synthesized in 1903.

Effects: Users report a decrease in anxiety level and a sense of relaxation and calm. But unexpected, unpredictable opposite effects, such as increased anxiety and hostility, are possible. At higher doses, drowsiness and loss of motor control occur.

Risks: There's a risk of overdose, with suppressed breathing or heart failure leading to death, usually when combined with other drugs, especially alcohol. Vertigo, lightheadedness, decreased memory and learning ability, and serious loss of coordination are possible. These side effects can last for a long time.

Do not combine with: Alcohol (which will dangerously impair coordination) or anything else that makes you sleepy (i.e., opiates, anesthetics, and other sedatives)—these combinations can lead to death from suppression of breathing and heart rate.

Addiction rating: Unknown.

Benzodiazepines

Found in: Valium, Xanax, Rohypnol (prescription anti-anxiety medications).

Source: The lab.

Legal code: Legal by prescription. (Mostly prescribed by doctors to treat anxiety and related disorders.)

History: Earlier sedatives synthesized by scientists were too risky to prescribe to patients because of the threat of overdose. In 1957 scientists synthesized the first benzodiazepine compound, Librium, which was heralded as a miracle cure for anxiety or depression.

Effects: Same as those for sedatives, barbiturates, and quaaludes.

Risks: Memory may be impaired for events that happen while under the influence of these drugs. Decreased learning ability, vertigo, and lightheadedness are other possible side effects. These effects can last for a long time.

Do not combine with: Alcohol (which will dangerously impair coordination) or anything else that makes you sleepy (i.e., opiates, anesthetics, and other sedatives)—these combinations can lead to death from suppression of breathing and heart rate.

"Roofies" (Rohypnol) have been slipped into people's drinks to cause a sedative effect, earning it a reputation as "the date rape drug." Be extra alert when drinking with people you don't know very well, and watch for strange effects like dizziness and confusion after a drink.

For more on date rape, see pp. 152–53.

Addiction rating: Low.

GHB (gamma hydroxybutyrate)

Available as a colorless, odorless, salty-tasting liquid. A capful of GHB provides users with a psychedelic high.

Source: The lab.

Legal code: Illegal, except by prescription.

History: First developed in the 1980s as a surgical anesthetic, it became popular as a muscle-building and weight-loss potion shortly thereafter and was sold mostly in health food stores. It was made illegal except by prescription in 1990.

Effects: Users report a sense of relaxation and mild euphoria. GHB reduces heart rate and can cause a depressed feeling. At high-

brain

levels, it can cause sedation, nausea, muscle stiffness, and respiratory collapse.

Risks: There's a risk of overdose leading to seizures, respiratory failure, coma, and death. Less severe side effects include headache, nausea, and drowsiness.

Do not combine with: Alcohol (which heightens the chance of overdose) or other drugs that make you sleepy.

Addiction rating: Unknown.

Nitrous oxide (anesthetic)

laughing gas poppers whippets rush liquid gold

A colorless, sweet-smelling gas that is inhaled.

Source: The lab.

Legal code: Legal, it's typically used for minor oral surgery and dental work.

History: Nitrous oxide was synthesized by scientists in the late 1700s as an anesthetic and pain reliever. It was quickly named "laughing gas" and was widely used in England in a recreational way. In the 1800s dentists started using it during painful procedures.

Effects: Giddiness, a dreamy or floating sensation, and a mild, pain-free state for a few seconds, followed by drowsiness.

Risks: Lack of oxygen is a major risk. When nitrous oxide is monitored in a doctor's office as an anesthetic, it's considered a safe pharmacological agent. But the gas comes from a pressurized tank and when it's used recreationally, it's freezing and can cause frostbite of the nose, lips, and possibly the vocal cords. Other immediate effects following use include nausea, fatigue, lack of coordination, disorientation, and loss of appetite.

There is some evidence that excessive or prolonged use of nitrous oxide can also damage the central nervous system (brain and spinal cord) and bone marrow.

Do not combine with: Anything else that makes you sleepy (i.e., alcohol, opiates, sedatives, and cold medicines).

Addiction rating: Low.

Inhalants

Found in: Solvents such as paint thinner, glue, and gas as well as some paints.

Source: Carbon-based substances such as glue, gasoline, paint, paint thinner, lighter fluid, model airplane glue, varnish, and nail polish remover are sprayed into and then inhaled from a bag.

Legal code: Legal. But even though these substances are legal for their manufactured use, they are not intended for inhaling and are extremely toxic.

History: As solvent compounds became available in household products, people began experimenting with sniffing them. Gasoline inhalation became a problem with the introduction of the automobile in the early twentieth century, and glue sniffing became a problem in the 1950s.

Effects: The effects are similar to those for alcohol and nitrous oxide—instant stimulation, then drowsiness and sedation. Perceptual distortions and hallucinations have also been reported. A mild hangover-like feeling (headaches, poor concentration, possible nausea) may last for about 24 hours.

Risks: Even one-time use can lead to overdose and death from lack of oxygen or "sudden sniffing death" (thought to be a result of cardiac arrest). Suffocation is a risk typically seen among inhalant users who use bags over their heads while sniffing to prolong the high; they may end up choking on vomit. Accidents while inhaling are very frequent, due to loss of motor control. Many solvents are flammable so there is also a risk of serious burns.

Inhaling solvents can also lead to nausea, nosebleeds, involuntary passing of urine and feces, dizziness, breathing difficulty, and heart palpitations. Long-term risks include irreversible brain damage and nervous system damage.

Do not combine with: Anything else that makes you sleepy (i.e., alcohol, opiates, sedatives, and cold medicines).

Addiction rating: High.

Herbal Drugs

Herbal drugs have been increasing in popularity in the 1990s. Because they are natural, people tend to think that they are safer. In reality, herbal drugs are dangerous, primarily because they are unregulated by the Food and Drug Administration and their effects and appropriate dosages are unknown.

Ephedrine/ephedra (ma huang) is the key ingredient in Cloud 9, Herbal Ecstasy, and Ultimate Xphoria, marketed as natural high-energy boosters. It is also found in decongestants, asthma medication, herbal formulas and teas, and dietary supplements. However, dosages of ephedra are not consistent across these products, and high doses can have very serious side effects, including death. Combining ephedra with certain medications, like decongestants and MAO inhibitor antidepressants, can be fatal. Even combining it with caffeine can put a lot of stress on the heart and circulatory system.

Yohimbe (Corynanthe yohimbe), from the African tree of the same name, is another "natural" drug marketed for boosted energy and sexual performance. But its major ingredient can cause fatigue, liver damage, and skin rashes. It can also cross-react with over-the-counter products containing phenylpropanolamine, such as nasal decongestants and diet aids, leading to seizures and death.

RESOURCES

National Organizations

AlAnon/AlATeen. Support for the family of alcoholics. Check the White Pages or their websites to find a chapter near you. Website: http://www.Al-anon-Alateen.org.

Alcoholics Anonymous (AA) at http://www.aa.org and **Narcotics Anonymous (NA)** at http://www.na.org. Check the White Pages or their websites to find a chapter near you.

Alcohol/Drug Abuse Referral Hotline: 800-ALCOHOL/800-252-6465. A 24-hour hotline provides referrals to treatment facilities.

National Clearinghouse for Alcohol and Drug Information. Phone: 800-729-6686. Website: http://www.health.org.

National Council on Alcoholism & Drug Dependence (NCADD). Phone: 800-NCA-CALL. Website: http://www.ncadd.org. Provides information on counseling services for alcohol or drug abuse.

National Drug Hotline: 800-662-4357. Offers confidential information on drug or alcohol abuse, as well as referrals.

Teen Help Adolescent Resources. Phone: 800-637-0701. Website: http://www.vpp. com/teenhelp. Information about teen drug prevention programs.

National Substance Abuse Hotline: 800-DRUG-HELP. A confidential helpline.

For information on specific drugs:

Cocaine: National Hotline for Cocaine Information and Help: 800-COCAINE.

Ecstasy and other club drugs: call the Do It Now Foundation: 602-76-0599.

Marijuana: call 888-MARIJUANA.

Online

Cascade at http://www.cascade.u-net.com. Straightforward answers about drugs.

Drug Education and Awareness for Life or DEAL at http://www.deal.org is a drug awareness site for and by youth.

The Drug-Free Resource Net at http://www.drugfreeamerica.com provides complete information about drugs.

Books

Buzzed: The Straight Facts about the Most Used and Abused Drugs from Alcohol to Ecstasy by Cynthia Kuhn (Norton). Nonjudgmental exploration of drugs and what they can do to you.

For more resources and information, see http://www.dealwithit.com

brain

PART 4

life

Life: how you spend your time, what you think about, and what you do with your body, sexuality, and brain. Life is in a constant state of flux—people are constantly evolving and readjusting to new situations. It's a process that doesn't stop, no matter how old you get.

Adolescence is by definition a time of transition, so changes to yourself and the people around you may seem particularly noticeable. Relationships with family, friends, love interests, and the rest of the world can create a complicated landscape for you to navigate. Although it may have its fair share of conflict and confusion, the journey from childhood to adulthood is a pretty amazing time in which you will learn many things, including a lot about who you are and how you want to live your life.

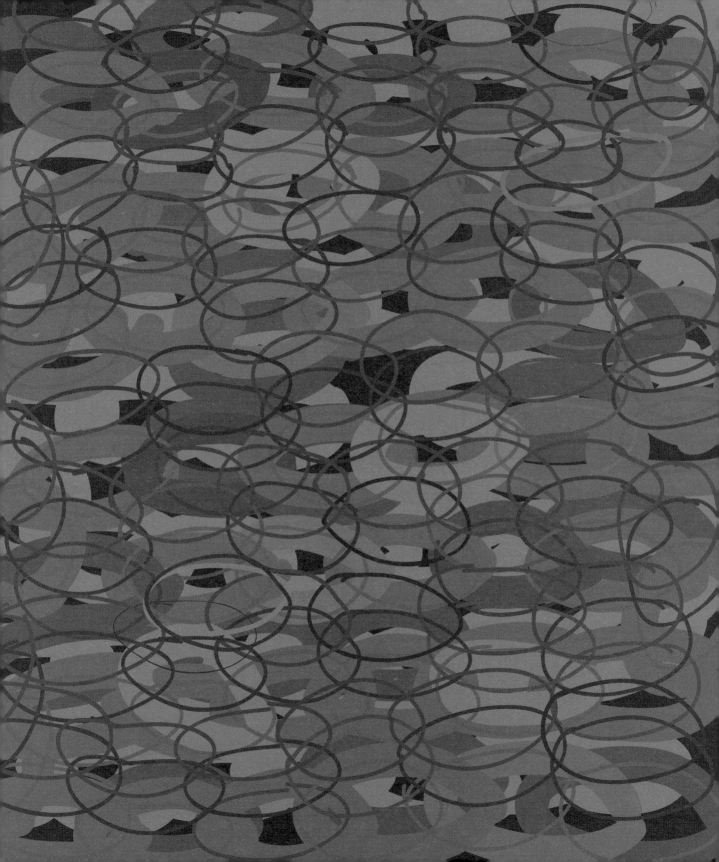

Chapter 1

FAMILY

You can pick your friends, you can pick your nose, but you can't pick your family...

Everyone has some family somewhere in the universe. Generally speaking, you're born into a family and you don't have much choice about who they are (at least until you're older).

At their best, families are a source of deep love, comfort, and support. At their worst, they're a source of great pain, frustration, disappointment, and anger. Often, they're a combination of good and bad.

As you become an independent person, you may start to see your parents (and siblings) as separate people with faults and virtues of their own. Also, seeing how other people's families function may give you perspective on your own family. You can begin to understand the ways in which you are influenced by your family, what you like and dislike about this influence, and what you want to change.

During all this, your relationship to your family may go through changes, conflict, and growth. As with any relationship, honest and open communication is crucial to getting through hard periods.

WHAT IS FAMILY?

Definitions of family range from very traditional to very broad...as do family experiences. A family can be thought of as:

- the basic unit in society, having as its nucleus two or more adults living together and cooperating in the care and rearing of their own biological or adopted children
- a group of people with common ancestry
- a group of individuals living under one roof—a household
- a group of people united by certain convictions

Whatever the definition or structure involved, every family is its own unique unit with its own unique set of relationships between people who are connected to each other in profound and intense ways.

My mom is German and my dad is African American.
So I came out mixed.

i live with my mom and an older sister. my dad died a long time ago; i don't even remember him.

My parents aren't married. They're together, just not married.

Ever since my mom and dad divorced when I was little I have lived with my dad, sister, grandma, and uncle.

I live w/ my grandparents.

my stepfather adopted me, but i'm having this problem about not knowing my real father.

My mom was with my dad for years and years, but now she's with a woman.

My mom is deceased and my dad is nowhere to be found, I don't remember even seeing his face at all. I stay with my aunt.

My parents are divorced, and I spend half the year with my mother and the other half with half-brothers, sisters, and my dad and stepmother.

PARENTS

No parent is perfect. But, in most cases, parents love you and care about you in a way that no one else in the world does, even when this isn't always clear. Relationships with parents at any age can be difficult and complicated. During the teen years, potential conflicts may be amplified by the changes teens go through.

Relationships in transition

As you become more of an independent person, you may start to see the ways in which you are different, or want to be different, from your parents. These differences (in tastes, behavior, expectations) can often become sources of conflict or embarrassment.

I am so tired of my parents expecting me to be someone I'm not. They want me to be a little prep. Plus, they hate the fact that I'm messy.
—LoisD

Emotional changes

You also may be going through emotional and physical changes in other areas of your life. Everything you're going through can have an impact on your relationships at home.

See Those Sucky Emotions, pp. 168–73.

> My mom and I have been best friends ever since I was a baby. Now I am in 10th grade and we are starting to break apart. My mom and I live alone, and it is tearing me apart. My mom says I complain way too much, and she's sick and tired of it. I don't know why I complain, it's just that I'm so pissy. Sometimes I'll just be sitting in my room and I'll start bawling because of all the emotions.
> —technicalme

PARENTAL MORTIFICATION INDEX

- **total mortification** — MOM DRIVES CARPOOL IN PAJAMAS
- **severe humiliation** — DAD WEARS AUSTRALIAN BUSH HAT CONSTANTLY
- **acute embarrassment** — DAD LAUGHS FUNNY IN FRONT OF CRUSH
- **mild distress** — MOM IS VERY LOUD

Trust

You and your parents may have different ideas about the rate at which you should achieve independence and even about what independence means. This can cause a number of different conflicts, as your parents are losing control over your life while you are trying to gain it.

The more your parents think you are able to take care of yourself in a mature, responsible fashion, the more likely they will be to allow you your freedom. Keeping your parents informed about what is going on in your life (as much as you and they will be comfortable with) can help to ease some of their fears. Simple things, like calling your parents to let them know where you are, can go a long way toward building trust. If you do something to lose their trust, the situation can become more difficult.

> my mom has NO trust whatsoever in me. so, i've lied and all that, but for over 5 months i have been a good kid. How do i earn her trust back?
> —Angelou

> My parents totally embarrass me. Whether it's my dad chasing me through Macy's or my mom talking to my dates and taking out the baby pictures, I don't know what to do. They embarrass me beyond belief! Sometimes I feel like crawling under a rock and staying there!
> —LeslieF

> The only way to earn back your parents' trust is to do exactly what you tell them you're gonna do. And maybe help around the house without being asked or get home early from a date or something. You will redeem yourself sooner or later...it just takes time.
> —AgnesV

> My mother seriously embarrasses me ALL THE TIME!!!! She'll be driving down the street and she'll suddenly start honking the horn and saying "Woohooo! Par-tay tonight! Part-ay! part-aaaaaay!!!!"
> —iridian

life

219

family

Overprotective parents

Lack of trust can play a huge role in how overprotective your parents actually act, as can cultural and religious upbringing.

> My parents are so unbelievably strict. I have a curfew for 11 o'clock! I'm 16 years old and most of my friends have a 1 a.m. or no curfew. I always have to leave before a party gets going. I've been thinking of sneaking out, but I'm really worried that my parents will find out and be really hurt.
> — **QueenH**

> I have parents who are just like that. You shouldn't sneak out because if you did get caught, they'd have a real trust issue with you. You should try to talk to them, to push your curfew to 12 or so. Don't push it too much. Tell them to give you a chance—just one. Compromise on a reasonable "punishment" if you break it. Give it a shot.
> — **stormyfriend**

> my parents are way too strict. they don't let me go out w/american people (i'm turkish), both girls and guys. i'm not allowed to go out by myself anywhere and i'm 16! i have absolutely no freedom, and i actually did try to talk, but they wouldn't listen.
> — **ellagreen**

> My mom is really nice and everything, but she is Japanese and she seems to think that raising kids the Japanese way (no makeup, no dating, and straight A's) is best. My dad agrees with her, even though he grew up in Nebraska.
> — **sigridy**

Privacy issues

Some parents are suspicious about or don't know what is going on in their children's lives and may try to find out by invading their children's privacy. This can be extremely annoying and upsetting. Invasion of privacy can cause or be caused by a serious breakdown of trust.

> My parents always look on the computer to see what sites I went to. — **iclash**

> my mom read my diary, and oooohmygod was i mad. it had stuff in there about me and some boy...and about me smoking. it really pissed her off, and she was saying stuff like "how can i trust you?" and it was like NO! how can i trust you?
> — **irridescent**

> Tell your mom that just because you're a teenager doesn't mean you don't have a right to privacy. If you can't stay composed talking, try to write her a letter, and leave it on her bed or something. She probably misses being the center of your life. — **hydrangeas**

Concerns about dating

It can be hard for parents to deal with their children getting involved in romantic, and especially sexual, relationships. Sometimes they need time to get more comfortable with the concept. Or they may have reservations about the people you're going out with and not trust you to handle yourself.

> My dad is really strict and I've been dating without his consent. This unfortunately causes problems in my relationships because I want to spend more time with the guy, but my dad won't let me. I'm about to turn 17 and he still has a problem with me dating!!??
> — **astapasta**

Concerns about friends

If your parents don't like your friends, the amount of time you spend with them, or the extent to which they influence you, this can cause conflict.

My parents make me feel guilty because they say I am never doing anything with them and I do too much with my friends!
— **reneerain**

about 2 years ago, i kinda changed the type of friends i hang out with. (i hang out with more of the "hardcore/ punk" type of people now.) my mom thinks they're really irresponsi- ble and she thinks I'll be like that. I stick up for my friends, and my mother and I end up getting into huge fights.
— **YolandaP**

you need to show your mom the good sides to your friends. tell her about how good of a friend so and so is. let her know that your friends are good people. let them get to know each other. it helps a lot! it worked w/me.
— **lowelld**

If you want your dad to loosen up, you guys should sit down and talk about what bothers him about you dating. Work out a set of compromises with him until he can feel at least a little comfortable with you dating. If he still refuses to let you date, drop the sub- ject and ask again in a few weeks. Be persistent but don't irritate him with stuff like "Everyone else's parents don't care. You are so unfair."
— **lilpetiteamie**

Parents and sexuality

It can be awkward to come face to face with the fact that your parents, like every- one else, are sexual beings with their own sexual lives and desires. The things you hear, see, or read may be embarrassing or traumatic and may force you to think about parts of your parents' personalities that you never had to consider before.

ATTENTION!
ATTENTION! The other night I was home and suddenly I heard weird noises coming from my mom's room. I went over and found her masturbating. I just ran out. She saw me, of course. I don't know what to say to her. I mean, I masturbate too, but it's so embarrassing. I think I should at least tell her that I'm cool with it, but I also just want to for- get it. — **pinkfuzzy**

I read my mom's e-mail, and she sent a message to my dad and he wrote back to lube up his hard drive. Now I can't look either in the face.
— **kukicha**

my mom usually makes me leave the house when her bf comes over. one time i was home while he was here (my mom knew i was home) and i heard her moaning through the wall!!! i'm so grossed out and totally disgusted with my mom's behavior...please help me get through this!
— **SharPei**

Know what? Your mom is only human and she has needs. But (as you have already found out) you don't want to be around while she is fulfilling them! — **topiary**

l i f e

Other things you may discover can have serious consequences for your entire family. Finding out that a parent is having or has had an affair is often an awful experience, involving feelings of betrayal, anger, sadness, and confusion. It may even lead to a big crisis in your parents' marriage.

> Oh my God, I feel horrible. My hands are shaking, I'm short of breath, and I feel dizzy. I just was at our family's e-mail looking at the out messages. There was one from my mom to this guy she knows from work. It said: "What shall we do this weekend? I'll answer businesslike if the kids are home." I feel like crying, but I'm so angry. — **pfenning**

If one of your parents comes out as gay or bisexual, it can also lead to a marital crisis and will most likely force you to confront your own and other people's feelings about bi- and homosexuality.

> My mom's just come out of the closet and people who have been saying for years that she's the nicest mom, have suddenly changed their minds! Having an opinion is great—imposing it on other people bites. Homosexuals have all the same things to deal with as heteros, and making them believe that who they love is wrong, sucks.
> — **sanddollars**

Conflict between parents

It can be really disturbing if there's conflict between your parents. (If it gets physically abusive, let someone else know ASAP.) Ideally, your parents' arguments should remain directed at and focused on each other. Unfortunately, sometimes the conflicts may grow to involve the rest of the family.

> I WISH my parents were getting divorced. All they do is fight! I can't sleep at night, and when I do I'm crying myself to sleep. I haven't told ANYONE that my parents hate each other. It sucks. They want a divorce, but they're staying together for me. They say that they want me to have 2 parents till I graduate from high school. — **hometowngirl**

> my parents have been seriously arguing off and on for about 6 years now, and every time they get in a fight, my mom swears that she's taking me and we're moving back to California. i want to go, but then i feel bad for wanting to leave my dad. they eventually make up, though, and then she doesn't want to move back...i can't take all this back and forth! i just want a stable, constant family life where i don't have to worry about what's going to happen the next day!
> — **Florenze**

Divorce

Divorce is really the breakup of a family.

No matter how common divorce has become, it is still extremely disruptive and distressing—the events leading up to it, the whole process itself, and the inevitable changes that occur in its aftermath.

In the best divorce scenario, both of your parents, however bitterly they feel toward each other, will keep their angry feelings separate from their continuing relationships with you. Parents should not force or encourage you to take sides in the conflict and should know better than to bad-mouth each other. Unfortunately, it does not always work out this way.

Family or individual therapy is often a good idea during or after a divorce because it can help you to make sense of your family's breakup, its aftermath, and your feelings.

See Therapy, **p. 175,** and **Family therapy, p. 227.**

My parents are getting a divorce. It is really hard for me and sometimes I just feel like lying down and crying myself to sleep. I haven't been writing in my diary because I am afraid I would just start bawling!
— lilFrancis

My parents got a divorce because my father had an affair. I was 6 yrs old and it is only starting to hit me now, 10 yrs later. This is a big deal and should not be taken lightly. You need to find supportive people who have been in your shoes...i suggest you go to therapy.
— draconian

My parents are divorced and they won't even talk to each other. Everything my mom wants my dad to know, I have to tell him. Every time I have to go to my dad's, he starts in on my mom. Any advice on how to tell him to quit?
— claraV

I didn't tell any of my friends about my parents splitting up when it first happened. I think it was a way of pretending that they were still together and everything was ok.
— MuTea

What I do when one of my parents is ragging on the other is, I tell that parent that it really hurts when they do that because I love them both.
— Beatrix

life

Post-divorce living

Custody

Where you live after a divorce depends on a number of factors—your relationship with each parent, the circumstances of their lives, and sometimes your own input. If you decide that you are not happy with your situation, it's important to talk to everyone involved to see if change is possible.

> My parents are getting divorced, and me and my mom are moving to California. I'm kinda upset I'm gonna have to leave the friends I've had all my life. — **ciTrine**

> I live in California with my mom and it's really nice. The cool thing is, even though I miss my dad A LOT!!!!! I get to see him for a long time in the summer, and then I get to see all of my old friends too. — **superfluity**

> Since my dad left my mom, she depends on me to watch my sister and I have a lot more responsibilities. It stinks. My mom asks too much of me and I don't have time for my friends. — **Alexpixie**

> my dad has me on wednesdays and every other weekend. i hate him. he calls me a bitch and a rude little shit. both of my parents say i can't not see him. what do i do? — **redcurrant**

> I was in a similar situation before I turned 18. You have to tell your mom about the things he calls you and ask her if there is something she can do. — **PenUltimate**

Parents and other relationships

Sooner or later, many divorced parents get involved with other people. In some cases, the fact that this has already happened is the reason for the divorce.

You may feel a whole range of different emotions about the situation, from anger to sadness to relief.

> My parents just recently got a divorce. And my mom has gone weird. She has started going out on dates almost every night. She has about 4 boyfriends. I don't think that this is why they got divorced. I don't know what to tell her or do... — **sneekypete**

> My mom is dating this guy I really hate. He tries to be my dad and HE'S NOT. It makes me so mad that she puts him before me. Always it's..."I'll be in late tonight because of Jack." It ticks me off and I don't know what to do. I cry every night because I feel like I don't have a mom anymore. It hurts me that she used to ask for advice and she used to care about my opinions and thoughts, but now it's Jack this and Jack that. Ooooooooooo I hate that jerk. — **suKii**

Stepparents

One or both of your parents may remarry, which will leave you with a stepparent and possibly an entire stepfamily. Relationships with stepparents can often be very difficult and complex and can bring up feelings of wariness, anger, and guilt.

Seeing your parent relate to a new spouse can be a very jarring experience, especially if his or her behavior is noticeably different from the way it was with your other parent.

Learning to deal (if not live) with "steps" is a process that will most likely involve conflict, transitions, adjustments, and hopefully, a certain level of acceptance and respect on everyone's part. Usually, things can settle over time.

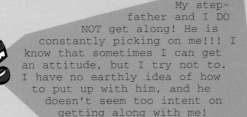

My step-father and I DO NOT get along! He is constantly picking on me!!! I know that sometimes I can get an attitude, but I try not to. I have no earthly idea of how to put up with him, and he doesn't seem too intent on getting along with me!
— **amatrix**

My dad just died and mom got remarried. It hurts my feelings about my dad being forgotten by my mother, plus the man she married is always rude to me. He says I have a bad attitude and has also turned my mom against me.
— **petitedeby**

My stepmom is trying a little too hard. I'm sure she is a little uncomfortable with this new situation, but she gets a little overbearing with all her niceness and concerns.
— **lakueva**

SISTERS AND BROTHERS

Sisters and brothers can be frustrating, fun, annoying, and inspiring. Learning to live with them is a process filled with ups and downs, love and hate. Conflicts arise over a number of issues.

Parental attention

Sometimes parents seem to favor certain siblings over others.

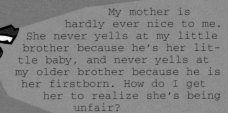

My mother is hardly ever nice to me. She never yells at my little brother because he's her little baby, and never yells at my older brother because he is her firstborn. How do I get her to realize she's being unfair?
— **bandee**

tell your mom how you feel. honesty has alwayz helped my relationship with my parents. :)
— **townes**

Troubled siblings

If your sibling is having serious troubles, emotional or otherwise, it can be very disruptive to you and your entire family.

My brother is in a depression, he drinks all the time, he smokes, and he won't talk to anyone about his problems. He has put this family through hell. My mom has pretty much had a nervous breakdown. My brother and my parents are going to counseling. I feel love for my brother and hate for his stupidity.
— **roryP**

Physical fighting

Physical fighting between siblings is pretty common, though always unpleasant. It is obviously better to try to work things out by talking to each other. Definitely let your parents know if the fighting becomes a pattern or if you feel really threatened by your sibling.

Younger and older siblings

Certain conflicts between siblings are specific to your order in the family.

if i just sit down and watch tv my younger brother will start beating me up for no apparent reason. i never fight him back cause i am afraid of him. he is really vicious. he always says, "i swear to god i am going to kill you." — **gothamgirl**

You need to tell your parents that your brother is violent and it scares you. Sounds like your brother could use therapy. — **Nadine14**

My kid sis is sooo annoying!!! She taunts my friends and says stuff about them when they are in the room. She also types in stuff when I am talking to my net pals. She has a life of her own but sheesh! Why doesn't she bug off? If this keeps up I will do something very drastic—like wrap duct tape around her mouth.

— **UrsulaH**

hey, i know what it's like...only i was the kid sister and i know what she's thinking: you are the coolest big sis that ever lived and this is the only way that she can get your attention...so what do you do? talk to your parents about it...set some boundaries. and if it's not impossible, include her sometimes. i know it's hard to compromise, but sometimes it's the only thing that works.
— **juliejr**

Sometimes I feel so suffocated when my sister's around!! All through school she was the straight A student. When I got to high school, the teachers would all smile at me and say, "You're Lizzie's sister aren't you?" They think I'll be a genius like her too. I'm not. I'm kind of average. — **frixx**

i have an older sister: she is 16 and i am 13!! sometimes we get along ok, but my problem is ever since she got her license she has been threatening not to take me places and stuff when she promised!!! it's really annoying because she can go wherever she wants and i have to find a ride, so i usually have to just stay at home!!! it sux so much!! what should i do?
— **irisM**

getting your license is a big ass deal...believe me...and sometimes older sisters don't want to be dragging their little siblings around, especially since they just turned 16. you can't expect so much. she has a life too, remember?
— **glittergurly**

226

DEALING WITH FAMILY CONFLICTS

Everybody deals with family conflict differently, depending on the personalities of family members and the situation that is causing trouble. Honesty and open communication are essential to finding a constructive way out of conflict.

Family therapy

If conflicts become chronic or out of control or there is a serious family crisis, individual or family therapy (or a combination of the two) is a good option.

See Therapy, p. 175.

Family therapy is a series of group therapy sessions with members of your family. The goal is to improve communication, reduce conflict, and change the way family members respond to one another.

Serious family issues

There are certain family situations that are particularly disruptive and can have very serious consequences for your family and your own life. Besides divorce, these include addiction, abuse, chronic illness, and death.

For more on Divorce, see p. 223.

Often, one difficult situation can lead to another (e.g., addiction leads to abuse leads to divorce...), so that some families are dealing with what feels like an overwhelming combination of challenges. If your family is experiencing hard times, life can be very tough. You may feel isolated, angry, depressed, and powerless over your environment. Different people have different reactions to these situations, and there is no single right way to handle painful circumstances.

When situations are as serious as these, it always helps to talk to people who can understand your difficulties. Talking about feelings with an adult you trust or with a therapist can help them to seem more manageable. Also, many schools and family agencies have groups for kids whose parents have divorced or died or are addicted to drugs. Keeping your feelings inside and not discussing them with anyone is generally not a good option.

See Resources, pp. 230–31.

Addiction in the family

If your parent (or sibling) is an addict, you may feel a combination of many different emotions—disgust, confusion, powerlessness, shame, anger, resentment, guilt, depression, fear, disappointment.

Parents who are severe substance abusers cannot be good parents almost by definition. You may end up taking on a lot of the responsibilities at home and possibly becoming their caretaker.

yeesh.
this past april
i moved into my
dad's place cuz i was
massively down on life, and my
mom was drinking more than usual
(if that's even possible). at my
dad's, it was gr8 cuz i could
just relax, and he NEVER
drank, and he let me get
a job.
— **miNimouse**

My dad
and I have
never gotten along.
All that I can remember is
the millions of times that he
has gotten drunk, and the results of
each. My mom went on vacation last
year for two weeks. Within that
period, my dad got drunk every night.
I was slammed up against walls, and I
even walked out of the house. I can't
stand him!!!!! He is making my
life a living hell.
— **randomqueen**

family

Their addiction may make them behave inappropriately, neglect their responsibilities, lose control, say incredibly hurtful things, and lash out. They may not remember it afterward, but you will. Physical abuse is often linked with substance abuse.

Once you understand that someone in your family is an addict (not an easy realization to face), your main concern has to be to take care of yourself. While you can try to express your concerns and feelings directly to the abuser, you probably already know that you won't be able to make a parent or sibling change until she or he is ready to admit that there is a problem.

It is important to recognize that the addiction is not your fault. But it is also important to deal with the addiction's effects on you sooner rather than later. Children of substance abusers are 50 percent more likely to hook up with an addict as an adult. Many more (70 percent) develop compulsive behavior patterns, such as alcohol or other drug abuse and/or overeating. There are many good support groups out there where you can meet other teens in the same situation and begin to get some perspective on what you're going through.

See Addiction, pp. 200–201, and Substance abuse Resources, p. 231.

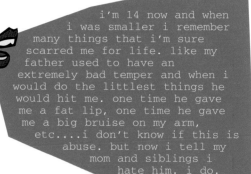

i'm 14 now and when i was smaller i remember many things that i'm sure scarred me for life. like my father used to have an extremely bad temper and when i would do the littlest things he would hit me. one time he gave me a fat lip, one time he gave me a big bruise on my arm, etc....i don't know if this is abuse. but now i tell my mom and siblings i hate him. i do.
— LaKeisha

I'm really sorry you're having to go through this. What your dad has done is definitely abuse. Go to a school counselor or a teacher you can trust. I'm sure that they will be glad to help you because something is definitely wrong when you feel hate for someone who is responsible for bringing you into this world!
— Xtraphat

A couple of months ago my dad got really drunk and he hit my mom and me. That was the first time it had ever happened and I doubt it will ever happen again. Since then, though, the whole bond between me and my dad is gone. He never even apologized or said anything about it and now I don't really feel like I want him in my life anymore.
— mezzaluna

Abuse

Abuse of all kinds—physical, emotional, and sexual—can occur between a parent and a child, between siblings, or between parents.

Physical abuse is any kind of behavior that inflicts physical pain. Most kids who are physically abused feel ashamed when others find out about it because they believe—incorrectly—that they must deserve it.

Emotional abuse can be very subtle, taking the form of repeated and severe criticism and put-downs or highly erratic behavior (loving one minute, screaming irrationally the next). It triggers the same insecurity as physical abuse—kids wrongly believe they deserve it. The damage it causes to your self-esteem can be real and lasting.

See Abuse Resources, p. 231.

228

Sexual abuse refers to any kind of sexual relationship between an adult and a child (legally defined as someone under 18). This covers any kind of sexual behavior, from kissing or petting to oral sex or actual intercourse. In general, if a girl feels strange or uncomfortable about the way she is being approached by a family member, she should trust her feelings and take action.

For more information on dealing with sexual abuse, see Incest, **p. 155.**

Illness

Having a seriously ill person in the family (or someone who's been in a severe accident or is suffering from mental illness) can cause various confusing feelings, including sadness, anger, resentment, and guilt.

Things are even harder when the ill person is a parent. People who are accustomed to thinking that their parents will always be there to take care of them have to confront the possibility that this may not be true.

There's no easy way to deal with this kind of pain and disruption to your life. It's important to acknowledge your feelings, even if they make you uncomfortable or embarrassed, and to talk to other family members about what's going on (and, if you need to, to a professional).

Death

The death of a family member changes life irrevocably. Your family structure will never be the same. When someone dies, you see how vulnerable everyone is. If your parent or someone else in your family commits suicide, this can be even more difficult to understand because there is a feeling that he or she has deliberately left you.

In addition to grief, there may be some guilt over thoughts or behavior before the parent's death. In many cases, children begin to worry about their own health, especially in those cases where the parent's death is caused by something that may be hereditary. Anxiety about this, about losing the remaining parent, about how life will be now, may preoccupy all surviving family members.

Grieving for a loved one, especially a family member, takes time, energy, and caring. Everyone grieves differently. Some people find talking to other family members helpful; others prefer being alone with their feelings.

Eventually, the intensity of the grief will subside—time really does help heal things. There will always be reminders of the death and your hurt, but there will also be good, comforting memories. As time goes on, the person you are mourning will become part of your everyday life in a new way, even though you will always miss their actual physical presence.

See Grief, pp. 171–72.

Four years ago, my mom died. It's still hard to deal with. I don't know how to handle it. My friend's mom died one year after mine did. She has a lot of problems too. Sometimes we can talk about it, other times we can't. My dad has a lot of problems too. He doesn't know how to raise a daughter going through this stuff all on his own. My sister already was through it when my mom died. She helps a lot, but she's also going away to college.
— KatieT

A little while ago my dad died. It was the toughest thing that I have ever been through. But my life has gotten worse. My mom thinks that she can't go on without him because he was her first boyfriend and the only person she was ever with (if you know what I mean). She feels sorry for herself a lot and gets very angry so fast. If a spoon is not where it is supposed to be, she blows up at us. I know that it is very hard because she is raising 3 teenagers and a foster son who is handicapped. — Tappi

life

family

The Mourning After:
The Aftermath of a Father's Death

My father died suddenly. He hadn't been sick or anything, it just happened one day. I am sure this is the single worst thing that I have ever had to go through in my life.

Because I was the first of any of my friends to have a parent die, most of my friends had trouble knowing "the right" thing to say to me. Ironically one of the more difficult aspects of his death was dealing with the reactions of other people around me. Watching others struggle with the whole WHAT TO SAY issue was painful and uncomfortable.

The small talk was the worst. The forward questions were the best. I respected the people who had the balls to ask me forthright questions about what I was going through. Unless I said that I "didn't" want to talk about it, I probably wanted to talk...desperately. Also, much comfort came from the condolence letters I received. Mail was the only thing to look forward to in the weeks that followed. When people I rarely spoke to anymore or I barely knew wrote to me, I was really touched because it meant they went out of their way to show they cared.

Two years later I still need people to ask how I am feeling. Lots of my friends say: "Call me whenever you need to talk." But it's not like that. I am always ready and wanting to talk. It's better if someone just comes right out and says: "So, how have you been feeling about your dad lately?" That gives me an open door.

The five stages of grief

Elizabeth Kubler-Ross came up with the five stages of grief to describe the different feelings that people experience after someone close to them has died. The stages are messy and can blend together or overlap.

1. **Denial:** This isn't happening to me.
2. **Depression:** I can't believe this is happening to me.
3. **Bargaining:** What can I do to stop this from happening to me?
4. **Anger:** Why does this have to happen to me?
5. **Acceptance:** It happened and I'll live to love and lose again.

RESOURCES

General families in crisis—National Organizations

Look under Social or Human Services or Crisis Intervention in the Yellow Pages for helping agencies in your area.

American Psychological Association: 800-964-2000. Website: http://www.apa.org/psychnet.

The National Association of Social Workers can recommend a therapist. Phone: 202-408-8600. Website: http://www.naswdc.org.

Call **1-800-THERAPIST** for the largest national mental health referral organization. Phone: 800-THERAPI(ST) or 800-843-7274.

General families in crisis—Books

Codependent No More and **Beyond Codependency** by Melody Beattie (Fine Communications). A guide to understanding—and breaking—the cycle of bad family relationships.

Divorce—National Organizations

The Children's Rights Council (CRC) helps children have meaningful and continuing contact with both their parents regardless of the parents' marital status. Phone: 202-547-6227. Website: http://www.vix.com/crc.

Stepfamily Association of America offers good information, advice, and support. Phone: 800-735-0329 or 402-477-7837. Website: http://www.stefam.org.

Divorce—Online

Stepfamily Network at http://www.stepfamily.net answers questions and provides support and advice.

Divorce—Books

The Boys and Girls Book About Divorce by Richard A. Gardner (Bantam). Guide to issues that arise when parents get divorced.

Teens with Single Parents by Margaret A. Shultz (Enslow Publishers). Explores the trials of living with one parent at a time.

Substance abuse—National Organizations

Alanon/Alateen: 800-356-9996 or 800-344-2666 (meeting information line). Website: http://www.al-anon.org.

Children of Alcoholics Foundation (CoF): 800-359-2623.

National Association for Children of Alcoholics (NACoA): 888-554-COAS. Website: http://www.health.org/nacoa.

Substance abuse—Books

Different Like Me: A Book for Teens Who Worry about Their Parent's Use of Alcohol/Drugs by Evelyn Leite and P. Espelan (Johnson Institute). Advice for teens whose parents are dependent on drugs or alcohol.

Inside a Support Group: Help for Teenage Children of Alcoholics by Margi Trapani (Rosen Publishing Group). Demystifies Alateen.

It Will Never Happen to Me by Claudia Black (Ballantine Books). Helps children deal with alcoholic parents.

Abuse—National Organizations

If you've been physically or sexually abused, contact the **National Child Abuse Hot Line** (800-422-4453), or call the police (ask for the juvenile department) or talk to a trusted adult.

Boys Town National Hotline works with children and families in crisis, active 24 hours. Phone: 800-448-3000.

KID SAVE offers information and referrals to adolescents in crisis 24 hours a day. Phone: 800-543-7283.

NineLine provides national referrals for youths for drug abuse, domestic violence, and sexual abuse 24 hours a day. Phone: 800-999-9999.

Youth Crisis Hotline helps teens with family issues. Phone: 800-HIT-HOME or 800-448-4663.

Sick or deceased parents—National Organizations

CancerCare and other organizations run support groups for loved ones of victims of chronic or terminal conditions. Check the Yellow Pages under the disease for a local chapter of a disease-specific organization.

Sick or deceased parents—Books

Death is Hard to Live With by Janet Bode (Laureleaf). A guide for young people who are coping with family and peer death.

On Death and Dying by Elizabeth Kubler-Ross (Collier Books). Discusses the effects death has on people and their families.

Straight Talk About Death for Teenagers by Earl A. Grollman (Beacon Press). Suggestions from a theologian on how to deal with death.

Fiction

Bastard Out of Carolina by Dorothy Allison (Plume). A raw and emotionally moving story of abuse.

A Door Near Here by Heather Quarles (Delacorte Press). A 15-year-old cares for her alcoholic mother and family.

A Ring of Endless Light by Madeleine L'Engle (Laurel Leaf). The summer that 15-year-old Vicky's grandfather dies of leukemia.

For more resources and information, see http://www.dealwithit.com

life

family

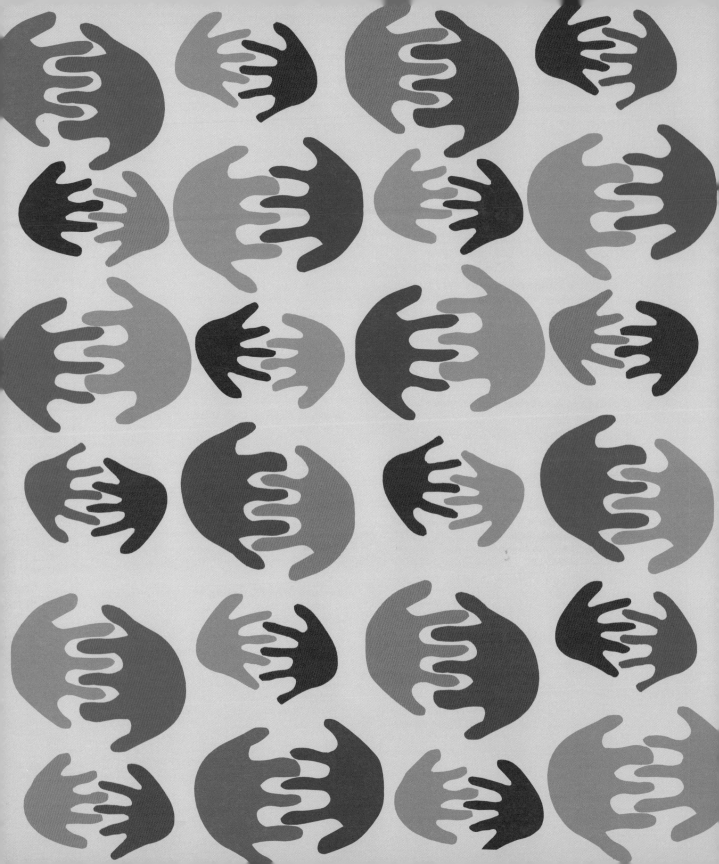

Chapter 2

Friends

As you become independent of your family, relationships with friends generally become increasingly important. They become a way to help you figure out who you are, what you're interested in, what you like and dislike, and how you relate to other people. Friends can often understand more of what you're going through than your family can because they're going through the same stuff at the same time.

No two friendships are the same. Some are casual, some are specific to a situation or activity, some are very close and deep, with all the variations in between. As with any relationship, trust and honest communication are key to a long-lasting friendship that can withstand the inevitable frustrations and conflicts that arise.

MAKING AND FINDING FRIENDS

Friends can be found almost anywhere you spend time. Circumstances or common interests bring you together with certain people. Everyone makes friends at their own pace and in their own way. Some people find it easier than others. People who are shy or self-conscious can find it difficult to open themselves up.

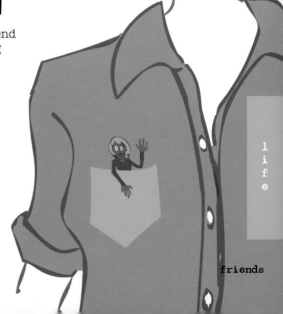

233

See Self-consciousness & shyness, p. 283.

it's already the 2nd or so month into high school and i have no friends. i didn't know anybody when i came here, and i still don't. i'm lost about making friends. — **flicka**

I know EXACTLY how you feel!!! In 9th grade, I had no friends and nothing to do at lunch so I'd just sit on the benches doing homework...sounds depressing, huh??? It was...I was really sad. Be friendly and ask people in some of your classes questions on work and then gradually ask if you can hang out with them. Try to talk about stuff besides school, too. And have fun! — **bugbutt**

i'm kinda shy when i first meet people. it takes me a bit but i start to talk a lot once you get to know me. the problem is since i'm kind of quiet, a lot of people just think that i'm really bitchy. — **yoyogirl**

Even though I have a lot of friends, I don't feel like I have anyone I can really talk to. I'm so afraid to show my deepest feelings about things because I know that then I would be vulnerable and I might get hurt by the person I tell something to. I want to have someone to talk to! I feel like my hopes and fears are about to explode out of me—I never reveal them! — **Bigkitty**

up until about a month ago, i was also afraid to really open up to ppl for fear of being vulnerable. finally i realized that if you don't open up and take the risk, you'll never be truly close to anyone. take the chance and say what you feel. if the person doesn't understand, they aren't worth keeping around anyway. :-) — **karenjr**

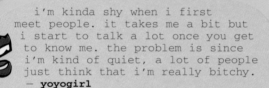

BEST FRIENDS

Everyone has a different idea of what being and having a best friend means. Sometimes a best friend can feel closer than family. Some people have a number of best friends; some have just one. Other people have no need to label one friend as best or better than another.

i really need help. my friend has been annoying me lately. she is the one that thinks i'm her best friend when i'm not. i don't think its really necessary for a person to have a best friend. — **kellylove**

Me and my friend really became close last summer. We were inseparable, and agreed on everything. But over the past year we have both changed, and we still hang out and call ourselves "best friends" but I think we both know it's not true. — **poppycorn**

COMPLICATIONS AND CONFLICT

There are many internal and external forces that can put pressure on a friendship. Withstanding conflict takes patience, trust, and communication.

Group situations

Friendships can be complicated by the fact that they often exist in a group context. When you're friends with a group of people, you have to deal with not only the ups and downs of each relationship, but also the flow of the group dynamic all at once.

i need some help. I think my friends are turning on me. i don't know what i did or why they are doing this but they just never include me in things anymore. they all go off and do things together, without me.
— TRIX

You might want to talk to all of your friends about this. Tell them how you feel about them doing things without you. Ask them why they do it.
— GaZella

When my group turned on me, I took action. I started talking to other people I wanted to be friends with. I found out that they wanted to be my friend too! I just had never seen it cause I was stuck on so few people!
— penny17

I have been in the same little group of friends for about 3 years. there are only four of us and it seems like all anybody ever wants to talk about is one of the other people. It's soooo annoying because I can't trust anyone. If you do one thing that they think is wrong or annoying, they will gang up on you. It's practically making me depressed.
— Nadine14

Peer pressure

Group situations can breed peer pressure. And sometimes it's hard to distinguish between what you really want to do, and what you think your friends want you to think or do or be.

For more on peer pressure, see **p. 288.**

Competition and jealousy

Competition and jealousy can arise between friends over many issues. People are good at different things—it can be very hard to see someone effortlessly doing something that is very difficult for you or vice versa.

See Jealousy, **p. 171.**

My friend is a good artist and pretty, but everyone thinks she is God's gift to earth. I know I should be happy for her that everyone notices her, but I feel so jealous and just in her shadow.
— maybelle

Try not to feel intimidated by your friend's talents. Be your own person, and try to be creative. Try not to make it feel like competition, though.
— vwxyz

my best friend is good at everything and all the boys i like like her. i mean, who wouldn't? she's pretty, skinny, athletic, and absolutely perfect!!!! i am so jealous! what should i do??
— drewgreen

heyyy, i used to spend all my time wondering why all the guys went after my friend instead of me, i mean, she had it all: looks, brains, personality, the works. i think it's natural to feel a little jealous of someone who apparently has it all together.
— SportyQ

My best friend gets jealous when I start spending more time with one of my other friends. I need other friends, too!
— tiziana

friends

l
i
f
e

Copycats

Friends can definitely influence each other's likes and dislikes, so a certain amount of similarity between friends is inevitable. Imitation is supposed to be flattering. However, sometimes the situation becomes extreme, and that can feel stifling.

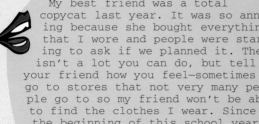

My best friend was a total copycat last year. It was so annoying because she bought everything that I wore and people were starting to ask if we planned it. There isn't a lot you can do, but tell your friend how you feel—sometimes I go to stores that not very many people go to so my friend won't be able to find the clothes I wear. Since the beginning of this school year, she hasn't really copied me. I think that talking about things helped.
— **robogrrl**

Friend or more?

If a friend starts liking you romantically (or the other way around) it can be exciting, confusing, and worrisome, especially because you can't be sure how it will affect the friendship.

I have a best friend that is a guy & I've been having feelings of more than just a friendship. I'm afraid to tell him cause I know it will ruin our friendship. I know most people would say, "Oh tell him, you'll feel better," but it will be worse. - **exercisequeen**

my best advice would be to ask the guy out, just for pizza or something. then you could casually ask him to a movie, and if he declines, don't act too bummed. some people are better off as friends. - **sugarysam**

Friends and relationships

It can feel bad when friends choose to spend time with their significant others instead of you, but it is a very common frustration. Talking to your friends about your feelings can be helpful.

lately i have been really jealous of my best friend's boyfriend. it seems that he is getting all of her time. she has even cancelled plans on me and decided to bring him w/her for plans that were supposed to be only the 2 of us. it seems like he has become everything to her and i am nothing anymore. she always says friends come first but since she has started going out w/this guy it seems she has forgotten her rule.
— **MetallicMary**

To me, friendship is extremely important and long-lasting and pure and can last forever, but going out with a guy in high school usually doesn't last forever. — **humbelina**

Betrayal

Good friendships are based in part on trust—two people opening themselves up and being vulnerable to each other. If this trust gets seriously broken, it can be very hard, though not impossible, to repair.

my best friend "accidentally" shouted out that i liked this certain guy, which was true. but it really made me mad and our friendship has only gone downward. she has apologized many times but i just don't feel that she is being sincere. also she has done this before and i trusted her not to do it again.
— **meowgirl**

See Getting involved?, p. 241.

Friends in need

Part of friendship is supporting or helping a friend when things aren't working out. It is very difficult to watch someone you care about getting hurt or harming themselves.

    If you have a friend with serious problems, it can be hard to know whether you'll be able to help on your own. If you think your friend is in danger, it's essential that you get an adult involved.

> Last year, my friend and I were totally depressed for the whole year. I don't exactly know why, but we were. Now, I'm getting better, but she's not. She's been having these dreams where she kills herself and she's even tried slashing her wrist. I think she truly wants to die. She doesn't have a great life at home and she feels like she's all alone. What can I do to snap her out of this? — **Korrie**

See Psychology, **pp. 167–81 and** Self-destructive Behavior, **pp. 183–99.**

> I know what that's like!!!! My friend did that to me and I have done it to her too. You should get her in private and tell her how you feel. I told my friend that I felt bad for telling a few of her secrets, and I was really sorry, but she needs to stop telling my secrets too. Friends shouldn't be doing that to each other. — **locoloco**

> I do fine with one rule of thumb—I NEVER EVER betray anyone by blurting out the secrets they tell me. People trust me more. — **Azura**

> Tell her that you're really worried when she talks like that. Ask if there's anything you can do to help her. Has something happened to her or her family to make her feel this way? Tell her mom or a school counselor that you're concerned. You can also call a help line or try to get her to call one if she doesn't want to talk to someone she knows. — **heliumfan**

> The thing is, no matter how damaged your friend may be, you are not a therapist and she has no right to put you in this sort of situation. She needs serious, clinical help—and you aren't the one to give it to her. You can always be there for her and help her, because that's what friends are for, but you don't have the training to truly help her. Get her to your guidance counselor FAST. — **lilbirdy**

GROWING APART

People grow and change at different rates and often in different directions. Sometimes friendships can evolve with these changes and sometimes they can't. It's always good to try to work through conflicts and misunderstandings with a close friend, but if too many bad feelings have gotten between you, it may become impossible to resolve things without first having some distance. When friendships end, whether it's the result of a big fight or just a long drifting period, it can feel extremely painful or it can seem like the right thing to do; often, it's both. In some instances, endings are not necessarily permanent. Given time, old friendships can return in new forms.

life

Chapter 3

There are many great things about being in a romantic relationship. There are also many great things about being alone. There is no right age, time, or way to become involved with somebody—the decision to be in a relationship is entirely your own.

There is a powerful myth that happiness is two people falling in love and living together forever, but most of us know that life and happiness are not as simple as that. No one can tell you exactly what love is. No two experiences of it are the same, not even to the same person. People fall in love at different times, with different people, for different reasons.

Romantic relationships may involve love, or they may not. They may involve companionship, support, intimacy, or sex. They definitely involve new and changing feelings about another person, and these feelings can often be confusing. Romantic relationships and the people in them grow and evolve over time, so it's important that both people involved communicate, trust each other, and work to resolve any problems that may arise.

BEING SINGLE

No one **needs** to have a boyfriend or girl-friend. There can be a lot of pressure from outside forces and from yourself to be in a relationship. This is true if you've never been involved with anyone or if you've had relationships but don't have one right now. At some times in your life, it may be better to be alone and open to the changes going on in yourself. Some valuable results of being single may include a sense of independence, a sense of freedom, and confidence that your happiness does not depend on somebody else.

 Is it OK to not have any boyfriends, even when you're in the 9th grade? I have tons of guys that are my friends, but no boyfriends. — **LaraC**

 i am really confused ...i haven't ever really dated anyone, and i really want to, but at the same time i do stuff to avoid guys, such as saying i already have a boyfriend.
— **teenEVE**

 I love being single! I've been boyless since last June. It's great. I don't hafta worry about my flirting habits or making someone jealous. It's the best! If I find a guy who treats me right, then maybe I'll like being taken, but until then I am "single and ready to mingle!" Rock on single ladiezzz!
— **basketballlover**

 I know not a lot of people love being single, but I just broke up w/my bf, and I can truthfully say I'M ENJOYING EVERY MINUTE OF IT. You have so much more freedom, and I never knew that so many guys liked me! It's like there's a whole new world out there. — **rodeogirl**

ATTRACTION

Why certain people are attracted to each other is sometimes obvious and sometimes completely mysterious. The factors that can play a role in the initial stages of attraction—looks, personality, interests, humor, intelligence, and chemistry, among others—are completely subjective. There are no rules of attraction. There is no list or combination of things that can be applied to a certain situation to make someone want to be with you or vice versa.

Can anyone give me some advice on how to get a boyfriend? I have never had one before and I want to start dating. — **riotrachel**

 There's no "way" to get a boyfriend, no technique or anything—it just happens. Be yourself, and don't hook up with some creep just because you want a boyfriend. Find someone who likes you for you. — **Alethea**

Crushes

Crushes can develop for lots of reasons. Some are more emotional than sexual; some are more about fantasy than reality. A crush always involves a certain amount of fantasy, since it is based on your idea of someone you like and not on a living, breathing relationship with another person. Celebrity crushes are common and strongly encouraged by the media and entertainment industries.

Crushes range from very mild to super intense. Having a huge crush on someone, especially when the reciprocity is questionable, can truly feel like being squashed like a bug.

You may want a crush to lead to something more or you may not. In either case, crushes can be an important part of the process of figuring out what you want and who you desire.

SPLAT!

Authority figure crushes

It's common for girls to develop crushes on significant adults in their lives. If the adult in question seems interested too, it can be very seductive. But the age and experience of the person you're interested in give that person a power over you that isn't healthy, no matter what you may feel. The adult is responsible for his or her actions both legally and ethically, and there can be repercussions in both areas. Understanding the power relationship and maintaining some level of distance from the situation can help you to process what's really going on.

Getting involved?

When you have a crush on someone, it can be hard to tell what that person is thinking, and it can seem to change from day to day. Trying to move from a crush phase or a friendship to a romantic relationship can be tricky and confusing.

There's this guy that I've been hanging out with, ever since he got dumped by his girlfriend. At first we were just friends, but now I'm not so sure. We hang out together when he's not working. He calls me and we end up talking for a while. We used to hang out with a whole group of people, but now we just see each other. I've had a lot of people ask if the two of us are going out, and all I can tell them is not that I know of. At first this whole thing was ok, but now it's really starting to bug me. — **marsgirl**

just bring up the subject of people asking you if you're going out and then ask him if he likes you like that. if you know him that well, then you'll know if he is lying. good luck!!! :)
— **GaZella**

Basically you know if a guy likes you, if he does just about anything to be near you, or looks at you a lot, or when you catch him looking at you—he smiles. Some guys show their attention in a different way. They try to annoy you, or make you mad, or whatever, so they can catch your attention.
— **prettysirus**

life

It can also be difficult to know what to do if you like more than one person.

there are two guys that like me. i really like both of them and i wanna go out with both of em, but i know i hafta choose one, or i will lose them both. i don't wanna hurt anyone either... — **poetrix**

Been there done that.
The first thing you need to do is think about what you like and don't like about both of them. What I ended up doing was trying to go out with both at different times and from there I had to figure out who I liked. It took time but it all worked itself out. — **luckylana**

RELATIONSHIPS

Hooking up hanging with going out seeing each other dating going steady boyfriend girlfriend

There's a certain amount of confusion that goes along with relationships. Figuring out how you feel about someone and what you really want are not simple tasks. On top of that, your feelings are likely to change over time.

If you get involved with somebody, it's a good idea to talk about what's going on and to make sure you're both comfortable with it. It can be hard to communicate when you are nervous that the other person won't feel the same way. But it's important to understand each other's expectations so you know what you are dealing with.

I have this problem that I can't keep a boyfriend. I've hurt so many guys this way. I like the guy until it starts getting serious, and then I suddenly decide that I don't like him anymore. I've never been with a guy longer than like 2 weeks. How can I fix this? Should I just swear off guys altogether so I don't hurt anymore of 'em? — **panama**

I don't see anything at all wrong with dating around. Just warn guys when you first start going out with them and tell them it's their choice to take the chance or not.
— **Peridot**

my boyfriend and i have been together 2 months and i really love the guy, but lately i can't tell what's up with him. he never calls or writes anymore, but he still says he loves me and we will never break up. he says he needs his space to get his life in check. i'm afraid he'll use it to party and never come back. — **Alexeyy**

Hey, last year, i asked my boyfriend for a little privacy too. He was just always there. Maybe your boyfriend also feels that he needs time alone with his guy friends, to talk about guy stuff and do guy things.
— **no-curfew**

There's this boy that I really like—but he is sending so many mixed messages. I am so CONFUSED. One minute he acts like he is so in love with me, the next he is a total jerk—he blows off dates, doesn't call...I don't know if I should drop him or give him a chance. We were supposed to be going together, but now I just don't know! HELLLLLP!! — **chopsticksue**

Dealing with difference

No matter who you're with, there will be differences in how the two of you do things and what you believe. Some people thrive on difference (hence the saying "opposites attract"). It's also one of the major sources of stress in relationships.

On top of everyone's basic individuality, there are some differences that can have a broader impact—culture, class, age, and disability, among others.

Cultural difference

If you choose to date someone outside your cultural background, you may encounter opposition, whether it's because of resistance to change, cultural pride, or racism.

I have grown up in a nearly all-white community for my whole life. So naturally, I like white guys (I'm black). Some guys don't have a problem dating me, but I know that most of the time if I get turned down, it's because they are a different race. I'd just like to say that I think it's okay for people of different races to go out and be happy.
— vintageme

I am white/Native American. I have gone out with Mexican guys, black guys, white guys, Native American guys, and Asian guys. I believe that it is really good to go out with people of a different race because you get to learn more about their way of thinking/lifestyles.
— Lugenia

My boyfriend is annoying, even though I love him to death. I really want to stay with him, but I think that he's too obsessed. It's really sweet, but it's starting to bother me! — jaCinth

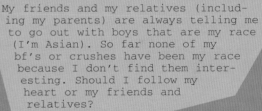

My friends and my relatives (including my parents) are always telling me to go out with boys that are my race (I'm Asian). So far none of my bf's or crushes have been my race because I don't find them interesting. Should I follow my heart or my friends and relatives?
— beepbeep

If a guy says to you "i would rather die than break up with u," does that mean he is really in love with you? Or does it mean that he is crazy?
— xylish

There is nothing wrong with interracial relationships, except that ignorant people have perception problems and can't see that we can love one another no matter what color we are. If your friends do not support your decision to date outside your race, they are not really your friends.
— naYa

I'd say it meant that he was really in love with you. But if he says, "If you break up w/ me, i'll kill myself," then he's crazy.
— kIwI_LuVer

243

Age difference: If you get involved with someone who is older (or younger) than you, it may require more patience and understanding on both of your parts. You may connect in a way that makes age seem insignificant, but it is important to remember that you are in two different places. If you are under 18, and are having sex with someone who is over 18, you may be in violation of the law.

> When I was 14, I was with a 20-year-old guy. I know, it sounds bad, and it was. He was way too pushy, and he expected WAY too much, and that was the only reason he was with me, because he wanted to be my first. As you get older, age difference doesn't matter as much as it did when you were younger. **— miasma**

Relationship issues

Real-life relationships breathe—sometimes you feel closer, sometimes you feel more distant. All relationships go through ups and downs. There are a number of things in a relationship that might cause anger, sadness, confusion, and/or conflict. In all instances, communicating about your feelings with the other person is a necessary step to getting past the problem.

Conflict
Conflict is a healthy part of relationships. It's important to air differences and resolve what might otherwise lurk and fester. People deal with fights and feelings in different ways. Finding a way of expressing your anger that you can both live with is one of the most challenging parts of a relationship. Physical fighting is never okay.

Your relationship and other people
No relationship exists in a vacuum. Friends and family affect and are affected by your romantic relationship.

Also see Parents' concerns about dating pp. 220-21, and Friends and relationships p. 236.

> Ok, I am really diggin' this guy, but he is really confusing me. One minute he wants to hold my hand and hang out, but the next minute when he's w/his friends, he doesn't even know how to say hi!
> **— farmerpatty**

> I think that guys just act different around their friends. It's not that he doesn't like you. He just maybe doesn't want his friends to tease him.
> **— springCHix**

> This is basically about your bf's own insecurities. You need to decide how much it bothers you when he doesn't acknowledge you as his gf around his friends. And, by all means, talk to him. Tell him how you feel. Hopefully, he'll understand where you're coming from. **— carolqueen**

Jealousy
Some people are just naturally more or less jealous than others. How you handle jealous feelings obviously depends on who you're with and the nature of your relationship.

> See, me and my boyfriend have been going out seriously for 4 months. We love each other a lot, and I'm a very jealous girl when it comes to him talking to other girls.
> **— sadiegirl**

Cheating

If you have an understanding that your relationship is exclusive and one of you does not respect that understanding, there has been a breach of trust and a betrayal that is potentially very harmful to the relationship. Some relationships are able to survive such betrayals without substantial destructive effect. Sometimes working through things can even help people learn to have better communication and improve their relationships. But love is built on trust, and damaged trust is difficult to repair.

> My boyfriend and I have been going out for a while now, and just recently he told me that he kissed another girl on the neck. Of course, I cried, then I forgave him. Should I just forget about him doing that and act like it wasn't a big deal? Or should I tell him it's over? Or what?
> — **bluebuggy**

> OK, he kissed another girl. Of course the natural thing to be is mad. You have two choices: either break up or talk about it. If you care for him, then you should talk to him about your feelings and his feelings. If he says he is sorry and really means it, then stay with him. But if he starts being a jerk to you, then break it off. — **iluvboston**

> my boyfriend and i have been together for a while now and i really love him. recently, i met another guy at work and we hang out once in a while. my boyfriend has been really jealous and has been giving me a hard time about seeing him and doesn't understand that I love him more than anything. how can I get him to trust me and know i wouldn't cheat on him?
> — **periwinkle**

> Tell him that you just want to be friends w/the other guy, and nothing goes on between you and him. If he loves you and you haven't done anything so far to betray his trust, then he should be able to trust you — **mica**

Sex issues

Romantic relationships often have a sexual component. Issues can come up when one person wants more physically than another. Of course, you should never do anything you are not comfortable with. And whatever you decide to do, be safe!

For more on sexual relationships, see To Do It or Not to Do It, pp. 95–101, and Protection, pp. 103–19.

> My boyfriend wants to go deeper into the relationship. He says he is sick of the making out....he wants to do more and experiment with things he has heard of. I don't know the best way to say "no" and end our 2-year relationship.
> — **HotPicante**

> i really like someone and he likes me, but there's one major problem. he has been sexually active with almost all his girlfriends. i am definitely not ready to have sex, but i don't know if he will expect me to have sex with him. he says he loves me, but i'm not sure if i should get together with him.
> — **dreamdream**

life

Abuse

Relationships take work, but overall they are supposed to feel good. If someone you're involved with consistently does things that make you feel bad about yourself or your relationship, something is wrong. You have a few options: you can try to change things, or you can end things.

It can be hard to admit that there is a problem. If you love someone, you may want to hang on, hoping that things will change. Unfortunately, however, abusive people hardly ever change no matter what promises are made.

There is never any excuse for physical violence, regardless of what you think you may have done to provoke it. When there is physical violence involved, it can be easier to realize you need to take action.

Abusive behavior also includes constant criticism, public humiliation, hurtful language, destruction of your property, and threatening behavior. If you are afraid of the person you're with, you need to get out.

my best friend & I have serious boyfriends now. my man treats me well & with respect. hers treats her like crap. he yells at her & calls her a bitch & a ho & fights with her at least 2 times a day & makes her cry & breaks up with her all the time & cheats on her. she even knows he is cheating on her. she loves him so much she just lets him do this to her.
— powerFLY

You should talk to your friend and tell her that her boyfriend is very controlling. If she doesn't get out of the relationship with him now, it's gonna be harder to end things the longer she stays with him. Tell her about abuse—physically, mentally, and emotionally. She needs your support and I know it's hard. Be a friend and stay by her side because she needs somebody to help her get through this. If you can, get her something to read (pamphlets or books) on abuse.
— glammaam

Breaking up

Feelings change over time, or problems can get worse and seem hopeless. At a certain point, it may be time for your relationship to end. Breaking up with someone is obviously different from being broken up with, but both positions are unpleasant.

Whether you are the leaver...

i finally decided that i'm gonna dump my boyfriend. i really don't wanna, cuz i know he'll be really upset, and he hasn't done anything wrong, but i just don't feel the same way towards him anymore...the prob is that i dunno how to do it...how do i get him to understand that i still wanna be friends? and i don't want him to hate me...cuz he's nice and so are all of his friends, and i sit beside him in 3 of my classes, so...what's the best way to break up with him????
— haZel88

There's no nice way to break up with someone. If you're sure, then tell him in a gentle way that you no longer have feelings for him. He may cry or scream at you. Whatever he does, just accept it as his way of dealing with having his heart broken. Don't rush him into the let's be friends thing cuz he might not be ready. Let him know that you still care for him as a friend, just not that way. — QofHearts

My b/f does drugs and drinks. The problem is he hits me and calls me names like "slut" or "whore" or even worse. Though, when he's sober and isn't on drugs, he's Prince Charming and he'll start crying when he notices all the bruises I have on me, and he promises me it won't happen again, but it does.
— patientchik

For information on dealing with an abusive relationship, see p. 248.

hey guys, my b/f of 16 mo. just broke up with me and all i wanna do is cry and die. he told me he still loves me, but will never love me the same way as when we were close. I've seriously thought about just ending it all, but i'm not sure I have the guts. can anyone help me get through this?
— **platform_shoes**

WHOA BACK THE TRUCK UP HERE!!! i'm sorry but no matter how much you digged this dude, do not end it, girl!! boys come and go, and it's not the end of the world. i mean i've been dumped a few times from major relationships, and i really think that in a little while you'll get over him. yeah, the breakups were painful. but killing yourself is never the answer. you may just need some time to relax.
— **CyCy**

The aftermath

No matter how long you've been together, breakups suck—but they can spur positive change. Each relationship you're in gives you experience and helps you to understand what you want and don't want in someone else, in yourself, and in a relationship.

And then there is the post-breakup fallout, which can range from no contact at all, to staying good friends with your ex, to obsessive behavior on someone's part, to a decision by both of you to try it again. Obviously, all breakups are unique to the people involved and there is no particular way to go about things.

Recovering from a breakup

People get over breakups at different rates, depending on individual circumstances. Some people think that, no matter what, everyone goes through some form of the five stages of grief (originally identified as the emotional process we go through to deal with death). The end of a relationship can be considered a kind of death.

See the five stages of grief, p. 230.

is the "ex" usually worth another try in your experience?
— **swelter**

Well, I think it depends on what the reason for the breakup was. If it was a measly little argument, maybe you should give it another shot. You probably just need some communication work. If it was something like he cheated on you, he isn't worth another try.
— **angine**

Marriage?

Legally, you can marry at 18 in most states without your parents' approval (and earlier in most states if your parents give their consent). Anyone considering the possibility of marriage should think hard about her reasons and motivations for doing so.

According to a report from the Bureau of the Census, people who get married before age 20 are more likely to get divorced than those who marry later.

Cyber romance

It can be very exciting to meet someone online. But there are a number of important things to keep in mind about being involved in a cyber romance.

1. There are predators out there. Do not give out personal information, such as your full name, address, phone number, or the name of your school.

2. Never meet someone you know online face-to-face except in a public place with other people present. Tell an adult where you will be and bring someone with you.

3. Be aware of the possibility that this person could be lying about everything. A person's online persona may have little or no basis in reality.

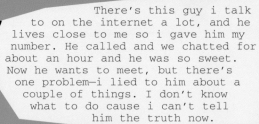

> There's this guy i talk to on the internet a lot, and he lives close to me so i gave him my number. He called and we chatted for about an hour and he was so sweet. Now he wants to meet, but there's one problem—i lied to him about a couple of things. I don't know what to do cause i can't tell him the truth now.
> — **suzxQ**

> Don't trust that this guy hasn't lied to you too. In fact I wouldn't even try to meet him. For all you know he could be a 90-year-old man. My guy friends do that all the time—they send a really hot picture of themselves and just play with people's minds.
> — **tardy_girl**

> Is it OK to have a relationship over the Net? I'm completely wigged out, but I really like this guy and he likes me too.
> — **victorialud**

> I had a problem with a guy on the internet that left me feeling the same way. See, I met someone in a chat room and we started e-mailing each other and then we started talking on the phone. We ended up telling each other that we loved each other. Then, all of a sudden, I get this e-mail from a girl saying she's his girlfriend for 2 years and they have a kid! He lied about all these things and probably lied about being in love with me.
> — **darianne**

RESOURCES

Abusive relationships

If you think that you may be in an abusive relationship, talk with a trusted adult, or call one of the hotlines on the next page. You can also go to the police or a lawyer to try and get criminal or civil restraining orders that prohibit your abuser from coming near you and/or people you live with (absolutely necessary if the abuser has threatened to kill you). You must carry the order on you all the time for it to be effective. Violating a restraining order is a crime punishable by imprisonment and/or a fine. However, enforcement can be tricky—especially if both parties go to the same school or work in the same place.

National Organizations

Boys Town National Hotline provides counseling about safety when you're in an abusive relationship and can refer you to someone for ongoing help in your area. Phone: 800-448-3000.

Domestic Violence Hotline is a hotline for dating-violence victims. Call if you think you are in an abusive relationship. Phone: 800-799-SAFE (800-799-7233).

National Coalition Against Domestic Violence (NCADV) is an activist, grassroots group seeking to end domestic violence against women and children. Address: P.O. Box 18749, Denver, CO 80218-0749. Phone: 303-839-1852. Website: http://www.webmerchants. com/ncadv/.

Online

Go Ask Alice website at http://www.goaskalice.columbia.edu answers a multitude of questions about health, dating, sexuality, drug use, depression, and more.

Teen Advice Online at http://www. teenadviceonline.org is devoted to answering teenagers' questions about a wide range of subjects.

Teen Net at http://www.teen-net.com is Teen magazine's site with lots of questions and answers about dating issues, among other topics.

Books

Changing Bodies, Changing Lives: A Book for Teens on Sex and Relationships by Ruth Bell (Times Books). A superb book covering all aspects of teen sexuality, relationships, and coping with life.

Dating Violence: True Stories of Hurt and Hope by John Hicks (Millbrook) tells the stories of teenagers involved in abusive relationships, both physical and emotional, with resources for help.

Go Ask Alice: A Guide to Good Physical, Sexual, and Emotional Health by Columbia University's Health Education Program (Henry Holt). Based on the website, the book answers questions about the whole range of health, sexuality, and emotional well-being concerns.

In Love and In Danger: A Teen's Guide to Breaking Free of Abusive Relationships by Barrie Levy (Seal Press). A guide designed to help with numerous relationship issues.

Mixed Matches: How to Create Successful Interracial, Interethnic, and Interfaith Relationships by Joel Crohn (Fawcett) discusses the difficulties in mixed relationships and talks about ways to negotiate the pitfalls.

For more resources and information, see http://www.dealwithit.com

l
i
f
e

Chapter 4

school

School is a unique universe, and it presents unique opportunities. Since it is the main place in your life where you exist independent of your family, school is where you begin to know yourself in the world—your goals, strengths, and weaknesses. It is where you start to figure out how you deal with responsibility, how you relate to other people, and even how you feel about yourself.

The universe of school can seem alternately mind-opening, oppressive, fun, traumatic, exciting, and monotonous. In any event, it is temporary. Life is much bigger than high school (or junior high). What school offers is a forum for beginning to discover and explore your interests and talents, while learning about the world outside your own reality.

TYPES OF SCHOOLS

Each type of school—public, private, coed, single-sex, boarding, homeschool—has its advantages and disadvantages, depending on your situation.

Public vs. private schools

In addition to personal preference, circumstances (such as where you live or your family's income) may determine whether you go to public or private school.

> i'm gonna be a senior next year, and i want to go to a public school. i have gone to really teeny tiny private schools (10 people in my class), so i have NO idea what a public school is like. i reeeally want to go, but i'm just kinda nervous. i guess i just want to know about public high school life.
> — **lilengine**

> Are you really sure that you want to go to a public school? I went to public school all my life up until my sophomore year, then I transferred to a private school. It was GREAT! I loved the closeness of it all. Although there are only 16 in my graduating class, we are all much like brothers and sisters.
> — **giga8pet**

Coed vs. single-sex schools

More than 95 percent of high schools are coed. But enrollment in private and religious schools for girls rose more than 15% between 1991 and 1997. Some studies have shown that single-sex schools are beneficial to girls' self-esteem and encourage girls' achievement, particularly in math and science.

Also see Self-Esteem, p. 174.

Homeschooling

More than 1 million young people in America are homeschooled. Homeschools are set up in a variety of ways, though all must work with the state's educational system. Some parents use public school curriculums and books, and others supplement or use more alternative sources, such as videos or websites.

SCHOOL SWEET SCHOOL

> I think coed schools are way better. For one: hot guyz. Also, we are going to need to interact with both sexes in our lives. We need to know what they're like, we need to be around them.
> — **mary2K**

> I'm not AGAINST coed schools, but I think single-sex schools give you a chance to learn in an environment without those oh-so-lush distractions called boys. By the time you reach college, you're a lot more mature and ready to learn without being distracted. You have all that time OUT of school to socialize with boys. — **harvesTmoon**

Homeschooling has a good side and a bad. Bad = we can't see our friends. Good = you learn more!
— **bellababy**

I'm homeschooled and I do have friends. My problem is just that I can't seem to figure out where to meet more people! I'm thinking of going back to public school once this year is over.
— **victoriousone**

I'm 16, and I've been home-schooled my whole life. I feel like I have learned a lot more things than most people my age would normally learn. For a while we were involved in homeschool support groups, and I had a lot of friends who were homeschooled too. But eventually we stopped going. To meet people, what worked for me was getting involved with just about anything. For instance, I joined the local teen leaders club at my YMCA. If there's a Y near you, then look into it.
— **denaB**

TRANSITIONS

Moving from school to school can be challenging. And changing grades can have its own related traumas, too.

 I'm going to be a freshman in September. I won't know anyone there and I'm so clueless about how to make friends cuz I've never been in a place where I didn't know anybody. I'm also kinda terrified of the whole high school experience itself.
— **T.G.I.F**

I know how hard it is to start out in a new school and not know anyone. You are probably wondering if they'll accept you for who you are. Well, try to be yourself, but keep an open mind toward the other kids and their ideas, and that will make it easier for them to accept you. But DON'T change yourself to be a little clone. Also, get involved in extracurricular activities like sports and after-school clubs and trips. It'll make meeting people who have something in common with you a lot easier.
— **astrid**

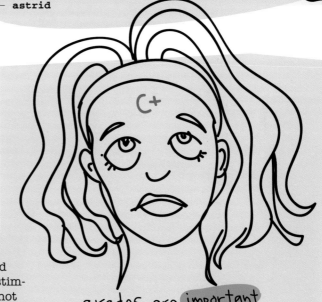

grades are important
(but they won't be tattooed on your face for the rest of your life)

ACADEMICS

In the end, school is about learning. And learning at its best can be interesting, stimulating, and mind-opening. Whether or not learning should be quantified is open to debate, but most schools do have a grading system and class rank.

Pressure!

School can be a very stressful and competitive environment. The pressure to do well, meet expectations, and make the right decisions about your future can seem overwhelming.

I feel soooooo much pressure at times that I don't know what to do. I have pressure to maintain my grades—in advanced classes. My parents don't like anything below a B. And then I have the pressure of sports. I am a starter on both the volleyball and softball teams. I have practice and then tons of homework. How do I handle the pressure, without giving up the things I love most?
— **spottieG**

I know that you have a lot of pressure and I know how it feels, but all you have to do is try your best, ok? Your parents can't yell at you if you get a B or something if you've tried your best all along. And maybe you can nicely tell your parents that you could probably perform better if they stopped pressuring you. — **GoldBeads**

I'm having mucho problems with my father. He constantly pressures me about my grades in math & science. Anything below an A- is completely unacceptable. Once I got a B+ on this science test that I studied REALLY hard for, and my father spent 3 hrs (I'm not exaggerating) yelling at me about how I don't try hard & then he grounded me for 2 weeks!— **septgirl**

I am always SO mad at myself for my grades. This time, I didn't get STRAIGHT A's like I usually do. I hate having to live up to what my brother is doing (getting straight A's ALL the time). I don't know what to do, but I HATE myself for getting lower than an A.
— **kookykate**

I didn't get straight A's, but I know that I tried my hardest. What are you more worried about, the grades or the way your brother always outdoes you? I think if you tried your hardest, you should be proud of yourself. You can't go back and change the grades you got, but you can show that you put a lot of effort into them.
— **aguana**

My mother puts so much pressure on me. I used to get straight A's, but this past year I got a C in religion and she totally freaked! This is what I told her and what I think you should tell your dad: One bad grade, possibly two aren't going to prevent me from succeeding or going to a good college, either.
— **gladyspat**

strengths & weaknesses

Obviously, everyone has academic strengths and weaknesses. Identifying your weaknesses and trying to figure out the best way to overcome or work around them is one of the main challenges of school, and every other aspect of your life. In some cases, people have learning disabilities, such as dyslexia, that make schoolwork much more problematic.

My problem is that I do really well on worksheets and assignments, but I come close to failing on the tests! I don't understand, cuz I'm an A student and I know the material almost word for word. I study for about an hour before tests!
— **smether**

I used to do pretty badly only on my tests too. I think one reason is the pressure. Also, if you practice solving problems at the end of the book or redoing homework problems you might be able to pinpoint weak spots before you take the test, so you can look out for them.
— **RaveOn57**

I have a BIG problem with grades. I've been getting C's and D's forever. I am very smart and know all the stuff—my problem is discipline. I get A's or B's on most tests. It's the homework that kills me! I get home and just blow it off, even if I have nothing else to do, and it reflects in my grades BIG TIME! — **scRawl**

See Resources for more information about learning disabilities, pp. 259–60.

I think all teachers suck and are there to be hated. I can't wait to finish school.
— **gotfreckles**

ever since i started high school (2 years ago) i've been horrible in science. i used to always get A's in science but not anymore. i just made it by in biology and chemistry, but next year i have to take physics.
— **polevaulter**

Hey, science is hard! The secret is (this earned me a 100 in biology): Do NOT be afraid to ask questions and don't stop until you understand! Who cares if people think you're dumb or slow or annoying? Where are they gonna be when you have to show your parents your report card? Where will they be when you go to college? I ask so many questions because I don't always understand everything immediately! It pays! Be confident.
— **PsandQs**

i procrastinate too. one of my teachers told me that i was the worst procrastinator she had seen in her whole teaching career. (i don't know whether to be proud or what...) i had to actually FORCE myself to do homework for at least a half hour every night. during the first few weeks it was hell on earth, but after awhile you get used to it, and it becomes easy. when that is no problem, increase the time.
— **sing-a-long**

Teachers

Teachers can really make or break a learning experience. A bad teacher can nearly ruin a subject for you and make school a miserable place. A good teacher can get you excited about something you thought you had no interest in.

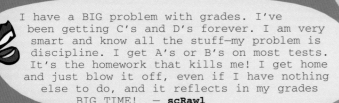

Don't preach the idea of hating teachers...they don't get paid a lot, but most of them do it for the students. I've had teachers who have changed my life. You just have to open up and find the right ones. — **ani_S**

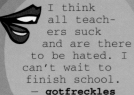

l i f e

school

I am taking first-year French and I'm not doing very well. Plus, my teacher doesn't like me and picks on me a lot. Other students have noticed it too.
— **moot-point**

I don't understand why my principal is mean. He will laugh at you if you ask him a question! Or he will make racist remarks about some people! Or he will touch your butt or your back, and it really SCARES me!
— **zoesmoey**

If you are having trouble with teachers, or they are harassing you, you MUST take it to a trustworthy authority. It may seem impossible, but your teachers have no right, whatsoever, to do anything in any way that makes you feel uncomfortable. SO please get help if you are being harassed.
— **mandycutie**

For more information about Harassment, **see pp. 147–49.**

Teacher crushes

Teacher crushes are pretty common, and they can range from minor to intense. It's easy to feel an attraction to someone who is making an impact on your life. Acting on a teacher-student crush is always inappropriate and can have serious repercussions. Teachers are legally and ethically responsible for their actions.

Also see Authority Figure Crushes, **p. 241.**

THE SOCIAL LANDSCAPE AT SCHOOL

School is a ripe breeding ground for cliques, labels, and other forms of categorization:

Brains. Jocks. Skaters. Grrls. **Druggies.** LOsers. Freaks. Sluts. Alternatives. **Nerds.** Geeks. Goths. **Straight edge.** Preps. Posers. **Punks.**

These categories can seem stereotypical, oppressive, and hurtful, or they can be a source of comfort and identity. Ultimately, cliques and labels can be limiting because they can prevent you from discovering new people, ideas, and points of view.

I am completely in love with my biology teacher. He is 41 years old, and he is not particularly attractive, yet I can't get him out of my head. This is not an obsession. This is not lust. I have never been in love before this. I am a fool for feeling this way, but I cannot help it. — **mintmilano**

my teacher is so cool! she is 28 and she is so pretty and so nice and i just watch her the whole class. i think i am in love with her! not as in "i am gay" love, but love that you have toward your mom. i think i like her so much because i have never had a true role model before. she is talented in many ways.
— **schmetterling**

i have had those kinds of crushes. by calling it a crush, i don't mean to imply that it's not love—i think in a way it is—but it probably has to do with loving the feeling of approval from authority/father-type figures.
— **manilavanila**

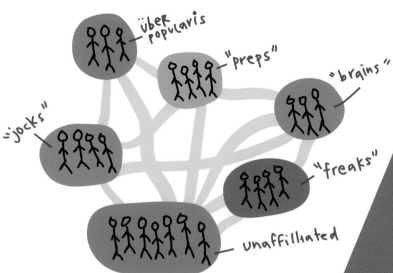

über popularis

"preps"

"brains"

"jocks"

"freaks"

unaffilliated

Popularity

Popularity is the state of being commonly liked or approved. Its pursuit can be an unavoidable aspect of school life. Wanting to be liked is definitely natural...but the popularity issue seems to go above and beyond that. It's connected to a whole host of other factors like cliques, labels, friends, peer pressure, money, and looks—just to name a few.

I am a freshman in high school and I am still good friends with my friends from elementary school and middle school, and I like them a lot, but they are so cliquey. I want to branch out and make new friends, but my friends categorize everyone (like the jocks, snobs, scrubs, and populars) and they only want me to hang out with our group.
— **greeneggs**

I have this theory about popularity. I think it's about the way a person carries herself. There's always this feeling of fear around every popular person. You feel scared to do anything against them. They're like these icons that everyone wants to be.
— **acollage**

It may be hard for some of your friends to deal with, but the best thing is just to tell them to chill out. If you talk to a different person and they ask, "Why were you talking to her?" tell them that you wanted to and that she is a pretty cool person. If they keep asking, just let them know you don't want to be limited in your friends or social skills. You do have a life ALL your own and should have some friends all your own.
— **applesaucey**

If you are happy with yourself, then you don't need to go searching for approval. I just graduated from a very cliquey high school, and I didn't belong to the most popular clique, but it didn't make me any less beautiful inside and out. It just meant that I was supposed to be friends with other people. At the same time, I know how hard it can be to be surrounded by cliques and want to fit in. — **caracara**

Why would you strive to be popular? The only way you can get everyone to like you is to be someone other than yourself. If you're not mean to anyone, and you keep an open mind, chances are more people will like you. Those who don't like you will be closed-minded people who judge by looks, clothing, race, religion...and those people aren't worth having as friends. — **shuli**

See Group situations, pp. 234–35.

See Peer Pressure, **p. 288**, and Labels, **p. 289**.

life

school

Violence in School

Ideally, school is a safe place. But, unfortunately, that's not always the case. And today, the level of violence in schools has dramatically escalated. Confrontations that once left participants battered and bruised are now ending in stab wounds, gunshots, and death.

If your school is a violent place, whether it's due to gang presence or individual acts, the environment can seem overwhelmingly negative. You may want to avoid it altogether. If switching schools is not an option, try to find positive outlets to counteract the environment—extracurricular activities, community involvement, or adults who can help you.

Even schools that have little history of violence can be vulnerable to violent outbursts from troubled students with access to weapons. If you're feeling like other students' threats or suspicious behavior could result in a serious incident, it's important to report this to school authorities.

I am having a really difficult time trying to decide between two colleges. One, my family can afford (and I'll have barely any loans); the other one is mucho more expensive and I'll have about 20 to 40 thousand in loans by the end of college. I don't want money to become the issue, but I feel it has. Also I like both schools about the same, although I like the more expensive one a little better. — **powderkeg**

See Resources for more information on finding the right college, **pp. 260–61.**

AFTER HIGH SCHOOL

It's definitely important to think about what you're going to do after high school well before you graduate.

College

Although college is not necessarily the right route for every person, it is a good idea for a lot of reasons. College:

- Is a great forum for exploring more of your interests, ideas, and opinions
- Is a good transition to adulthood and independence
- Allows you to come into contact with a lot of different people with varying backgrounds, attitudes, and beliefs
- Gives you better career prospects
- Opens doors that would otherwise remain closed

Making a decision about college can be an agonizing process. In general, it's a good idea to understand what makes one college different from another—academics, social life, size, competitive admissions, campus location, etc.—and then to figure out what you are looking for. You can do this through research and campus visits, which are particularly helpful because they give you the chance to talk to students. It also may be

First I went to a small (expensive) college that gave me a lot of money. I ended up not liking it at all and leaving (grants and everything), and going to a different (expensive) school that gave me no money. I finished with about a $15,000 debt, and it was the BEST decision i could have made. I'm not telling you to go to the expensive school, but i am telling you that you probably should not base your decision on the money. There is always a way to pay for it. — **cpcake**

helpful to talk to your guidance counselor, who theoretically should have a good base of knowledge about schools that will be appropriate for you. Even with careful consideration, some people end up dissatisfied with their college choices. In these cases, transferring to another school can be a good option.

For people who are concerned about finances, there are many opportunities available—from government subsidies to private grants—that require some research.

For financial aid resources, see pp. 260–61.

Exploring other options

If you know or think that you want to go to college, there's nothing that says you need to do it right after high school. Some people want to work for a while before they go on to more school; others are interested in exploring travel or internship opportunities.

Sometimes living in the real world, or exploring the world beyond the one you grew up in can help to clarify your interests or future goals.

For information on study abroad and internships, see p. 261.

RESOURCES

Homeschooling—Online

2Cool4School at http://www. 2cool4school.genxer.net/ is an online magazine with message boards and chats for homeschooled teens.

Homeschool Fun at http://www. homeschoolfun.com has articles, help, and message boards for homeschoolers and their parents.

Homeschool World at http://www. home-school.com contains comprehensive homeschooling information.

Teen Homeschoolers at http://www. eatbug.com/homeschool is on online magazine and site for teen homeschoolers with message boards, pen pals, chats, articles, and more.

Learning disabilities—National Organizations

Council for Exceptional Children (CEC) Division for Learning Disabilities (DLD), 1920 Association Drive, Reston, VA 22091.
Phone: 703-620-3660.
Website: http://www.cec.sped.org.

Learning Disabilities Association of America (LDA), 4156 Library Road, Pittsburgh, PA 15234.
Phone: 412-341-1515.
Website: http://www.ldanatl.org.

National Center for Learning Disabilities (NCLD), 381 Park Avenue South, Suite 1420, New York, NY 10016.
Phone: 888-575-7373.
Website: http://www.ncld.org.

Learning disabilities—Online

The Daily Diffs at http://www. dailydiffs.com/dop000.sy.htm is a great resource for news on schools and resources for students with learning disabilities.

life

The Interactive Guide to Learning Disabilities for Parents, Teachers, and Children at http://www.ldonline.org is a comprehensive resource about learning disabilities, the newest research, and relevant links.

LD Pride at http://www.ldpride.net is a resource for youths and adults with learning disabilities and attention deficit disorder.

LD Resources at http://www.ldresources.com provides information for the learning disabled, including valuable advice for selecting an appropriate college for students with a learning disability.

Teens Helping Teens at http://www.ldteens.org is by and for dyslexic teens.

Violence in school— National Organizations

National Crime Prevention Council can give you information on how to stop the violence. Address: 1700 K Street NW, Washington, DC 20006. Phone: 202-466-6272. Website: http://www.weprevent.org.

Students Against Violence Everywhere (SAVE) can help you get started mobilizing your school against gun violence. Phone: 800-789-1274.

Violence in school—Online

The Center to Prevent Handgun Violence at http://www.handguncontrol.org has information on how to combat violence.

At Peace It Together Community Center at http://phoenix.mcet.edu/peace allows you can chat with peer leaders and violence prevention agents.

College—Online

College Board at http://www.collegeboard.org is the place for online SAT registration and links to test prep materials for the SAT and other standardized tests.

College Net at http://www.collegenet.com includes financial aid information and a comprehensive college search by such categories as specific states, regions of the country, size of student body, and tuition.

College Quest at http://www.collegequest.com is the place for submitting your school application online to 1,200 different colleges.

The Educational Testing Service Network at http://www.ets.org is a gateway to definitive information about college admissions and placement tests, with links to SAT and ACT sites, as well as other educational resources.

The Financial Aid Information Page at http://www.finaid.org is a comprehensive annotated collection of information about student financial aid on the web.

Financial Aid Resource Center at http://www.theoldschool.org provides comprehensive, basic (and not so basic) directions regarding financial aid resources.

Peterson's Education Supersite at http://www.petersons.com covers a whole range of useful college information. The site also includes information on job searches, internships, and study abroad.

Project EASI—Easy Access for Students and Institutions at http://www.easi.ed.gov assists students and their families in planning for postsecondary education, choosing among alternatives, and financing these choices.

The Student Guide—Financial Aid from the U.S. Department of Education at http://www.ed.gov/prog_info/SFA/StudentGuide/ is a must for anyone planning to apply for financial aid. Order from The Federal Student Aid Information Center, P.O. Box 84, Washington, D.C. 20044 or call 800-433-3243.

Individual college handbooks are a good source of information about the schools, though they often give a rose-colored view of what's offered. The best way to really get the flavor of a place is to visit it and speak with the students there. But that isn't always practical.

Generic college guidebooks can be a good source of practical information like the size of the place, whether it's single-sex or coed (and the male-to-female ratio), what departments it excels in, if it has a strong religious or sorority emphasis, teacher-to-student ratio, if it offers much in the way of culture, how many freshmen return the following year, how diverse it is ethnically, median ACT and SAT scores, class size, cost, most popular majors, and stats on how many people apply and how many are accepted each year. Your local bookstore or library has a slew of college books, as does your school's guidance counselor office.

Two of the better college references are the **Princeton Review's Complete Book of Colleges** and the **College Entrance Examination Board's The College Handbook.**

Cash for College: The Ultimate Guide to College Scholarships by Cynthia Ruiz McKee and Phillip C. McKee, Jr. (Hearst Books) has solid information on the wide variety of financial scholarships that are available.

Directory of Financial Aid for Women 1997–1999 by Gail Ann Schlachter (Biennual). The most thorough women's financial aid resource available.

Dollars for College: The Quick Guide to Financial Aid for Women in All Fields. A 90-page booklet, revised every 12–18 months, with new listing of financial aid programs. There is a whole series of dollars for college books for a variety of fields. Available for $6.95 from Garrett Park Press, P.O. Box 190D, Garrett Park, MD 20896. Phone: 301-946-2553.

The Smart Girl's Guide to College by Christina Page (Noonday). First-hand accounts of a variety of college experiences.

Study abroad and internships—National Organizations

Your school guidance counselor and local library will have information on study-abroad programs. Your local Rotary Club may offer study-abroad fellowships (you can find its number under the Business section of the White Pages). Or call the American Field Service (800-AFS-INFO/800-237-4636) or Youth For Understanding (800-424-3691).

Study abroad and internships—Online

International Internship listings at http://jobsearch.miningco.com/msubintlint.htm is a great list of international internships and study abroad programs.

Internships Online at http://www.internjobs.com is an international database of jobs and internships.

For more resources and information, see http://www.dealwithit.com

school

life

Chapter 5

beliefs

i believe in myself!

Everybody believes in something...even if that something is nothing. Belief systems help us to make sense of ourselves and the world around us. They help us to think about the big questions—who are we? why are we here? how can we contribute? They give us a way to define ourselves, to figure out what is and isn't important to us, and they can help to provide a framework for our actions.

i believe in the power of love.

What you believe can and does change over time. Attitudes and opinions evolve as you meet new people, learn and experience new things. People's beliefs are greatly influenced by their families and upbringing. We pick up our family's attitudes and opinions, as well as those of our friends and teachers, sometimes without even realizing it. Often, the process of figuring out who you are includes questioning the beliefs you've grown up with and coming to terms with your own ideas, whether they are in sync with your family's values or not.

i believe in rock 'n roll.

i believe in one nation under God.

i believe that children are our future.

life

beliefs

jainism sikhism hinduism
buddhism catholicism
paganism shamanism
christianty islam judaism
unitarian confUcianism
taOism shintoism
quaker bahai

Religion brings up some of the biggest questions of all. Is there a God? What is God like? How did we get here? What happens when we die? The answers (or non-answers) we come up with affect our actions and attitudes toward other people, politics, and the earth, among other things.

There are so many religious and spiritual paths to go down. Some people feel comfortable with organized religions and follow just one path, whether it's a system they've grown up with or one they've chosen for themselves. Others find ideas in a variety of religions that speak to them, and they prefer to worship in individual ways. Here is a quick description of some of the world's major organized religions, their beliefs, and holy writings. This list is just a sampling of what's out there.

Judaism

Beliefs: Judaism was the first monotheistic religion, and it is the religion from which both Christianity and Islam developed. Jews believe in a single, incorporeal (bodiless) God, who is the creator of all that exists. Judaism affirms the inherent goodness of the world and everything in it as creations of God. Believers are able to sanctify their lives and draw closer to God by fulfilling mitzvahs (divine commandments). Jews believe that God monitors the activities of humans, rewarding individuals for good deeds and punishing evil. There are three main branches of Judaism today: Orthodox Jews believe that the Torah is the word of God revealed to Moses and cannot be altered. Conservative Jews believe in the sanctity of the Torah, but believe that it should be adapted to today. Reform Jews believe that the Torah was simply inspired by God, and is therefore open to more widespread interpretation. Based on these beliefs, practice and ritual by Jews differs accordingly. Jews believe that at some point in the future the Messiah (the anointed one of God) will arrive and return Jews to the land of Israel, and that there will be a general resurrection of the dead at this time.
Texts: The Tanakh (the Torah, the Prophets, and the Writings) and the Talmud (the Mishnah and the Gemara).

Buddhism

Beliefs: The Buddha's Four Noble Truths may be described (somewhat simply) as (1) suffering is universal; (2) the cause of suffering is the desire to have and control things; (3) suffering ends with the final liberation of nirvana, when the mind experiences complete freedom; and (4) the way to this enlightened state and the cessation of suffering is through an eightfold path, consisting of right views, right intention, right action, right speech, right livelihood, right effort, right mindfulness, and right concentration. Buddhists practice tolerance toward all others.

Buddhists believe in reincarnation: the concept that one is continually reborn into a new life. After going through many cycles of birth, living, and death, if one can completely release any attachment to desire and the self, one attains nirvana (and the cycles end).
Texts: About two and a half centuries after the death of the founder, Buddha, a council of Buddhist monks collected his teachings and the oral traditions of the faith into a written form called the Tripitaka. This includes a large number of discourses called sutras.

Catholicism

Beliefs: Catholics are Christians who believe that there is one God who created the universe; that the Holy Spirit is the method by which God communicates with humankind; and that Jesus Christ, God's only son, was born of a virgin, was executed by crucifixion, rose from the dead, and ascended into heaven. They also believe in original sin, as well as the forgiveness of sins and the possibility of people achieving sainthood. Catholics regard the pope as the representative of Christ, and the pope's teachings are to be obeyed. Catholics are expected to take part in various sacraments—confession, communion, and confirmation, for example. Their spiritual leaders are not allowed to marry.

Catholics believe in the resurrection of the body after death and eternal life, in heaven or hell.
Texts: The Bible.

Taoism

Beliefs: The Chinese word "tao" can be roughly translated into English as "path" or "way" (of the universe). Tao is thought to be a force that started the universe and that flows through all life. A key characteristic of this force is effortless action (taken without striving). Taoists aim for a simple life, without striving, and they believe that inner quiet is the way to understanding. They value compassion, moderation, and humility as essentials to a virtuous life. One aspect of Taoism is the belief in the harmony created by balancing opposites, expressed in the concepts of Yin (dark, female, passive) and Yang (light, masculine, active).
Texts: The most important text is Tao-te-Ching ("The Way of Power," or "The Book of the Way"). Supposedly written by Lao-Tse, it describes the nature of life, the way to peace, and how a leader should conduct his (or her) life.

Mormonism

Beliefs: Followers of the Church of Latter-day Saints are called Mormons or Latter-day Saints. They believe that their church is the true, restored church of Jesus Christ on earth, and that God still reveals himself to those seeking revelation. They practice baptism by immersion at the age of eight or older, and emphasize family solidarity. The Church officially ended the practice of polygamy in 1890. Mormons commonly act as missionaries for two years, and they are forbidden to smoke or partake of alcohol or caffeine.

Mormons often practice vicarious baptism and marriage for the dead because they believe that the gospel can be accepted even after death. They believe in an afterlife where the resurrected will be rewarded.
Texts: The Bible; the Book of Mormon, a history of the early people of the Western hemisphere which supplements the Bible and was translated by the founder of the Mormons, Joseph Smith; Doctrine and Covenants; and the Pearl of Great Price.

Protestantism

Beliefs: The Protestant Reformation was a religious revolt during the sixteenth century against the authority and doctrines of the Roman Catholic Church, and led to Christian diversity. The four major Reformation movements—Lutheranism, Calvinism, Anglicanism, and Anabaptism—led, in turn, to the development of virtually all the 1200 Protestant denominations that exist today. As a further distinction, many Anglicans or Episcopalians do not consider themselves "Protestants," but as a group in between Protestantism and Catholicism.

Protestants believe in a monolithic God; the Bible as the word of God; the Trinity of the Father, the Son, and the Holy Spirit; and Jesus' role as the Savior, including his resurrection and imminent return to earth. Protestants' spiritual leaders are allowed to marry; their leaders and members are allowed to divorce; and they do not usually believe in saints or all of the sacraments.

Protestants believe in an afterlife of heaven and hell.
Texts: The Bible.

Islam

Beliefs: Followers of Islam are called Muslims, after an Arabic word referring to those who submit themselves to the will of God (Allah). Muslims' duties, as described in the Five Pillars of Islam, are:

1. To recite at least once during their lifetime the shahadah (the creed: "There is no god but Allah and Muhammad is his Prophet"). Most Muslims repeat it at least daily.
2. To perform the salah (prayer) five times a day, facing toward Mecca.
3. To donate regularly to charity through zakat, a 2.5 percent charity tax, and through additional donations to the needy as the individual believer feels moved.
4. To fast during the month of Ramadan—believed to be the month that Muhammad received the Qur'an (Koran) from God.
5. If economically and physically possible, to make at least one hajj (pilgrimage) to Mecca.

Muslims are strict monotheists who believe that God, the creator, is just, omnipotent, and merciful. They practice abstinence from alcohol, gambling, and the eating of pork.

Muslims believe in hell (where unbelievers and sinners spend eternity) and paradise (a place of physical and spiritual pleasure, where the sinless go after death).

Texts: There are two texts: the Qur'an (Koran), the words of God; and the Hadith, collections of the sayings of Muhammad.

Hinduism

Beliefs: At the heart of Hinduism is the belief that the entire universe is one divine principle or soul "who" simultaneously is at one with the universe and transcends it. As a result, Hindus believe in the sacredness of all living things. Hundreds of Hindu gods and goddesses are worshipped as various aspects of the divine unity. Among the most important deities is a triad consisting of Brahma the Creator; Vishnu (Krishna) the Preserver; and Shiva the Destroyer. Another important figure is Kali, who is Shiva's consort and takes on both good and bad aspects, serving as both the goddess of motherhood and a fierce destroyer.

Humans are perceived as being trapped in samsara, a meaningless cycle of birth, life, death, and rebirth. Karma, the accumulated sum of one's good and bad deeds, determines how you will live your next life. The goal is, through good deeds, eventually to escape from samsara and become inseparable from the divine principle.

Texts: The Vedas, a collection of hymns and other writings, is the oldest religious scripture in the world, dating to more than 3,000 years ago.

Unitarian Universalist

Beliefs: The Unitarian Universalist Association is a liberal religious movement that accepts basic Judeo-Christian teachings and emphasizes each person's "inherent worth and dignity." Although its main source of spirituality is Christianity, it also draws from earth-centered religions (African religions and Native American spirituality, among others), Judaism, other major world religions, and humanist philosophy. Unitarians believe that spiritual enlightenment is a personal exercise based on life experience. The prime function of a congregation is to help the individual, through cooperation with others, to grow spiritually. Members are encouraged to direct their efforts toward human rights and fostering peace, liberty, and justice throughout the world.

Texts: Unitarian Universalists are generally guided by the Bible, but they also refer to the teachings of the Christian philosopher Origen (circa A.D. 185–254), the sixteenth-century Spanish theologian Michael Servetus ("On The Errors of the Trinity"), and other writers, scientists, activists, and theologians who have promoted religious tolerance.

Religious Society of Friends (Quakers)

Beliefs: Quakers rely heavily upon spiritual searching by individual members. They believe that through the "inner light," every man and woman has direct access to God (so no priests or churches are needed), and that every person is of equal worth. They are opposed to war and are involved in promoting peace. In both their services and lifestyles, Quakers stress simplicity. Quaker worship usually takes place in an unadorned "meeting house," where members sit silently, essentially meditating on God, until someone feels "moved" to speak.

Texts: Quakers follow the Christian Bible, though much of its interpretation is left up to the individual. In addition, they use Faith and Practice, a collection of readings that includes statements of belief or doctrine.

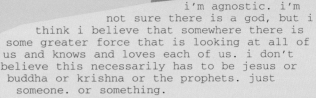

i'm agnostic. i'm not sure there is a god, but i think i believe that somewhere there is some greater force that is looking at all of us and knows and loves each of us. i don't believe this necessarily has to be jesus or buddha or krishna or the prophets. just someone. or something.
—**IamShana**

Agnosticism

Agnostics believe that God is unknowable. They cannot prove or disprove the existence of God. If you can prove it, they'll believe it. In the meantime, they'll remain open to the question of whether God exists or not and may even pray occasionally.

Atheism

Atheism literally means without any god. Having investigated the various options, atheists believe that there is no possibility of an eternal being or savior.

Wicca

Wicca, legally recognized as a religion since 1985, is based on elements of a pre-Christian religion of northern Europe.

Most Wiccans believe that a creative force—sometimes called "The One" or "The All"—exists in the universe. They regard the Goddess and the God as representing the female and male aspects of this creative force. Wiccans often meet in covens (groups), preferably outdoors. Meetings can include healing, divination, teaching, discussion, or other nature-based ceremonies, rituals, and activities. Wiccans also perform their rituals alone.

I call myself Wiccan only because i believe the basic principles—we have the responsibility to preserve nature, the earth was formed by a mother goddess, but there may be other gods and goddesses, and that magic exists within us all.
— **smoonie**

I don't believe in God. I believe that God is just a thing that humans made up to comfort them in a world full of hate.
— **Holisticgirl**

Women in religion

Many Western organized religions have recently begun to allow (if not embrace) female leaders. There are Baptist, Methodist, Presbyterian, Unitarian, and Congregationalist female ministers. There are female Episcopal bishops and Lutheran pastors. And the Reform and Conservative branches of Judaism allow women to be rabbis. Although women cannot be Roman Catholic priests, they are increasingly taking on leadership roles within the church that were previously unavailable to them.

life

beliefs

Exploring your faith

Exploring and understanding religions and beliefs different from your own can be very enlightening. It can help you to understand and respect where other people are coming from. If you find yourself interested in ideas that are at odds with or are unfamiliar to your family's, it can be awkward, though.

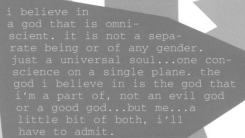

i believe in
a god that is omni-
scient. it is not a sepa-
rate being or of any gender.
just a universal soul...one conscience on a single plane. the
god i believe in is the god that
i'm a part of, not an evil god
or a good god...but me...a
little bit of both, i'll
have to admit.
— littlevera

Personally, at this
stage in my life, some of
the more modern, organized religions sound like a lot of brain-
washing to me. I don't believe
that we need one almighty
figure to tell us how we
live.
— goaliegirl

I was raised to go to
church and all of that,
but lately I just can't
understand the church's views
and I have stopped attending,
which puts stress on my family. My
mom wants me to "commit" myself
to the church, and I don't want
to. I guess what made me not like
my church was that it was putting
down other religions. I can't
understand how they can do that
when God teaches otherwise.
— pHraNC

I want to go to church and
youth group, but nobody in my
family is Christian, and it is
hard to ask them to take me.
They don't believe in God or
anything. It's pretty sad.
I don't know how to let
them know that I
really want to go.
— Sleepie

i like
to believe
for myself, mean-
ing this: i simply take
the bits i like from
whatever religion, bits
from the Bible, the medi-
tation rites of the Bud-
dhists, the symbolism of
the earth religions, and
turn it into my own per-
sonal faith. it means a
lot more than just going
and sitting on a bench
each Sunday.
— viceversa

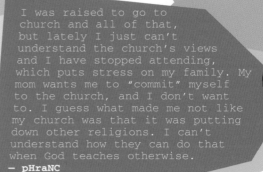

Cults
The differences between a cult and a religion are not necessarily obvious at first glance, except that cults are outside of the religious mainstream. However, this is not enough of a distinction, as many major religions began outside of the religious mainstream of their time.

Other differences are more subtle and dangerous. Cults generally seek to brainwash people into becoming members by using unethical and manipulative techniques such as purposeful misinformation, isolation from friends and family, fasting, sensory deprivation, and/or drugs to get their point across. Cults sometimes prey on college students who are away from their parents and homes for the first time and may feel isolated. Often, they ask people to make sacrifices to truly belong, like abandoning nonbelieving family members and friends and making contributions (financial) to the organization.

SPIRITUALITY

Spirituality is broader than religion in a sense. Where religion is more of a particular set of beliefs (individual or organized), spirituality has to do with the life of the spirit and the soul within each of us. And there are ways to explore this that don't involve any religion at all...

 Yoga means "to yoke" so it's a harnessing of your mind, body, and spirit. It combines deep stretching with breathing exercises and meditation.
— **JstdandY**

i used to meditate all the time—i think it's one of the best things people can do because it really deepens your mind. Meditation made me so aware of everything and so excited because it changed my outlook. i felt so open and nothing mattered except what was really important.
— **BekkaBo**

My mom and I just got back from a 45-minute walking/jogging/running thing we do every second day now. That's when I feel the most spiritual, when I'm out in nature. All I have to do is start at a steady pace, close my eyes, and just feel everything flowing in a combination that makes me fly. It's amazing. I can feel my blood pumping, my veins filling and pushing the blood, and my heart beating, the real engine beneath my strength in everything I do.
— **rrriot**

 I love candles and incense. I used to just sit in my room for hours, in the light of candles, with incense burning, just staring nowhere and thinking. It was so relaxing. I reached this point where I just...WAS. I felt so energized afterward. I realize things about myself while burning them. I just can't even begin to describe the feeling.
— **gunshy**

i view dreams as highly spiritual. i think they reveal a part of how you feel deep down. they can give you insight into what to do or how you feel about things. for me, it's similar to meditation, where you see parts of yourself that would never come out in your conscious mind. — **fastrhythm**

life

POLITICS

People's beliefs (religious and otherwise) can and do have a big impact on their politics. Many political issues raise moral questions about the way we treat each other and the world around us. The beliefs we have developed and continue to develop throughout our lives provide a framework within which we consider issues and figure out where we stand on them. Political positions are works in progress that can change and evolve over time as we encounter new ideas and learn through new experiences.

Acting on political beliefs can be an empowering and exciting process. No matter what resistance you run into and what the naysayers say, change is possible. And it has to start somewhere.

> "Never doubt that a small group of thoughtful committed citizens can change the world: indeed it's the only thing that ever has."
>
> — Margaret Mead

Student Activism

History has shown how potent student movements can be. The antiwar protests of the sixties and seventies in America, the 1968 demands for reforms in France, the attempted overthrow of the Communists in Czechoslovakia during the "Prague Spring" of 1968, the calls for democracy in Tiananmen Square in China in 1989, the 1998 protests in Cambodia, the ongoing Palestinian liberation movement—all have been fueled by students, many under 20.

There are lots of ways to act on your political beliefs, from voting and/or campaigning for candidates who agree with your positions, to boycotting companies whose policies you don't like, to becoming actively involved with causes or groups that you support. The following pages discuss some political issues that people feel strongly about. This is not an all-inclusive list. If you have strong feelings about issues that aren't addressed here, by all means figure out how to get involved!

For ideas on how to become politically active, see Resources pp. 276–79.

Abortion

People (especially women) have exceedingly strong beliefs on the subject of whether a woman legally should be allowed to terminate her own pregnancy and under what circumstances.

Those who advocate "choice" say the decision of whether or not to carry a pregnancy to term rests with each individual woman and is private in nature.

Those who oppose a woman's right to choose abortion say that abortion is murder, that human life starts at conception, and that the right of the unborn fetus to live supersedes the right of a woman to choose whether or not to carry a pregnancy to term.

Religious beliefs can play a huge role in where people stand on this issue. The Roman Catholic Church, and many other Christian fundamentalist organizations, are involved in the anti-abortion (also called "pro-life") movement. Muslims accept abortion until the 40th day of pregnancy, because Islam teaches that the fetus has not received the "breath of life" until that time. Most Jews support abortion rights—especially when the mother's health is in danger—and the Presbyterian and Unitarian churches strongly support abortion rights.

For more information on abortion, see pp. 127–28.

270

The abortion debate

Americans generally favor choice but are conflicted about it:

- **64%** say it should be legal in the first trimester.
- **26%** say it should be legal in the second.
- **13%** say it should be legal in the third.
- **50%** say they believe abortion is murder, even some people who have had abortions.

I am pro-choice. This does not mean I am an advocate of abortion, it just means that I think it should be left up to the individual. Some people are against it for religious reasons, and that's cool with me. Religion can be a very important part of one's life. But this country has something called *freedom of religion.*
— **hazelq**

Because a baby has a soul, a mind, feelings, that baby is a PERSON...and an abortion is MURDER. In Christianity, abortion is a mortal (very bad) sin, as bad as murder. Once a baby is conceived, a soul is placed there, becoming part of God's Kingdom, and you shouldn't take that away. ADOPTION is the ONLY option.
— **dogcat**

Abortion is not something that can be classified as right or wrong. I think it's your decision. Personally I know that if I got pregnant right now I would most definitely have my little butt up at the abortion clinic. BUT that's just me. It should be about what's right or wrong for me. Because in the long run it's not going to matter who said what, all that will matter is that you did what you knew you needed to do for yourself. — **ToFuLover**

Environmentalism

Many people are concerned that we do not take good enough care of our environment and that unless we conserve our natural resources, the earth will no longer be habitable for our grandchildren. Environmental issues range from protecting endangered species to fighting industrial pollution to preserving the rain forest or even your local swamp.

Animal rights

There is a long-standing debate about whether it is right to use animals for scientific experimentation or product testing, to eat animals, or to use their by-products for things like shoes.

For information on health issues related to vegetarianism, see **p. 60.**

I am a vegetarian and disagree with animal testing. People say that animals don't know what's going on, that we have to use something to test on, but to me, this seems so wrong. Animals are mortal beings just like we are. I think they have all the emotions we do. They feel fear and pain, sadness and anger. Who are we to inflict these emotions on them?
— **atallone**

I think if god (or nature) made us omnivores, that's how we should be. I don't think it's right to test stupid stuff like hairspray on animals. But if killing 1,000 rats might find a cure for cancer, then I'm for it. And if...let's say...tigers were the enlightened race, then what's not to say they wouldn't do it, too? — **merry-go-up**

271

life

Equal rights

Equal rights is the general notion that people should be treated the same regardless of sex, race, class, sexual orientation, disability, or other differences.

Women's rights

Women have truly come a long way in the United States in the last 150 years. In 1848 the first women's rights convention met in Seneca Falls, New York. About 80 women and men signed the Declaration of Sentiments (based on the Declaration of Independence) demanding equal rights for women, including the rights to vote, own property, divorce, have custody of children, go to college, work in any profession, and be considered independent people in their own right (as opposed to the property of their fathers and husbands). Now women have virtually all of these rights in the United States. Many of these changes came about because of legislation and court cases pushed by tenacious individuals and women's organizations.

Today, many of the things that advocates of women's rights fight for are quality-of-life issues: racism, pollution, poverty, health care, child care, and family leave, to name a few. There are obviously plenty of issues that women don't agree about, including abortion and women in the military. There are many organizations advocating individual positions on these and other issues.

Women of color: The history of the women's rights movement in America has often been criticized as the history of white, middle-class women's issues. In general, this is a criticism that rings true for many women of color—African-American, Asian-American, Native American, and Latina women, whose gender issues are compounded by issues of ethnicity and race.

In addition to pushing the feminist movement to address issues such as racism and violence, women of color have come together to fight for their rights as women and minorities. In 1895, 100 African-American women formed the National Federation of Afro-American Women. The group fought violence (particularly lynchings) against black men and women—and also joined the white suffragists in the battle for women's right to vote.

Rights of African-American, Latina, and other women of color have lagged behind those of white women. As recently as 1992, women were paid 71 cents for every dollar paid to men, on average. At that time, black women earned an average of 65 cents and Latinas 54 cents to the male dollar.

Civil rights

The Emancipation Proclamation of 1863 freed all American slaves. It did absolutely nothing to ensure African-Americans equal rights either under the law or in practice. The Fourteenth Amendment (passed in 1868) attempted to establish equal protection for all U.S. citizens, but it was never fully enforced. For the past 140 years African-Americans have had to fight for their civil liberties through the efforts of

272

organizations such as the NAACP (National Association for the Advancement of Colored People, founded in 1909) and the National Urban League (founded in 1911 to help southern blacks migrating to urban centers in the north).

ERA

"Equality of rights under the law shall not be denied or abridged by the United States or by any State on account of sex." The Equal Rights Amendment was orginally drafted (in a slightly different form) by Alice Paul and introduced into Congress in 1923. In 1972, it was finally passed by the Congress and sent to the states for ratification. By the end of 1973, a total of 30 states had passed the amendment and 8 more were needed to make it part of the Constitution. At that point, conservatives began a very effective propaganda campaign against the ERA, designed to play on people's irrational fears—that passage of the ERA would lead to rampant homosexuality, integrated bathrooms, the destruction of marriage as an institution, and more. The ratification period expired in 1982 and the ERA was never passed.

WE SHALL OVERCOME

Equality under the law: In 1866 Congress passed the first Civil Rights Act, guaranteeing citizenship to African-Americans. The second Civil Rights Act, enacted in 1875, recognized "the equality of all men before the law" and assigned stiff penalties for denying any citizen "full and equal enjoyment" of hotels, public transportation, theaters, and the like.

It wasn't until the 1950s, however, that the Supreme Court acted to ban segregation—in schools (in the 1954 landmark case of Brown v. Board of Education of Topeka), on buses (in 1956, largely as a result of the Montgomery bus boycott inspired by Rosa Parks), and in other public facilities (prompted by sit-ins at "white-only" lunch counters in the South in the 1960s).

In 1965, Martin Luther King, Jr., led the famous march to Selma, Alabama, to protest the denial of black voting rights in the South, and Congress passed the Voting Rights Act, but enforcement problems remained.

life

beliefs

More recent civil rights issues have included: affirmative action, the controversial practice of favoring equally qualified minority candidates in schools and in the workplace; the related issue of quota systems, legally forcing schools or corporations to admit or employ a representative number of minorities; poverty; health care; and economic empowerment. Since the 1960s, the scope of civil rights has expanded to include many different peoples—Latin-Americans, Asian-Americans, Native Americans, Arab-Americans, and so on—each group with its own struggles.

Gay rights

The twentieth century has brought cataclysmic changes in terms of the attitudes, beliefs, theories, and politics of homosexuality. Influenced by the civil rights movement, gays as a group increasingly saw themselves as a persecuted minority that needed to organize politically to gain and defend its rights. Things came to a head in 1969, when the gay liberation movement was officially born during the famous Stonewall riots, in which gay people took to the streets to protest a police raid on a gay bar in New York City's Greenwich Village.

Now quite formalized, gay rights is a political movement whose goal is equal rights for gay people under the law.

For more on gay issues, see Sexual Preference, pp. 133–45.

These rights include:

1. Protection from discrimination in the workplace.
2. Abolition of sodomy laws, which ban oral and anal sex.
3. Legally recognized domestic partnerships, in which gay spouses would receive the same benefits as heterosexual spouses.
4. Rights of gay parents to custody, visitation, and adoption.
5. Protection from hate crimes.
6. Legal protection against discrimination for people with HIV.

The struggle for gay rights is most strongly opposed by homophobic religious conservatives, who have actually organized to some degree around an anti-gay platform. The conflict between the two sides is likely to continue in a heated fashion.

Disability rights

Over the last few decades, the disability rights movement has raised awareness about the injustices faced by people with disabilities. This required the reversal of the centuries-long history of complete segregation of people with disabilities.

The disability rights movement adopted many of the strategies of the civil rights movements and gained their first large victory after a tremendous effort from The American Coalition of Citizens with Disabilities (ACCD) who staged the longest sit-in of a federal building to date. The Rehabilitation Act of 1973 states that no program receiving federal funding or assistance could deny participation to or discrimate against a disabled person.

The Americans with Disibilities Act (passed in 1990) made the accomodation of a person with a disability an issue of civil rights. The ADA prohibits discrimination on the basis of disability in employment, programs and services provided by state and local governments, goods and services provided by private companies, and commercial facilities.

Before this act was passed, a very effective national campaign was initiated to write "discrimination diaries." People with disabilities were asked to document daily instances of inaccessibility and discrimination. The diaries served not only as testimonials of discrimination, but also to raise awareness of the numerous barriers to daily living which were simply tolerated as a part of life for the disabled.

There is still a great deal of work to do in the area of disability rights—there are significant limitations of the ADA and numerous places and experiences that are not accessible to a great number of people.

RESOURCES

Religion and spirituality—Online

Finding God in Cyberspace at http://gabriel.Franunivedu/up2/fgichtm.

The Pluralism Project at http://www.fas.harvard.edu/~pluralism is a Harvard University project to document the vast religious diversity of the United States.

Research on Religion at http://www.columbia.edu/cu/religion/research.html is a fairly comprehensive list of online religious organizations.

Religion and spirituality—Books

The Hitchhiker's Guide to the Galaxy by Douglas Adams (Ballantine Books) provides (not always serious) answers to questions like Why are we born? and Why do we die?

Leaves of Grass by Walt Whitman (Bantam Classics) is a universal favorite.

Selected Writings of Ralph Waldo Emerson (Modern Library) and **The Portable Emerson** (Viking Press) provide good introductions to the transcendentalist thinking of Ralph Waldo Emerson.

Zen and the Art of Motorcycle Maintenance by Robert M. Pirsig (Bantam Books). Set as a story of a cross-country trip on a motorcycle by a father and son, it is more a journey through 2,000 years of Western philosophy.

Check out these highly accessible non-judgmental dictionaries for reliable and fair information on religious groups, figures, ideas, and rituals:

Dictionary of Cults, Sects, Religions, and the Occult by George A. Mather and Larry A. Nichols (Zondervan Publishing House).

life

beliefs

The Encyclopedia of Eastern Philosophy and Religion: Buddhism, Taoism, Zen, Hinduism by Ingrid Fischer-Schreiber, Franz-Karl Ehrhard, Kurt Friedrichs (Shambhala Publications).

The Illustrated Worlds Religions : A Guide to Our Wisdom Traditions by Huston Smith (Harper San Francisco)

The Oxford Dictionary of World Religions, edited by John Bowker (Oxford University Press).

Politics—National Organizations

To become a page, check with your guidance office for applications or contact your local congressperson online at http://www.congress.org.

National Teenage Republican Headquarters will help you get involved in Republican politics. Address: P.O. Box 1896, Manassas, VA 20108. Phone: 703-368-4214. Website: http://www.rnc.org.

Young Democrats provides information about the Democratic party and how to get involved. Address: 430 South Capitol Street SE, Washington, DC 20003. Phone: 202-863-8000. Website: http://www.democrats.org.

Politics—Online

E the People at http://www.e-thepeople.com is a free, nonpartisan service that helps you connect with over 140,000 federal, state, and local officials nationwide.

ELECnet at http://www.iupui.edu/~epackard/eleclink.html is one of the most comprehensive Internet listings of U.S. federal, state, and local elections offices with 400 links to election-related sites, including state, county, and city elections offices.

Rock the Vote at http://www.rockthevote.org is an organization dedicated to inspiring political action in teens and provides online voter registration.

ToolKit for activists at http://www.2020vision.org/tools.html is a useful site about getting your message heard.

Web White & Blue at http://www.webwhiteblue.org is the largest online public service campaign promoting the use of the Internet in democracy.

The White House Project at http://www.thewhitehouseproject.org is a group working toward establishing a balance in democracy by electing a female president.

Abortion rights—National Organizations

Feminists For Life of America believes that nonviolence (including ending what they view as the violence done to women by abortion) is one of the core principles of feminism. Address: 733 Fifteenth Street NW, Suite 1100, Washington, DC 20005. Phone: 202-737-FFLA (3352). Website: http://www.serve.com/fem4life.

National Abortion and Reproductive Rights Action League (NARAL), 1156 Fifteenth Street NW, Washington, DC 20005. Phone: 202-973-3000 or 202-973-3018 (legal, library, and information line). Website: http://www.naral.org.

Abortion rights—Online

Abortion Law Homepage at http://hometown.aol.com/abtrbng/index.htm helps people, regardless of their political beliefs, to understand the background and state of abortion law in America, and to access related legal material.

Abortion Rights Activist Page at http://www.cais.com/agm/main/ gives up-to-date information on the fight to guarantee the choice of abortion to all women.

National Right to Life at http://www.nrlc.org/ is a pro-life site.

Environmentalism—
National Organizations

Greenpeace USA is dedicated to protecting endangered species, banning the bomb, among other worthwhile causes. Address: 1436 U Street NW, Washington, DC 20009. Phone: 202-462-1177. Website: http://www.greenpeace.org.

People for the Ethical Treatment of Animals (PETA) is an animal rights organization that provides free information about protecting animal rights. Address: 501 Front Street, Norfolk, VA 23510. Phone: 757-622-7382. Website: http://www.petaonline.org.

Sierra Student Coalition is an offshoot of the Sierra Club for high school and college students. Address: 223 There Street, No. 2, Providence, RI 02906. Phone: 401-861-6012. Website: http://ssc.org.

Environmentalism—Books

The Eco-Club Environmental Activist Guide. Specifically for high school and junior high students, this comprehensive guide includes advice on recruiting members, publicizing your activities and holding productive meetings. Write: Global Response, Box 7490, Boulder, CO 80306-7490, or call 303-444-0306.

Women's rights—
National Organizations

Center for the American Woman and Politics (CAWP) provides information about women in politics and public office. Address: 90 Clifton Avenue, Rutgers University, New Brunswick, NJ 08901. Phone: 732-828-2210. Website: http://www.rci.rutgers.edu/~cawp.

The Feminist Majority provides information about the current status of women and women in politics. It also has a student internship program. Address: 1600 Wilson Boulevard, Suite 801, Arlington, VA 22209. Website: http://www.feminist.org.

The League of Women Voters is a multi-issue organization whose baseline mission is to encourage involvement in politics. Address: 1730 M Street NW, Washington, DC 20036. Phone: 202-429-1965. Website: http://www.lwv.org.

National Organization for Women (NOW) is the largest feminist organization in the United States. Address: 1000 Sixteenth Street, NW, Washington, DC 20036. Phone: 202-326-1921. Website: http://www.now.org.

Office on Civil Rights. Contact this agency if you think you are a victim of discrimination. Phone: 800-368-1019.

Women's rights—Online

Femina at http://femina.cybergrrl.com/ is a searchable database of education sites for, by and about women. Includes links to women's studies programs plus activist information.

Resources for Feminists Who Want to Get Politically Active at http://www-unix.oit.umass.edu/~emcallah links to feminist political organizations, news about current legislation, general info about American politics, instruction manuals for beginning grassroots activists, and info on how to write to your elected officials.

Women's rights—Books

Ain't I A Woman: Black Women and Feminism by Bell Hooks (South End Press) is a smart, historical treatment of race and gender politics.

In Search of Our Mother's Gardens by Alice Walker (Harcourt Brace) is a collection of essays exploring race, gender, and what it means to be human.

Outrageous Acts and Everyday Rebellions by Gloria Steinem (Henry Holt) is a collection of humorous political essays.

Timelines of American Women's History by Sue Heinemann (Perigee) is a comprehensive resource for all aspects of the U.S. women's rights movement.

l
i
f
e

beliefs

Anti-Defamation League of B'nai B'rith monitors the activities of hate groups and publishes books, bulletins, and reports on the state of race relations. Address: 823 United Nations Plaza New York, NY 10017. Phone: 212-490-2525.

National Association for the Advancement of Colored People (NAACP) is one of the nation's largest and oldest organizations dedicated to racial equality. Address: 4805 Mount Hope Drive Baltimore, MD 21215. Phone: 410-358-8900. Website: http://www.naacp.org.

National Civil Rights Musuem, located where Martin Luther King, Jr., was killed, provides an educational overview of the civil rights movement. Address: Lorraine Motel, 450 Mulberry Street, Memphis, TN 38103. Phone: 901-521-9699. Website: http://www.midsouth.rr.com/civilrights.

U.S. Commission on Civil Rights, 624 Ninth Street NW, Washington, DC 20425. Website: http://www.usccr.gov.

U.S. Department of Education Office for Civil Rights (OCR), Customer Service Team, Mary E. Switzer Building, 330 C Street, SW, Washington, DC 20202. Phone: 800-421-3481. Website: http://www.ed.gov/offices/OCR.

Finding Common Ground at http://www.enviroweb.org/fcg is a network of organizations and individuals trying to figure out how to achieve racial, sexual, and socioeconomic justice and equality as well as preserving and protecting the earth's environment and resources.

The Civil Rights Movmement: A Photographic History, 1954–68 by Steven Kasher, with a foreword by Myrlie Evers Williams (Abbeville), provides an overview of the civil rights movement through famous, moving photographs.

Eyes on the Prize: America's Civil Rights Years, 1954-1965 by Juan Williams (Penguin USA) is an oral history of the first ten years of the civil rights movement.

Parting the Waters: America in the King Years, 1954-63 by Taylor Branch (Touchstone Books) is an excellent history of the civil rights movement and its major players.

Gay & Lesbian Alliance Against Defamation (GLAAD) is a membership organization promoting fair and accurate portrayal and representation of gays and lesbians to challenge stereotypes and discrimination. Phone: 800-GAY-MEDIA (800-429-6334). Website: http://www.glaad.org.

Lambda Legal Defense and Education Fund is the most well-established advocacy and legal organization fighting for the rights of gay people and people with AIDS. Address: 120 Wall Street, Suite 1500, New York, NY 10005. Phone: 212-809-8585. Website: http://www.lambdalegal.org.

The National Center for Lesbian Rights is a legal center dedicated to advancing the rights and safety of lesbians nationwide. It provides free legal advice and counseling, among other services. Address: 870 Market Street, Suite 570, San Francisco, CA 94102. Phone: 415-392-6257. Website: http://www.nclrights.org.

Parents, Families and Friends of Lesbians and Gays offers advice, general information, support groups for friends and family, and coming-out support. Address: 1101 14th Street, NW, Suite 1030, Washington, DC 20005. Phone: 202-638-4200. Website: http://www.pflag.org.

OUTPROUD!, the National Coalition for Gay, Lesbian, Bisexual, and Transgender Youth is at http://www.outproud.org.

Disability Rights Education and Defense Fund Inc. (DREDF) at http://www.dredf.org is a national law and policy center dedicated to furthering the civil rights of people with disabilities.

National Association of Protection and Advocacy Systems at http://www.protectionandadvocacy.com/ is a federally mandated system in each state and territory which provides protection of the rights of persons with disabilities through advocacy.

U.S. Department of Justice Americans with Disabilities Act Home Page at http://www.usdoj.gov/crt/ada/adahom1.htm provides information on rights and legislation for people with disabilities.

The Council for Disability Rights at http://www.disabilityrights.org advances the rights of people with disabilities by influencing public policy and legislation and by increasing public awareness.

Disabled Peoples Direct Action Network at http://www.disrights.org campaigns for accessible public transport and full civil rights for disabled people.

disABILITY Information and Resources at http://www.eskimo.com/~jlubin/disabled.html provides links to other resources for the disabled.

The Disability Social History Project at http://www.disabilityhistory.org/ is a comprehensive look at the history of the disability rights movement.

For more resources and information, see http://www.dealwithit.com

life

beliefs

being YOURSELF

Everyone is different.

Figuring out who you want to be and how you fit into the rest of the world is not an easy task, but it is an interesting one. Your identity is a unique, complicated, ever-evolving thing that only you can define (and redefine) over time.

Every person has her own ways of defining herself. There are many different options and messages out there, telling you what to do and who to be. Family and friends may have ideas about what you should wear, like, think, or do. Or people may want to define you in a certain way based on only one or a few aspects of your life that don't reflect the sum of who you are.

It is important to explore your interests and pay attention to yourself and what feels right for you. Being true to what you want and believe in is essential to the lifelong process of becoming you.

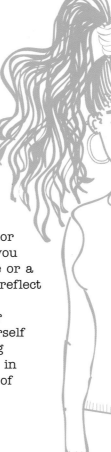

life

281

being yourself

EXPRESSING YOURSELF

A big part of being who you are is expressing yourself to other people and to the world.

There are an infinite number of ways you can do this: the stuff you get involved in (whether it's sports, arts, crafts, writing, computers, clubs, etc.), your body, your clothes, your likes, your dislikes, and more.

i'm a goth and i flaunt it.

My days are filled with writing and html coding. oh! and thinking! lots and lots of thinking!!

I am not a girl skater but I am a documenter/ commentator and huge supporter of the sport.

I love skiing, going to plays, shopping in cities, and listening to music.

I'm a walking contradiction.

I am a vegetarian rock-climber & soccer player.

I'm creative, romantic, stubborn, passionate, compassionate, and best of all...I'm WEIRD.

I guess I am pretty much a jock.

I love drawing, painting, looking at art, doodling, the works.

I do a zine, mostly because I have a lot to say.

I love, love, LOVE writing poetry.

I'm a geeky girl, who just works on the computer all day.

I am really a film lover. I want to write a screenplay before I finish high school.

Self-consciousness & shyness

It can be hard to express yourself when you are feeling overly aware of the fact that other people are watching you or judging you.

I'm always worried that I'll get embarrassed and I mean everywhere I go and everything I do. From school to the dinner table. I blush over everything!!!! If a guy talks to me I'll turn bright red, same when I have to read in class or do an oral presentation, even when I eat lunch at school. - **Hawaii50**

I used to be painfully shy. When I was a kid I'd hide when people came to the house. The only way to get over it (and YES, you can! I did) is to get out and face your fear. The more activities you are involved in, the more you have to talk about so you'll meet more people.
- **Veghead**

Being shy can be tough, but I've known a lot of people who have overcome it! It's truly, not that hard. All you need to do is face your fears. What makes you not want to say Hi to people? Maybe you should consider taking up a drama class. It'll be really hard, but kinda push you in the direction you wanna go!
- **Bettzel**

getting a job really helps boost your confidence. i was dead shy before i bagged myself a job in a shop a year ago. working with people and dealing with other people's problems really helped me get over my shyness. i am really enjoying work. the people i work with are great too. i know that this isn't going to cure your shyness just like that but it's a step in the right direction.
- **iLLuminator**

I feel for you, I really do. The first thing to do is when you're talking to a person, imagine that they're not there and think of the things you would say if you weren't shy. Just kind of pretend that you're rehearsing for a play alone in your room. Keep on doing this and sooner or later it will become so natural. The other thing to do is try to imagine that everyone you talk to is someone you've already known for a long time. - **MissV**

Experimentation

It is hard to figure out who you are without trying some things on for size.

Having an open mind about different ways of thinking and being can allow you to determine what you like and what you don't, what feels right and what feels wrong, and what combination of things will make you who you are at any given time and place.

Experimentation is a big part of understanding yourself. Testing how it feels to act or dress a certain way might give you perspective on other ways of looking at the world, even if you decide that the ideas you have been trying on are not for you.

as far as who i am? i haven't figured that out yet. all i know is that i'm confused. everything i do, say, think, wear, everything!! confuses me.
— **Ladybuggie**

Ok, I really hate my style. I wear my hair up, sometimes down if it's freshly washed and stuff. But I'm not a real prep or anything. I wear flare pants sometimes, big baggy jeans other days, dress shirts, tight sweaters...Am I the only one in here who's confused about how to decide which style to be? Or is it better to have all these different styles, which means being all kinds of different people at once?
— **myaimistrue**

STANDING OUT

Everybody stands out in some way. No matter what the distinctions—race, disability, appearance, religion, family situations, attitudes, or anything else—most people do feel different from the people around them at some point in their lives. Depending on your circumstances and the reactions of people around you, it may feel good to stand out or it may feel incredibly frustrating or embarrassing.

If you are having trouble with people accepting your difference, it can be more challenging to hold on to positive feelings about yourself. You can try to educate people so they will understand why your difference is something they should learn to accept. Or you can just decide it isn't worth your trouble to try to change someone's mind, and go about your business, comfortable with who you are. If closed-minded people can't deal with your differences, it's their problem.

When the reaction from other people is negative, it is important to let out your emotions. Anger can be useful in these cases. Even though you can't control people's stupid comments or reactions, you can learn to understand and deal with your own emotions surrounding their behavior. Talking to other people in similar situations about how they handle intolerance can be very helpful.

i've got some troubles on my mind. I'm the kind of girl who likes to play a lot of sports. i guess you could say i'm pretty strong and that's supposed to be good right? wrong! these guys would call me butch as i walked down the halls in school. at first i didn't let it bother me but then they did it everywhere i went.
— **icarius**

I know exactly what you are going through. i am into sports and i am strong too. most of the time I was stronger than the guys. they used to call me she-man, rambo, hercules, oh there were just so many things i really can't remember. it really hurt my feelings, but they really didn't give a crap. don't worry about it, they will eventually leave you alone. they stopped saying stuff to me. — **jigsaws**

I'll be 15 soon...and I don't ever want to grow up. Guys have been my only friends since 1st grade. I'm a major tomboy. Now I'm going to a new, bigger high school...how will I cope? And more importantly, does this mean I have to become a girl again? — **the_mystery**

See anger, **p. 168.**

A lot of people won't hang around me cuz i'm too "weird." What i've learned to do is say "forget you!" and it helps me get over everything. If people treat you mean just cuz you're different then just say "forget u! i don't need u!!" totally just be proud of who and what you are and other people like you will start to come around and want to be your friend. believe it or not, i think a lot of people get jealous of people like us because they are the ones who aren't brave enough or have enough confidence to be different.
— **sincerely**

I have friends and everything, but I am often right on the outside of what's going on. My real problem is my sarcasm. Lots of people don't get it, and they are intimidated by that and my grades. But you know what? Good at school and sarcastic are who I am. I like it, and my friends get used to it.
— **roBotix**

l
i
f
e

285

being yourself

Racial and cultural differences

The United States is the most culturally and racially diverse country in the world. This is one of our biggest strengths as a nation, and one of our greatest challenges.

People have varied feelings about standing out because of their ethnicity, ranging from pride to anger to isolation. When people are prejudiced or rely on cultural stereotypes to judge you, it can feel very frustrating. Fear of difference and lack of knowledge can make for a very narrow view of people with different backgrounds. Getting to know and communicating with people from other cultures is an invaluable part of being a citizen of the world. And exploring your own ethnicity can be an important part of understanding who you are.

See civil rights, pp. 272–74.

I'm Asian and it seems as though some people shun me and look down on me. There are not that many other Asians at my high school. What should I do about it? — **fun-fun**

Hey - I'm Asian, and I get some of that crap too. But you've got to hold your head up high and act as if you are way better than those who put you down for what you are. Because - YOU ARE!!! I know its hard to do this, but you've got to totally ignore what people think of you. (It's easier said than done, I know.) Focus on what you think of yourself rather than on what other people think. —**maryDixon**

I go to a school that is mostly black (I am black too) and I do not have a problem with that. My problem is that I am lighter than most of the black students at my school and I have curly hair. People tell me that I try to act white and that I only have white friends, but this is not true. I have black friends, just not many of them because some of the black students don't want to accept me for who I am. My mother has told me many times not to let those people get to me and just to go on. — mewmew

i'm half black and half white. at my school there aren't very many minorities (there's one black guy in my grade) and people don't really have a problem with it, but since there are so few minorities, and many times the races are separated, some people are intimidated at the idea of hanging out with someone who is "different". — Isew

That is so ironic. I have that same problem. The only difference is I go to a culturally diverse school (about 1/3 are black, 1/3 hispanic, 1/3 asian.) They make fun of me cause I'm the only flat-chested black girl and because I talk "white." I also have a small amount of black friends too. Just wanted to let you know you are not alone. — cHirp

286

Disability

There are currently 30 to 40 million people in the United States living with a disability. Disabled people have a diverse set of situations that can set them off from other people, from a limp to the loss of a sense to a degenerative disease. Reactions from other people can range from unwanted sympathy to an assumption of incompetence to comfort to overzealous interest. Negative reactions might be based on people's fear of difference or their fear of disability affecting their own bodies. Some places or activities may be inaccessible to people with disabilities, which can lead to a sense of isolation and get in the way of being yourself. But there are ways to work around these obstacles.

See disability rights, p. 275, and Resources, p. 279.

hi. i'm 15 years old and a great girl (at least i think) my friends think i'm funny and i think i have a really pretty face. i'm not stuck-up, please don't judge. the thing is, i'm in a wheelchair and i feel that hinders my making friends. i'm really insecure. i am in great shape mentally, but physically i have a severe muscle weakness called muscular dystrophy. i feel like people ignore me and don't want to be friends with me. would you guys be friends with a person in a wheelchair? do you have any suggestions for me? PLEASE UNDERSTAND—I DON'T WANT SYMPATHY, JUST TO BE TREATED EQUALLY — **MartaH**

I stutter and some people make fun of me. I feel like I'm the only one in the world who stutters. — **imperialgrrl**

i mean, what does it matter? if people in your school are that judgmental i feel sorry for them! — **idlegURL**

See, i'm profoundly deaf, which is a big problem for me. I feel left out. When I first moved to Hawaii in 6th grade (i'm a senior now), i was an outcast. I still feel like one. Deafness has always been an obstacle. But i'm not embarrassed, i speak out my true feelings. But when i try to join a conversation, i'm always excluded, because see, I lip-read and everyone's talking to someone else. and it really hurts me when no one invites me to go out. I know I'm supposed to invite them too, but i would, if they'd invite me! — **3elves**

287

life

FITTING IN

Most everyone wants to be accepted on some level by friends and/or certain groups, and this desire to fit in can definitely influence how people express themselves.

Fear of what others will think can sometimes stop people from following their interests and desires (this isn't necessarily bad if it discourages people from hurtful behavior), or it can inspire people to do things they wouldn't otherwise do. In either case, it can hold you back from expressing yourself fully.

I am at a seriously religious high school, but that is not the problem because I am a Christian myself. But I dress a little differently. Do not get me wrong; I LOVE what I wear (if you are curious, my style is baggy pants. theirs is cowboy boots and tight jeans)! They (the students and even my teachers!) think I am "bad" for wearing what I do, and I actually am not. I make good grades and go to church regularly. But they still like to turn up their noses when me and my small posse walk down our halls. Someone even asked me if I practice black magic one day! Should I dress like them & "clean" up my closet? Help me!
— **fuschiapanther**

I am the type of person who likes to pretend I don't care about what other people think, but I really do. Recently, after school let out, I got this really awesome haircut, but it isn't the kind that everyone is going to like. I am really scared of what everyone will think. It is making me crazy. School starts in two weeks, so I can't cut it back the way it was or anything. It is short, and I am scared everyone is going to think I am a lesbian.
— **jojokale**

Peer pressure

Inevitably, there will be some people who will think you should be or act a certain way and may try to influence you to change to fit their concept. This can be confusing, especially if it's coming from someone you care about and if you aren't so sure of who you are yourself. Advice and suggestions from others can be helpful, and can give you ideas for experimentation. But if you are being pushed in a direction that doesn't feel right to you, by all means listen to yourself!

Hey, I have a problem. It's got a lot to do with music. At my school I'm always the one who is the loser just cause of the music I like. Ya know, punk + ska. I mean it's like music nowadays is the most important thing. You can only be friends with people who listen to the same music. Don't get me wrong, I love people that I can talk with about my favorite type of music, but when it gets to the point where you're an outcast don't you think it's going a little too far?
— **fringechix**

See Altered States, pp. 200–213.

See To Do It or Not To Do It, pp. 95–101.

See Friends, pp. 233–37.

Peer pressure affects many areas of your life.

i can't decide whether to go out for tennis or volleyball this year (they're at the same time) cause i am good at tennis but none of my friends are doing that—they're all going out for volleyball, but i'm not that good at volleyball...
  – **Babbette**

I've been labeled as "Uncool" because I was nice to a girl whom everybody hates because she's poor. I don't like bitching about other people because I know I wouldn't like it if others did the same to me, but that seems weird to my friends.
  – **erinmaria**

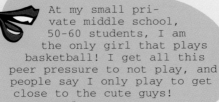 At my small private middle school, 50-60 students, I am the only girl that plays basketball! I get all this peer pressure to not play, and people say I only play to get close to the cute guys!
  – **emptyglass**

As a child growing up in the 80's it was really rare that you see a girl playing basketball! I would always try to play with the guys but they wouldn't let me! And then they would tease me and all the girls started calling me a tom boy and made me sit with the boys, well now I have a full tuition scholarship for b-ball at Oklahoma State. Just don't care what people say.
  – **moiracat**

Labels and definitions

loser misfit goth fat
loner outcast loser smarty
punk prep cool dork
geek skater hippy popular

One way that people deal with the whole fitting-in concept is to put themselves and others into particular categories. Finding people or a group that you identify with is, for some people, an important part of the process of defining who they are.

However, defining someone by the way they look, what they believe, or something they like or do is usually an insult to the many dimensions that make up a person. No one thing, no matter how much it means to you, is the whole of who you are.

For more on cliques and labels, see **pp. 256–57.**

being yourself

life

EVERYDAY I walk through the hallways and people will talk and laugh about me. I mean all I have to do is say hi or look at them and they seem to think it gives them a right to discuss me. I mean I dress uniquely sometimes and I LOVE MY CLOTHES!! LOVE. But I HATE being judged because of what I wear. Clothes don't make the person. One day I'll be goth the next I'll be a trippy hippy. I get labeled as a wanna be, but I'm not. I wear and do and act the way I CHOOSE. MEAN PEOPLE who judge suck!
  - elainychix

Finally I've found someone that is the same way I am, I used to think I was the only one. For example, one day I'll wear a green skirt (up to my knees), a brown and green striped shirt and these really funky dockers. People will be like "oh she's a freak." Then the next day I'll wear wide legs and a Marilyn Manson shirt and I'm a headbanger or a goth. I happen to really like making my own clothes like I'll take a pair of jeans that don't fit, cut them into shapes and sew them onto other clothes. **- artista**

I'm a cheerleader, so everyone assumes "all cheer-leaders are snobs, bimbos, sluts, airheads, and popular." ok but i'm not a slut, bimbo, air-head or a snob the only thing i am is popular but i was popular before i was a cheerleader! I get really good grades and am nice to everyone!! So why does everyone automatically think all cheerleaders a bad!! Please help me **- margeyann**

when someone asks me what music i like, they expect me to say something like alternative or techno or rap or whatever, but i actually like some of everything. i like some alternative, some rap, some punk (ok, most punk), some metal, some rock, some clas-sical, hell even some coun-try. but there are some groups that don't fit into any category. so when i'm asked what i like, i say "a little of everything." i don't like having to be within these little bor-derlines society has made. **- ellenfrank**

well how exactly do you define a prep? by the way they act or by the way they dress. because if it's just a certain way a per-son dresses, how can you say you hate them or they are all snobby. and how can you criti-cize they way they dress yet at the same time hate it when other people criticize the way you dress.
  - RNBlover

i am sick of people giving music stereotypes. i like nirvana, nin, hole, marilyn manson, metallica...all those bands. some people would look at that and label me as a skater, a skid, a punk, among various other things. but, i also listen to mariah carey, shania twain, n'synch, usher, and 2pac. i am not a prep, and i'm not a skater. i'm just me. so to all you stereotyping people...fuck you!!! **- quinnquix**

290

RESOURCES

Online

Do-It-Yourself Search at http://www.diysearch.com/ is a search engine dedicated to the DIY music, e-zine, and the arts community.

Hues at http://www.hues.net/ is an online zine created to promote self-esteem among women of all cultures, shapes, religions, and lifestyles.

Gimpgirl at http://www.gimpgirl.com is a great zine and community for younger girls with and without disabilities.

Tash at http://www.tash.org/ is an international association of people with disabilities fighting for a society in which inclusion of all people in all aspects of society is the norm.

Books

Between Voice and Silence: Women and Girls, Race and Relationship by Jill McLean Taylor (Harvard University Press) is an exploration the cultural differences that affect girls' coming of age.

Finding Our Way: The Teen Girls' Survival Guide by Allison Abner, Linda Villarosa (Harperperennial Library) is a guide for teenage girls that addresses self-image, personal identity, relationships, family problems, activism, and much more.

From Girls to Grrlz: A History of Women's Comics from Teens to Zines by Trina Robbins (Chronicle Books).

Girl Goddess #9: Nine Stories by Francesca Lia Block (HarperCollins) is a wonderful collection of short stories for and about girls.

The Girl Pages: A Handbook of the Best Resources for Strong, Confident, Creative Girls by Charlotte Milholland (Hyperion) is a resource for girls to discover and explore their interests.

Girl Power: Young Women Speak Out by Hillary Carlip (Warner Books). Girls from ages 13 to 19 express themselves through letters, poems, interviews, and stories about their lives and experiences.

Ophelia Speaks: Adolescent Girls Write About Their Search for Self by Sara Shandler (HarperCollins).

The Perks of Being a Wallflower by Stephen Chbosky (Pocket Books). The novel offers a unique look into of one 15-year-old boy's awkward struggle to be understood.

Real Girl Real World: Tools for Finding Your True Self by Heather M. Gray and Samantha Phillips (Seal Press). This book strives to give girls the power to choose for themselves.

Reviving Ophelia: Saving the Selves of Adolescent Girls by Mary Pipher (Ballantine Books).

Stay True: Short Stories for Strong Girls by Marilyn Singer (Scholastic) is an anthology of short stories about growing up.

Sugar in the Raw: Voices of Young Black Girls in America by Rebecca Carroll (Crown Publishing). Interviews with 50 girls about their lives.

Wake Up, I'm Fat by Camryn Manheim (Broadway Books). In this memoir, actress Camryn Manheim chronicles her journey from a discouraged, "overweight" teenager who desires to fit in, to a self-loving, proud, fat activist.

Zine Scene: The Do It Yourself Guide to Zines by Francesca Lia Block, Hillary Carlip (Girl Press). Zine Scene is celebration of the zine culture and a guide to producing your own zines.

For more resources and information, see http://www.dealwithit.com

being yourself

l
i
f
e

Special Section

Money

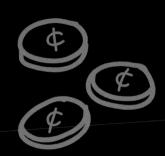

Money is far from the be-all, end-all of life, but inevitably, it is important. Having money can allow you to do the things you want to do; it can help you gain freedom, independence, and self-sufficiency. But not having money can limit your options dramatically. Working out your relationship with money—how you earn it, spend it, and save it—is a process filled with trial and error. While almost everybody has to work for money, the more you know about it, the more you can get your money to work for you.

EARNING IT

When you are young, a lack of work skills, experience, or higher education can limit your job opportunities. But you still have many options to earn money or gain experience, from baby-sitting to working in a store or office to starting your own business.

Eventually, everyone must grapple with how to support herself. Asking people you know about the work they do can give you some interesting perspectives on your career choices. Since you'll have to work anyway, if you find a job doing something that interests you, working will be a much more pleasant and rewarding experience.

Part-time work

A part-time job can be a great opportunity to earn money and gain experience and responsibility. One benefit of working is that you'll get a tangible benefit as the result of your time and labor—a paycheck. And if you work with other people, you can open your world to personalities and ideas that you might otherwise never come into contact with. Before taking any job, it's a good idea to think about what you want to get out of the experience and whether your work will interfere too much with the rest of your life (especially school).

Laws and Regulations

In 1996, Congress created a special "opportunity wage," or youth minimum wage, which applies to employees under 20 years old. As of 1999, employers are permitted to pay teenagers $4.25 an hour, as opposed to the minimum wage of $5.15, for the first 90 calendar days after their initial hire. Once the 90 days are up, teenagers must be paid at least the current minimum wage.

To find out the law in your state, contact the Labor Department (see Resources, p. 296).

Some states have laws determining the total number of hours and how late teens are allowed to work. Depending on where you work, these restrictions may protect you from exploitation, or they may just feel limiting.

My friend works at a pizza place, and she got me a job there two days a week. I really want to take it, but my mom doesn't want me to. I absolutely HATE baby-sitting and I need (well...want) money. Plus, a lot of my friends work there so it wouldn't be that bad. Any ideas on how I can convince my mom?
— **bobbette**

U can tell your mom:
* The reasons you deserve to take this job.
* Promise her that you will keep your grades up and help around the house more without being asked.
* Promise to quit if your grades start to drop or if you can't do what you're supposed to do around the house.
— **ladyliberty**

Some parents will never change. But you could tell them that if you don't have a job, they will be the ones paying for your clothes, car, school supplies, and personal stuff because u have no way of making money. Without taking a job, u can't become independent and learn how to be responsible. Good luck with your parents.
— **shannonT**

I know you may think this is lame advice, but getting a job really helps boost your confidence. Maybe you can tell your mom that this is one of the benefits of working. I was dead shy before i got a job a year ago. Working with people and dealing with other people's problems helped me get over my shyness. I am really enjoying it, and the people I work with are great too.
— **erinmaria**

Starting a business

Work isn't limited to finding pre-existing jobs. Many people create their own jobs by identifying and selling products or services that other people want or need. It can be very interesting to research the origins of companies you admire. Starting your own business can be incredibly exciting and can give you a great sense of personal satisfaction. But, it will most likely be a lot of hard work.

If you intend to get serious about your own business idea, it's a good idea to create a business plan, which can be a fun and interesting exercise in and of itself.

My best friend suggests we try being party planners (I like the title "Occasion Planner" better). We would organize everything for other people's parties and charge them for our time and creativity, in addition to the cost of the supplies. We wouldn't necessarily do all the cooking and decorations ourselves, but we would find the resources for all the party details. Does anyone think there is a market for this type of thing?
— **lorettaspy**

I think party planning might be a good thing to try, but it depends on the area where you live. I know that people in my neighborhood wouldn't go for it because nobody has big, extravagant parties. But in a big city or a wealthy suburb it would probably work. — **mayBcranky**

life

SAVING IT

Saving your money—whether it is for your college tuition, or for something you want to purchase in the distant future—takes a bit of discipline and some force of habit. Often, delayed gratification can be well worth it. Creating a savings account and understanding the way interest works is always a good idea.

Investing it

There are smart ways to invest your money so it will work more efficiently for you throughout your life. There are a number of ways in which to do this: savings bonds, mutual funds, IRA's, investment clubs, and stocks. You can also choose to invest in ways that coincide with your values by choosing companies that have sound personnel or environmental policies.

Even if you don't have much money to invest, it can be fun to play the stock market just for the experience (check out the Young Investors Guide or the finance area on Yahoo.com).

See Investing resources, p. 297.

Investment Glossary

Blue chip stock: Stock of a large, well-known national corporation that has performed well historically. Blue-chip stocks tend to enjoy steady growth in earnings as well as reputations for solid management, products, services, or all three.

Bond: An IOU that companies or the government sell to the general public to raise money.

Bear Market: Time when the financial market is down and companies' stock prices are falling for a period of months or years.

Bull Market: Time when the financial market is up and companies' stock prices are rising for a period of months or years.

Broker: An "agent" who handles the purchase of stocks and bonds and makes recommendations for you in exchange for a fee (commission). A broker acts as an intermediary but does not actually sell you stock or buy stock from you.

CD (Certificate of Deposit): A form of savings deposit that yields a higher rate of interest than a savings account, but cannot be withdrawn before its set date of maturity, at which point you receive the interest also.

Dividend: A portion of a company's profits which are paid to shareholders on a regular basis.

The Dow Jones Industrial Average: An index of 30 stocks that provides an indication of how the market is doing as a whole.

FDIC (Federal Deposit Insurance Corporation): A federal agency that insures banks and guarantees that people cannot lose the money they deposit (up to $100,000) into a bank account if the bank fails.

IRA (Individual Retirement Account): A tax-deferred retirement plan in which you earn interest without paying taxes on it until you withdraw the money at legal retirement age.

Interest (rate): The charge for borrowing money. You may receive interest from a bank when you put money in an account, because the bank borrows your money and lends it to other people. (If you borrow money from the bank, you will pay interest on the loan to the bank, usually as part of a monthly fee.) Interest rates for money you owe on a credit card can be very high.

Mutual Fund: A company that pools money from many people to invest in stocks or bonds. Mutual funds are usually less risky than buying shares in a single stock because your investment is diversified over many companies.

NASDAQ (National Association of Securities Dealers Automated Quotations): The computerized network run by the NASD providing price quotes on over-the-counter and other securities.

NYSE (New York Stock Exchange): The largest of the securities exchanges. Located on Wall Street, the NYSE is sometimes referred to as "The Exchange" or the "Big Board."

The Standard & Poor's 500: An index of 500 major companies whose value reflects how the market as a whole is performing.

Stock: A part or share of a company that the general public can purchase, also known as a share.

Stock Market: Place where shares of many companies are bought and sold.

SPENDING IT

Regardless of what you can afford or what you choose to purchase, you live in a consumer culture where advertisers and marketers want and need their customers to believe that purchasing the right products can lead to happiness. Some people believe this and think that the more they can afford to do and buy, the more satisfied they'll be, but this just isn't true. Unfortunately, people

are sometimes judged by how much or how little money they have.

You are powerful as a consumer. Currently, teenagers are the largest growing demographic group in the United States with disposable income of over $157 billion. What you do and don't spend your money on—from movies to music to clothes—has a huge effect on the economy. So carefully choosing where and how you spend your money can make a difference. You can find out quite a bit about the companies you patronize, from their politics to their environmental and social policies. It is also interesting to notice how many of the things you purchase from different music or clothing labels often are owned by the same large corporation.

Credit

Credit cards can be very seductive because they allow you to buy things that you otherwise couldn't afford. But, things that you buy on credit cards often end up costing you significantly more. If you don't pay off the full balance every month, you could end up paying a lot of money in interest and finance charges. And if you don't pay the minimum balance on time every month, you could ruin your credit rating, which could make it difficult for you get approved for loans for things like college tuition or a car for years. If you get a credit card or if your parents get one for you, find out about the interest rates and payment terms, which differ from card to card.

My family says that I am totally self absorbed. They don't wear brand name stuff and aren't in to their looks. I am only trying to carry myself in a good way. I'm not a makeupface, but the fact that I am 14 and I wear makeup bothers my parents. I can't really talk to them, because whenever I do, they come out and say that I am so self absorbed and that I am wasting money.

— **pippiL**

if it's any consolation at all, i know how you feel. we don't have a lot of money in my family, so i have to buy a lot of my own stuff (shampoo and soap). the really stupid thing is that i feel like i'm always being scrutinized by my mom even for spending my own money on such "trivial" things as nice shampoo! your priorities are obviously different from those of your family and so of course they don't always understand why some things (like makeup) are important to you. maybe try telling them that wearing makeup helps you to feel good about yourself and remind them that it IS your choice after all.

— **estaticgrrl**

About every person I see at school wears expensive sneakers. I like them a lot more, but they are $50 and up. My mom won't pay that kind of money. I feel like the only one that doesn't have them. — **sQuidy**

Well, you aren't the only one to feel that way. Everyone at my school wears Nike and Tommy shoes and Doc Martens and everything. I mean, I even have Nikes, several pairs but my mom wont buy shoes over $80. Everyone at my school is rich. You'll just have to live with it. Those brands are really in style and most everybody will do anything to be in style and popular.

— **TaraGirl**

Paying for college

Many people's parents pay for their college education, but some parents are unable or unwilling to afford this or can only contribute part of the amount. If this is your situation, you need to do as much research as possible to find additional funding. There are great resources for learning about scholarships, financial aid, and other grants at your school's guidance office, the library, and on the Internet. Money is available in the form of federal loans and grants, merit scholarships from your community or the college of your choice, college financial aid, scholarships sponsored by organizations your family may belong to, and church or synagogue groups, among others.

Also see financial aid resources, pp. 260–61.

RESOURCES

To find out about your state's age requirements for employment, contact the Labor Department (look in the White Page's Blue Section). If you think you are being unfairly treated, you can make official complaints to the Employment Agency of Complaints (also in the White Page's Blue Section).

Online

Fleet Financial Group at www.fleetkids.com has interactive games that tackle saving and budgeting.

The Independent Means at http://www.
anincomeofherown.com is for women
under twenty to find out about starting a
business; making, saving, and growing
money.

Junior Achievement at http://www.
ja.org has been educating teens about eco-
nomics since 1919. Check out the site to
find a branch in your area.

Liberty Financial's Young Investor at
http://www.younginvestor.com teaches
about money and how to invest wisely.

MainXchange at http://www.
mainXchange.com is an interactive stock
game where you can win prizes.

Salomon Smith Barney at http://www.
smithbarney.com produces a "Young
Investors Network."

The Savvy Student at http://www.
savvystudent.com/ is a website for high
school and college students focused on
managing and saving money.

She's on the Money at http://www.
girlsinc.org/money helps girls learn to
manage money.

Stein Roe Young Investor Fund at
http://www.steinroe.com is a mutual fund
for youth that has its own newsletter with
teen-friendly financial stories.

The Stock Market Game at http://www.
smg2000.org lets you play the market
with this electronic simulation of Wall
Street trading.

Wall Street giant Merrill Lynch at
http://www.plan.ml.com/family
(or-800-MERRILL) runs an online family-
saving website and produces literature
for teens.

Working Solo at http://www.
workingsolo.com/ is a resource for the
self-employed, home-based business
owner, free agent, e-lancer, telecommuter,
consultant, or other independent professional.

Wristies at http://www.wristies.com is
about a young entrepreneur who created
her own successful wrist warmers.

YoungBiz.com at http://www.youngbiz.
com/ shows how business is not just for
adults anymore and includes investment
and portfolio information and advice.

Young Investor Guide at http://www.
investyoung.com/ has lots of good links,
including profiles on successful young
investors, book suggestions, and hard-
core business information.

Books

Companies with a Conscience by
Mary Scott and Howard Rothman (Citadel
Press).

Gain by Richard Powers (Farrar Straus &
Giroux) highlights the danger of living in
a consumer-driven society through the
tyranny of an American household-prod-
ucts corporation, and its cost in human
suffering.

Girl Boss by Stacy Kravetz (Girl Press).
Entrepreneurial skills, stories, and
encouragement for modern girls.

**Girls and Young Women Entrepreneurs:
True Stories About Starting and Running
a Business Plus How You Can Do It Yourself** by Francis A. Karnes (Free Spirit
Publications).

What Color Is Your Parachute Workbook
by Richard Nelson Bolles (Ten Speed
Press) is a practical way to help you
figure out what turns you on work-wise.

**Will the Dollars Stretch? Teen Parents
Living on Their Own—Virtual Reality
Through Stories and Check-Writing Practice** by Sudie Pollock (Morning Glory
Press) contains stories of teen parents
accompanied by exercises providing practice in writing checks and in meeting the
real challenges of living within a tight
budget.

**Wise Up to Teens: Insights Into Market-
ing and Advertising to Teenagers** by
Peter Zollo (New Strategist Publications)
shows teens that they have power in the
consumer market.

For more resources and information,

INDEX

Bold indicates a diagram

DEAL
WITH
IT!